Immersive Theatre and Audience Experience

"Rose Biggin offers a richly nuanced model for understanding immersive practice that will be applicable well beyond the example of Punchdrunk. Interweaving theories of interactivity, aesthetics and ludology, the careful frame Biggin establishes lets her skilfully unpick the structures of theatre events and probe the nature of 'immersion' at the level of audience experience. Punchdrunk's pioneering work emerges vividly in this discussion, with the author's research into audience response demonstrating why their practice has drawn criticism as well as extraordinary devotion. This energetic, imaginative and intelligent study will be a catalyst for further scholarship in the field."
—Dr. Frances Babbage, *Reader in Theatre and Performance, University of Sheffield, UK*

"Alongside the fascinating, in-depth study of the company, this volume offers us a new framework for analysing immersive experience in performance. This is something I can use in the studio with the next generation of theatre-makers, helping them think about how and why they might create immersive experiences."
—Professor Jane Milling, *Associate Professor in Drama, University of Exeter, UK*

"This is a distinctive and very useful study, with detailed analysis and original theorisation, challenging as well as celebrating the work of this important company."
—Dr. Gareth White, *Reader in Theatre and Performance, Royal Central School of Speech & Drama, University of London, UK*

Rose Biggin

Immersive Theatre and Audience Experience

Space, Game and Story in the Work of Punchdrunk

Rose Biggin
Independent Scholar
London, UK

ISBN 978-3-319-62038-1   ISBN 978-3-319-62039-8 (eBook)
DOI 10.1007/978-3-319-62039-8

Library of Congress Control Number: 2017944604

© The Editor(s) (if applicable) and The Author(s) 2017
This work is subject to copyright. All rights are solely and exclusively licensed by the Publisher, whether the whole or part of the material is concerned, specifically the rights of translation, reprinting, reuse of illustrations, recitation, broadcasting, reproduction on microfilms or in any other physical way, and transmission or information storage and retrieval, electronic adaptation, computer software, or by similar or dissimilar methodology now known or hereafter developed.
The use of general descriptive names, registered names, trademarks, service marks, etc. in this publication does not imply, even in the absence of a specific statement, that such names are exempt from the relevant protective laws and regulations and therefore free for general use.
The publisher, the authors and the editors are safe to assume that the advice and information in this book are believed to be true and accurate at the date of publication. Neither the publisher nor the authors or the editors give a warranty, express or implied, with respect to the material contained herein or for any errors or omissions that may have been made. The publisher remains neutral with regard to jurisdictional claims in published maps and institutional affiliations.

Cover credit: © REUTERS/Alamy Stock Photo

Printed on acid-free paper

This Palgrave Macmillan imprint is published by Springer Nature
The registered company is Springer International Publishing AG
The registered company address is: Gewerbestrasse 11, 6330 Cham, Switzerland

Acknowledgements

I am very happy to be able to thank members of Punchdrunk: in particular Felix Barrett, Rebecca Dawson, Maxine Doyle, Peter Higgin, Jennie Hoy, Colin Marsh, Colin Nightingale, Jen Thomas and the *Crash of the Elysium* actors, for generously giving me access to their time and expertise at various stages of the project. Punchdrunk's interest and enthusiasm remained steady and encouraging throughout the process. Of course, all errors and opinions are my own. Particular thanks are also due to the always brilliant Jane Milling, who has been supportive from the start.

An earlier version of Chap. 4 was initially published as "Reading fan mail: Communicating immersive experience in Punchdrunk's *Faust* and *The Masque of the Red Death*" in *Participations* (Volume 12, Issue 1: May 2015). Reprinted here with permission of the editors, Kirsty Sedgeman and Martin Barker.

Contents

1 Immersive Theatre, Immersive Experience   1

2 Interactivity and Immersion: Theoretical Approaches   59

3 Interactivity and Immersion in *The Drowned Man*   79

4 Fan Interactivity: Communicating Immersive Experience   97

5 Follow the Story: Narrative and Immersion   113

6 Exploring Multistories: Narrative, Immersion and Chronology   135

7 Play the Story: An Approach to Narrative in Immersive Theatre   157

8 Environment and Site-Specificity: Space, Place and Immersion   177

9 Conclusion 207

Bibliography 213

Index 219

CHAPTER 1

Immersive Theatre, Immersive Experience

GENERAL INTRODUCTION

The essence of Punchdrunk is that you have to *feel* it.

(Barrett in Machon 2013: 163)

How exactly to define immersive theatre? In 2012, Lyn Gardner called *immersive* "theatre's new buzzword" and joked that, as a result of various associations with trendiness or cutting-edge experimentation, or promises of excitement and wonder, in marketing terms *immersive* had come to mean "practically anything that isn't a play by David Hare" ("Theatre Roundup: Advice for Playwrights"). But some people can, and presumably do, become highly engaged while watching a Hare play: so while this definition is, of course, too broad to be useful, it is also not quite broad enough.

This book proposes a distinction between immersive theatre and immersive experience as a new way of looking at audience experience in a form of theatre that is often characterised by certain aesthetic signifiers or audience configurations. I draw from philosophical aesthetics, cognitive science and computer games to define immersive *experience* as a graded, fleeting, intense and necessarily temporary state defined by an awareness of its temporal and spatial boundaries. Immersive theatre, then, is a genre of theatrical work in which certain audience configurations might be expected, but in which immersive experience itself can only be allowed for, not guaranteed. With this distinction in place, it is

© The Author(s) 2017
R. Biggin, *Immersive Theatre and Audience Experience*,
DOI 10.1007/978-3-319-62039-8_1

possible to consider how different aspects of an immersive theatre production might achieve various effects on its audience.

My discussion is broadly divided across three areas: environment and space; narrative and story; and interactivity and game. These aspects make much immersive theatre visibly different to (for example) a proscenium arch production: the ability of an audience to wander with apparent freedom through a spatially innovative environment, usually scenographically rich and multisensory; a non-chronological and/or impressionistic approach to narrative; and interactive elements or characters, often with an emphasis on empowerment, choice or freedom for the spectator. Each chapter in the book considers the relationship(s) between these areas and immersive experience.

Throughout the book, my discussion is framed using productions by the theatre company Punchdrunk. They are a prominent company working in the form: in 2008 when speaking of "the kind of work that is being called 'immersive theatre' [...] the leading company working in this idiom is probably Punchdrunk" (Nield 2008: 531); by 2011 they could be called "immersive theatre pioneers Punchdrunk" (Arnott 2011: n.p.). Or at least, pioneers of a current interest in the form: the traits listed earlier regarding space, narrative and interactivity can be traced at least to the early twentieth century in terms of performance history, and immersive experience per se goes back long before that (as does my own definition of *immersion*.) Punchdrunk's work has an international reach: *Sleep No More*, which premiered in London in 2003, continues to run in New York (2011–) and recently opened in Shanghai (2016–). Punchdrunk's prominence in the contemporary theatrical landscape, and their continued association with immersive theatre as a form or genre, makes their work ideal for providing extended case studies of immersion and audience, and keeping my analysis to a single company gives this project a focus for its theory. There is also a practical reason for the Punchdrunk focus which is worth declaring at the outset. The process of research that informs much of this book was made possible due to my having continued access to the company, giving me the means to consider their work closely.

This book is the product of research conducted as part of an Arts and Humanities Research Council (AHRC) Collaborative Doctoral Award (CDA) between Punchdrunk and the University of Exeter between 2010 (when the company were celebrating their ten-year anniversary) and 2014. As an embedded CDA researcher, I was able to explore audience immersion with access to Punchdrunk's archives and through interviews with company members, as well as through maintaining an extended presence at rehearsals and performances. In this way this book sits in the tradition of Spectator-Participation-as-Research (SPaR) approaches (Heddon et al. 2012), a methodology in which writers draw on first-person accounts of their own experience as audience members alongside more theoretical writing (Babbage 2009; Machon 2016; Alston 2016a). I remain extremely grateful to Punchdrunk for their openness and enthusiasm throughout the process of my research. It is important to stress, however, that although I spent time embedded within the company, I have never been a member. My research conclusions are my own, and my arguments do not reflect the opinions of Punchdrunk.

Nor is my focus on Punchdrunk intended to suggest that their work is in any way the definitive example of any theatrical form, technique or trope. *Punchdrunk* and *immersive theatre* are not synonymous, and any research into the wider genre of immersive theatre must of course take in more examples than the productions of a single company, however influential or "pioneering" (Hoggard 2013) that company may be perceived to be. My being embedded with Punchdrunk for a time enables their work to be considered here in detail, as well as drawing on exposure to ongoing processes and archive material: and a long-form critical study of their work is overdue. However, this book's other (and to some extent primary) aim is to develop theoretical perspectives on immersive audience experience that will be of use for considering other immersive-identifying theatrical forms. Focusing on one company allows this book to propose approaches to analysing immersive work—in reference to interactivity, narrative and environment—that I hope will be of use to other researchers, students, artists and makers.

Sophie Nield's definition of the "kind of work that is being called 'immersive theatre', in which the audience inhabit the space of the play alongside the actors" (2008: 531) makes spatial and structural elements key to whether a piece of work might be defined as *immersive* or not. A pragmatic outline of what happens in terms of performer action and movement—the basic structure of audience logistics and layout—makes a show immersive in terms of its shape. Nield's definition continues to specify that actors and audience jointly inhabit "a tricked-out space [...] perhaps infused with smells, sounds" (2008: 531). This kind of emotional/visceral/multisensory experience is often cited as what makes Punchdrunk's work uniquely exciting, as in Barrett's emphasis on *feeling* it at the beginning of this chapter. The form of an immersive production and the sensory experience aimed for within it are closely linked, the former facilitating the latter: Punchdrunk's own statements of intent emphasise emotional, visceral and sensory excitement rather than offering a pragmatic description of their shows' logistics, as being what makes a Punchdrunk experience a truly *immersive* one ("this work only functions if there's a sense of mystery [...] It's about a heightened state of awareness. The more real it is, the deeper it becomes." Barrett in "Burn the Seats," 2013). The word *immersive*, therefore, might describe the shape or genre of a production, or the emotional quality of experiencing it. And immersive experience can be felt within any theatrical form: it is just as possible to become highly emotionally engaged in a piece of end-on proscenium arch performance as it is to feel indifferent or bored while moving through a production that described itself as *immersive* on the posters.

> Your productions seem to center around this idea of "mystery." Why?
>
> [Barrett:] I think it's because mystery instigates a state of tension in the audience and there's an apprehension and a sort of nervous excitement that comes from not knowing what's going to happen next. And because that's the state you're in when you're exploring, or adventuring, or maybe doing something that's illicit, it's totally charged. *That's why Punchdrunk could never do a comedy, because it's a totally different state.* We're trying to empower the audience by making them feel like they're the most important person in the space, and that they're doing something they shouldn't be and the more they work the more they'll discover. You need that tension to be there in order for that to work. (Barrett interview in Godbout 2012: n.p.; my emphasis)

In this quote, Punchdrunk's Artistic Director explicitly locates immersive experience as a primarily *emotional* phenomenon, a product of instinctive emotional response. Immersive theatre, framed in this way, is all about audience effect, and formal decisions are made with a view to how they will produce these effects (rather than being made simply for novelty's sake). For Barrett, being "immersed" in a Punchdrunk show is all about experiencing a specific, limited set of emotions—fear, mystery, "nervous excitement," apprehension—and a sense of transgression and danger: "illicit" activity that goes against (unspecified) rules. Immersive experience can certainly be facilitated by an atmosphere of menace, by drawing on tensions of secrecy or mystery and the illicit excitement of apparent rule-breaking. In the quote above, Barrett expands this into a wider statement about genre. By explicitly excluding comedy, immersive theatre and its emotional effects are by default tied to drama and tragedy; and many of Punchdrunk's productions do sit firmly, aesthetically and atmospherically, in the trappings of tragedy and its sub-genres of mystery, horror, and crime.

In this book, I argue that this is a fundamentally limiting way of theorising immersive experience, and one which, by association, impoverishes our perceptions of immersive theatre's potential.

Immersive experience is not a felt/not-felt binary but a graded and temporary state, defined (somewhat paradoxically) by the existence of its boundaries. By uncoupling "immersive experience" the sensation and "immersive theatre" the form, I argue for a distinction between content, form and effect. Ultimately, immersive experience must be facilitated by an interplay between content and form: one is not the natural and automatic result of the other. The "totally charged" excitement Barrett describes previously is not the inevitable result of a production taking a certain form: the question then becomes one of *how* content, form and effect might facilitate immersive experience. The sensation of breaking rules that Barrett champions might actually be adherence to a new set of rules. The distinction between "immersive theatre" and "immersive experience" also helps us escape the (ultimately unhelpful) truism that all theatre can be immersive in one way or another.

This book considers various aspects of immersive experience—the emotional, the physical, the *sensation* of immersion in place, space and story—to examine in detail what is actually meant by being "immersed" across these different contexts. I argue that immersive experience might be facilitated by a production's form or its content, or through the reciprocity of both: atmosphere/mood and logistics can be manipulated to facilitate immersion. But they do not guarantee it. A feeling of repetition might prevent immersion much faster than innovation within that repetition can allow for it. Implicitly, then, running throughout this book is the suggestion that it would indeed be possible to make an immersive comedy.

Founded by the alumni from the University of Exeter in 2000, Punchdrunk's early work showed several now-established spatial and experiential trademarks. Often drawing on classic texts (*Romeo and Juliet* in 2003's *The Firebird Ball*; *Macbeth* in *Sleep No More* [England

2003; Boston 2009; New York 2011-]), these productions turned large non-theatrical spaces into design-rich environments through which the audience was allowed to wander, arriving upon scenes out of the text's original order, and finally gathered together to witness the finale. *Faust* (21 Wapping Lane, 2006–2007) and *The Masque of the Red Death* (Battersea Arts Centre, 2007–2008) were commercial and critical successes: Gardner called *The Masque of the Red Death* "undoubtedly the theatre event of 2007" (2007b), and its run was extended due to demand. These productions established a physical grammar for "typical" Punchdrunk shows concerning use of space and story, and movement of audience (as summarised in Nield's definition previously). Later productions would be compared to these, in terms of both structure and logistics and the quality of their visceral emotional punch. *Tunnel 228* (Old Vic Tunnels, Waterloo, 2009), *The Duchess of Malfi* (Great Eastern Quay, London, 2010) and *The Drowned Man* (31 London Street, 2013–2014) all followed this format, as well as shows that deviated from it—*It Felt Like A Kiss* (Hardman Square, Manchester: 2010), *The Crash of the Elysium* (Salford Quays: 2010) and *The Borough* (Aldeburgh: 2013)—could be considered unusual by their linear narratives, their lack of performers or their occurring outside. But these productions can still be considered from the perspective of creating immersive experience in their audiences. And if experience is what makes for a Punchdrunk show, rather than the physical signifiers, these latter productions are not as atypical as a description of their deviances from the template might suggest.

Over the course of the company's work there has been a huge rise in Punchdrunk's prestige and visibility, both nationally and internationally. In the 2011 Arts Council England funding reshuffle (where many companies faced substantial cuts), Punchdrunk received "a hefty rise" of 141% (Higgins 2011: "the great axe falls"). At the time of writing *Sleep No More* is still running in New York after premiering in 2011, and in Shanghai from November 2016 (Hemley 2016). Punchdrunk Enrichment continues to produce successful work for children and communities; Punchdrunk International provides bespoke commercial projects to national and international audiences; Punchdrunk Travel, an expansion of the one-on-one form for individual participants, is still in experimental stages.

Regrettably, this book does not focus on the company's enrichment and commercial strands; these aspects of Punchdrunk's work merit detailed consideration elsewhere.

Since its founding in 2008, Punchdrunk Enrichment has undertaken a series of superb projects with and for communities, schools and children, including *The Uncommercial Traveller* with local communities; installation-based *Under the Eiderdown* for primary schools; and family adventure shows *The House Where Winter Lives* (Story Studio, 2013) and *Against Captain's Orders* (National Maritime Museum, 2015). This branch of the company's work deserves a book of its own.

Punchdrunk's commercial projects have seen experiences and theatrical experiments tailored for brands including *The Black Diamond* for Stella Artois (2010), a Louis Vuitton store launch (2010) and W Hotel (2011). While one way of negotiating the contemporary theatrical landscape ("theatre and business are discovering ways of working together that may bring money into theatre in a way that [Arts Council] subsidy no longer can" Gardner 2006a: n.p.), this work has attracted considerable criticism, particularly regarding the ethics of this form of immersive advertising. (Further accusations of succumbing to economic imperatives have been levelled at *Sleep No More*: "Is this a sell out I see before me?" Gillinson 2012: n.p.) The intersection between immersive experience, commercial imperatives and audience care is one of particular tension, and this area is a continual source of interest in scholarship of immersive media (see Rose 2012; Alston 2013, 2016a; Gordon 2013; Frieze 2017). This book does not engage in this dialogue directly; rather, its aim is to lay out theoretical concepts for approaching immersive theatre and audience experience to provide a toolkit for further exploration that can include this area.

Immersive theatre has become a popular area for study as well as an oft-used phrase: in 2014 Lyn Gardner referred to "the much overused term 'immersive'" in her review of an unsuccessful production that seemed "more of an aimless wander" than the environment-sensitive theatrical adventure implicitly promised by the term (2014: n.p.). There is an increasing academic interest in the topic of immersive performance, and these studies often use Punchdrunk as a point of focus (Nield 2008; Babbage 2009; Machon 2007, 2013; White 2005, 2012, 2013; Eglinton 2010; Shaughnessy 2012; Gordon 2012; Purcell 2013; Worthen 2012; Alston 2016a; Dinesh 2016; Frieze 2017). There is an increasing interest in how to create immersive theatre (such as Warren 2017), and journal issues that focus on audience studies are likely to feature a strand on immersive or interactive theatre, such as *Participations* Volume 12, Issue 1 (although I myself supplied one of these); and the

Journal of Contemporary Drama's special immersion issue (Volume 4, Issue 1), which featured multiple entries on Punchdrunk. The fashion for theatre describing itself as *immersive* has led to backlash on occasion, a sense of immersion fatigue: in 2009 Charlotte Higgins asked, "Immersive Theatre—Tired and Hackneyed Already?" and described feeling "unmoved; bored, even" at finding herself being "blindfolded *again*" (n.p.; original emphasis). The question of whether all immersive theatre is tired and hackneyed aimless wandering is founded on an assumption that immersive theatre and immersive experience are one and the same, and that to be awake to the gimmicks of the former is to be immune to the magic of the latter.

Contemporary celebratory discourses around immersive theatre tend to emphasise audiences as a group of separate individuals having unique experiences:

> No two audience members within the spaces have the same show and every evening the experience you've had is yours and yours alone, and in fact even if you're holding hands with your loved one when you arrive we'll make an effort to try and separate you because you'll have a better time when you're fighting for yourself and you're selfish for once. (Barrett 2014: talk at "Experience Economy" Remix Summit)

The relationship between participation and passivity in theatre is already in question: Freshwater suggests that "the belief that participation empowers has become a compelling orthodoxy in theatre and performance studies […] it often seems to be applied reductively and uncritically" (2009: 36); Shaughnessy (2012) draws on Rancière to question whether physical inactivity automatically equates to passivity; referring to a history of unsuccessful promenade productions of Shakespeare's *As You Like It*, Dusinberre rightly notes that "physical participation does not necessarily create imaginative participation" (2006: 67). This book proposes a vocabulary and set of theoretical concepts for approaching immersive experience while remaining aware of this distinction, in order to consider how it is claimed to manifest in immersive theatre, and who is doing the claiming.

Here are two introductions to the two main areas in which this book sits. The first looks at approaches to audience in theatre, film, television and cultural studies. Much analysis in this book comes from observing idealised spectator perspective implied by the work, to discuss how

Punchdrunk craft and facilitate immersive experience in their productions, and drawing on my own presence at rehearsals and performances (SPaR) in order to place individual accounts in the context of that implied audience member. The second section considers current understandings of *immersion* in other fields—cognitive science and psychology, philosophical aesthetics, virtual reality (VR) and computer gaming—to build a working (re)definition of immersive experience that will be used throughout the body of the book.

Approaches to Audience

> Since 2000 Punchdrunk has pioneered a game changing form of immersive theatre in which roaming audiences experience epic storytelling inside sensory theatrical worlds. ("Punchdrunk", description on the *Sleep No More* New York website)

The importance of the audience has always been a theatrical truism. In Brook's famous formulation a theatrical experience is defined by human connection created by the act of spectatorship: "A man walks across this empty space while someone else is watching him, and this is all that is needed for an act of theatre to be engaged" (1968: 9). The description of Punchdrunk above appears on the website for the New York production of *Sleep No More*—a site and production that establishes the company's international profile. While this description contains language of innovation ("pioneering"; "game changing"), it also places Punchdrunk firmly in a tradition of making work that explicitly emphasises its relationship to audience. This tradition has precedents in other fields than performance history: Bishop (2006) charts a trajectory in contemporary fine art away from viewer as passive spectator and towards active participant. The description given previously defines the "immersive" form by its spectator-performer dynamic (the audience get to "experience" the company's "epic storytelling") as well as its spectator-space dynamic, with the description of "sensory theatrical worlds" and the way audience members (are invited to) experience them. It is particularly important to pay critical attention to the relationship between tradition and innovation when work describes itself as "game changing," as it pre-supposes an understanding of the implied original game.

This section considers three areas of exploration regarding the question of audience: methodological approaches in theatre scholarship; in film, television and cultural studies; and in studies of immersive theatre and Punchdrunk. These fields provide the frameworks for the approaches in this book. It is also important to note that the criticism considered in this section occupies a landscape that is also populated by a more informal blog/fan site discourse. The result is a rich ecology of discussion, analysis and interaction on, and with, immersive theatre: Chap. 4 is situated within these wider discourses.

Approaches to Audience: Theatre and Performance Studies

Studies of theatre audiences have begun to use methodologies drawn from the social sciences and cognitive studies, using a mixture of data collection (often interviews or the writer's own attendance) and the application of theoretical concepts to case studies. The tension between individual experiences and writing about "the audience" as a single group becomes particularly relevant to theatrical events designed to facilitate individual journeys.

Freshwater has pointed out that theatre academics rarely consider asking theatregoers what they thought of a show: "audiences are beginning to be trusted by practitioners and by industry. But it seems that theatre scholars have yet to develop this trust" (2009: 74). She notes that theatre studies have historically had a low level of engagement with the methods of cultural studies. It is usually theatre marketing departments that conduct any audience research; not many academic studies of theatre ask people who aren't practitioners, scholars or critics, as television and film studies do. Theatre and film/television studies can even appear mutually exclusive in their interest in audiences: Bennett's study of theatrical spectatorship (1997) deliberately omits television; Freshwater notes that in Brooker and Jermyn's (2003) summary of historical approaches to audience, "Theatre is notable by its absence" (2009: 79). Barker suggests "Academic study of theatre audiences has been, to put it kindly, spasmodic and discontinuous" (2003: 1). There is a gap to be bridged between theoretical constructs and descriptions of actual audience experience.

Bennett's influential *Theatre Audiences* (1997) traces a history that begins with democratic Ancient Greek amphitheatres, where theatre attendance overlapped with civic duty, and moves through to nineteenth-century naturalism with its clear separation and darkness between audience and performance. The move is towards an increasingly passive audience, a historical narrative that would be seconded by Punchdrunk: "they [the masked audience of a Punchdrunk production] are removed from the traditional role of the passive, hidden audience" (Barrett in Machon 2013: 160). Carlson states that "much theatre theory still regards the theatre performance as something created and set before an essentially passive audience," which fails to consider "what demands and contributions it [the audience] brings to the event" (1989: 82). Carlson was writing in opposition to much theatre scholarship at this time, which was overly literary and relied heavily on analysis of text instead of considering the live event as a whole. However, the assumption that traditional theatregoing is inherently passive remains persistent today, not least in the rhetoric of immersive theatremakers.

Bennett suggests that the business of buying a ticket, agreeing to watch the action, and so on constitutes a "social contract" (1997: 204) between spectator and production. This concept of the social contract can be used to interrogate the way immersive theatre promises (either implicitly in being so-called or explicitly in its promotional rhetoric) an "immersive experience"—an adventure of heightened emotions, of visceral, sensory intensity—before the production has even been attended. Much criticism of immersive theatre comes about in response to a perceived gap between the promise of experience implicit in calling a production "immersive" and the reality of physical pragmatics in the space: a fundamentally *dishonest* social contract. Hence, Worthen comments negatively on ushers who "intervene to police the spectacle" (2012: 95) and Shaughnessy suggests that

> [the] rigorous and sometimes coercive, stewarding, or policing, of the behaviour of participants in immersive performances means that their freedom of manoeuvre can be quite severely restricted, their range of interactive possibilities relatively limited, and their freedoms more rhetorical than real. (2012: n.p.)

The pragmatic necessities of immersive theatre get in the way of the promised pleasures of immersive experience. For Goode this is a gap with damning political implications:

> The most immersive theatre now being made—or the most interactive, or that in which the audience is most mobile, or that in which actors and audience most concertedly share the same "space"—may very well in the

> event replicate and even reinforce the power structures of "conventional" theatre; it may offer carefully crafted simulations of freedom and power-sharing that, once tested at their borders, turn out to be the most disappointing apparitions. Indeed, it's these supposedly free-range experiences that often have to operate under conditions secured by extremely precise and accurate control mechanisms in order to achieve the audience's sense of fluency in movement and curiosity. (2015: 223)

Any meaningful distinction between "immersive" and "traditional" theatre dissolves: both forms can replicate the flattening conservatism of Brook's "Deadly Theatre."

> … it would be a mistake to imagine that [Deadly Theatre] moribundity is the sole preserve of the "traditional" fourth-wall narrative play, drooping under hot lights and cumbersome costumes and blocked to death. The amount of executive control and hypernaturalistic detail required by some immersive theatre productions is not only deadly in itself but flashily deceitful in the simulation of liveness it sells (far from cheaply) to its flattered audiences, who are no more creatively or meaningfully exploring the syntax and parameters of their freedom than are bored frightened teenagers drinking themselves daft in a city centre precinct on a Friday night. (Goode 2015: 284)

The dishonesty of the social contract, framed here as inherent to immersive theatre's form, amounts to a betrayal of its audiences from which it seems difficult to recover.

Bennett's "Theatre Audiences, Redux" (2006) identifies a sociological turn in theatre and performance since 1997's publication of *Theatre Audiences*, and an increasing interest in the field in using methodologies from the social sciences. However, she suggests the most significant advances in audience studies continue to occur outside of academic research. Studies conducted by marketing departments or audience research reports by government bodies are where any real attempt to understand an audience can be found: "the audience has become an important object of study, not necessarily or even frequently motivated by the discourses of theatre studies, nor by our theatre history making, but by the economic realities of the cultural industries" (226). Bennett notes that "The study of audiences has also reminded the theatre scholar of his or her own implication in the production-reception framework" (226). The situatedness of the writer is of particular interest in this project, as the tension between the absent idealised spectator for whom the shows are created, and the individual actual participants, is important to bear in mind when studying immersive performance and the creation of immersive experience.

Knowles (2004), Tulloch (2005) and Reason (2006) express an awareness of the need to include audience response, rather than relying only on theatrical reviews, to build up an idea of a production's theatrical effects. Tulloch has also written on television fan audiences (Jenkins and Tulloch 1995), and his study of audience response(s) to the theatrical event (2005) bridges a gap between these two fields with different histories of audience research: discussing audiences from the theoretical perspective of theatre studies and drawing on methodologies from cultural and media studies such as focus groups and individual case studies. Reason (2010) also uses sociological methods such as interviews to obtain primary data, aiding a discussion of the theoretical theatrical event with specific details from audience members. Megson and Reinelt (2016) undertake empirical audience research into audience value and Dinesh's (2016) qualitative experiment contrasted the effects of an "immersive" production with a more "conventional" one. This book has a similarly twinned approach of primary data and theoretical concepts (the SPaR model). While discussions draw on my own presence at Punchdrunk rehearsals and performances, any personal readings and responses are not intended to be definitive but to provide a focus for discussing how *immersive experience* manifests in relation to the three main themes of this book.

An interesting recent approach to immersion in theatre is the "cognitive turn" identified in McConachie and Hart (2006). McConachie's cognitive approach to theatre audiences argues for "conceptual blending as the cognitive basis of spectating" (2008: 18). This book proposes a definition of immersive experience that is strongly linked to an awareness of boundaries. Although I do not draw on cognitive studies directly, *conceptual blending* (discussed in more detail in the section on immersion later in this chapter) is useful for demonstrating immersive experience as a state that is able to be aware of its boundaries and forgetful of them at the same time. Immersive experience can be defined as a sensation of complete engagement to the point of forgetting anything outside the immediate moment: "…we never want anything to happen that breaks the spell. If they [the audience] suddenly remember they're in London in 2007, then we've failed" (Barrett in Gardner 2007a: n.p.). This book proposes a more nuanced definition of immersive experience that is founded on an awareness of their boundaries and can exist in the interplay between the "spell" of the performance and the reality of "London in 2007."

Many concepts familiar to drama—including doubling and empathy in the business of spectating—when seen through the lens of cognitive science, are given a neurological basis and, through it, an evolutionary purpose:

> Our muscular, chemical, and neurological responses to others' emotions are often so small that they escape conscious recognition, but they can have a significant impact on our behaviour. In other words, evolution has equipped us to attune our bodies to the emotions of other people; this basis for our sociality as a species is inherited and embodied. Embodying other's emotions produces emotions in us, even if the situation is an imagined or fictitious one. (McConachie 2008: 67)

This reading of emotional empathy defines theatrical spectatorship as a set of embodied cognitive processes. Bogart also offers a description of theatrical spectatorship that blends cognitive activity with emotional/visceral affect:

> [Affect is defined as] the thrill of being in the presence of actors who are radiantly experiencing the present moment [...] Affect means "feeling associated with action." Our blood rushes faster, our mirror neurons spike new synaptic activity throughout our bodies, adrenalin courses throughout the system [...] This visceral experience, one of the leading attributes of all encounters with art, is a large part of why we bother to engage with art in the first place. The increased adrenalin resulting from the experience sharpens the mind and focuses the attention. (in Hurley 2010: xii).

And a similar conflation of the physical and the emotional—the form and the effect—can be found in the way immersive theatre is framed by makers. Describing the questions and considerations that led to the creation of Punchdrunk and informed its early productions, Barrett suggests that the physically *immersive* shape of a show is connected to the emotional *immersive* experience of it, and that the manipulation of environment and space results in emotional (cognitive, even) responses in an audience member:

How can I make theatre dangerous again? How can we take an audience out of their comfort zone and put them in a space that's charged, that's got no safety net, and so that suddenly they're adrenalin-fuelled and their synapses are firing and they receive everything tenfold so the theatrical experience can be better received and a show can be higher impact – so we started taking the action outside of theatres and taking it into empty buildings [...] and suddenly an audience is learning on the trot, they're living it, they're in it, and it resonates in a deeper place. (2014: talk at "Experience Economy" Remix Summit)

Many of the atmospheric and spatial trademarks of Punchdrunk's immersive form came about from experiments in creating the sensation of a very particular audience experience. Running throughout this book is the contention that immersive experience in an audience member is something that can be constructed, allowed for, and/or facilitated by theatre productions but that can never be guaranteed. Cognitive behaviour is part of theatrical experience, and in the quote above they have a direct relationship. A problem with perceiving these aspects as being so closely linked is it prevents an approach towards immersive experience as a construct that is the product of makers' choices. An analysis of a cognitive studies approach to empathy will illustrate the difference.

Krasner's "Empathy and Theatre" suggests that audiences need to have an understanding of the story or world of a performance, and to have suitably focused their attention on it, before any empathy occurs (2006: 257). McConachie suggests Krasner is conflating empathy with understanding, compassion and sympathy: "Spectators do not wait to deploy empathy, but engage it unconsciously right from the start of every performance to help them figure out where to focus their attention, who these characters are, and what their story is about. Empathy is a proactive search engine that is always ready to engage intentional onstage action and mirror it for meaning" (2008: 72). McConachie's approach is extremely useful for considering the cognitive functions that occur in theatre spectatorship. But from the perspective my definition of immersive experience, what Krasner is pointing out are *barriers to immersion*. Barriers to immersion are discussed in more detail later (in the section on immersion in computer games later in this chapter): simply put, they are aspects that might manifest in either the content or form of a work, that must be overcome to allow for immersive experience. Krasner's suggestion is therefore useful for conceptualising immersive experience as a series of graded states which must overcome various barriers in order to create and then maintain that state. Drawing on these models, rather than the immediate unconscious engagement of cognitive science, also allows immersive experience to be considered from the perspective of artists who seek to create work that enables or facilitates certain experiences or responses in their audiences. Auslander (1999) argues that the live moment is still ultimately mediatised: McConachie rightly points out that this perspective understands the two to be a binary, whereas "live" and "mediated" actually exist on a continuum, not a dichotomy—a live singer wearing a microphone is both live and mediated (2008: 209). Similarly, this book argues for a definition of immersive experience existing as a series of graded states rather than a felt/not-felt binary. Applying cognitive studies to theatrical experience reminds us that empathy and emotional engagement are processes that are rooted in embodied consciousness. However, considering immersive experience from this perspective risks a reductive or essentialist analysis that defines any experience as immersive if it results in the right kind or amount of cognitive activity. This book is interested in how immersive experience is situated in theatrical production, rather than how it physically manifests in the brain.

The quotation from Brook that began this section placed human connection as central to spectatorship and, via spectatorship, to theatrical experience itself. However audience members in immersive productions may often find themselves alone, in spaces empty of both performers and fellow spectators. In a discussion of audience experience and scenography in immersive space, McKinney describes the scenography of Punchdrunk as one that "challenges and problematizes notions of audience, who are no longer distant spectators of images and pictures that are laid out before them." When considering work with immersive/participatory scenography it is necessary "to consider both the audience as a collective entity and the responses of individual spectators within those audiences" (2012: 221). The tension between considering audiences as a whole group and a collection of individuals has long been identified in audience studies (Bennett 1997) but this arguably becomes even truer in the case of immersive forms, where audience members encounter different moments at different times and literally see the same moments from different perspectives. Nield's "The Rise of the Character Named Spectator" (2008) draws on this paradox by combining the results of a small number of interviews into the creation of a single voice that speaks of varying experiences within Punchdrunk's *The Masque of the Red Death*. Nield's method illustrates the possible tension between talking about the effect of a performance on an absent "idealised spectator" and considering individual responses to immersive work through interview or survey. From the perspective of creating work, immersive shows—like any other form of work—are created without exact knowledge of audience movement or reaction. This book considers the creation of immersive experience for the absent idealised spectator, which is how productions are conceived, designed and rehearsed; but my approach is also aware of the ways individual experiences change and vary. Personal experiences are used to illustrate but not to represent the "correct" response to being in a Punchdrunk space. McKinney also suggests that kinaesthetic empathy might be useful for considering the empty room, since "empathy, stimulated by kinaesthetic perception, might arise between spectators and scenographic objects as well" (2012: 225).

When there are performers in the room, it is possible they will be dancing. Maxine Doyle's distinctive choreography has appeared in many Punchdrunk shows and is a valuable part of the company's aesthetic. A helpful recent study considering audience methodologies in the field of dance is Reynolds and Reason's *Kinesthetic Empathy in Creative and Cultural Practices* (2012), which draws on the cognitive turn in performance studies to consider how performance (and dance in particular) makes meaning for spectators. Reynolds (2012: 121–136) apply kinaesthetic empathy to spectatorship, emotion and affect when watching dance, coining the phrase "the dance's body" to signify "a body that is not identified with a fixed subject position of either performer or spectator, but which is both 'here' and 'there', invested as subject and object in the shared materiality and affective flow of choreographed movement" (123). Kinesthetic empathy is useful for considering immersive experience in interactions that are not naturalistic one-on-ones (where the audience member may more explicitly participate), but spectatorship in the presence of contemporary dance.

Approaches to Audience: Film, Television and Cultural Studies

As mentioned previously, some scholars have commented on a failure in theatre studies to discuss audiences with any great degree of rigour or trust. Abercrombie and Longhurst (1998) identify a sociological turn in audience studies, proposing it is no longer appropriate to think of an audience as one body, but as a diffuse entity made up of individuals. Media and cultural studies approach audience research from a sociological perspective: about television audiences (Gorton 2009; Seiter 1999); film audiences (Jancovich et al. 2003; Stafford 2007; Staiger 2000); theatre audiences (Ruddock 2007); ethnographic studies of media audiences (Moores 1993; Nightingale and Ross 2003; Nightingale 2011); historical studies of general trends across theatre and television (Butsch 2000; Spigel 1992); and cultural studies on new media audiences and digital technologies (Ang 1991; Jenkins 2008). The particular audience type of the fan has been considered mainly in regard to film and television (Jenkins 1992, 2012) but can be applicable to theatre. This highly engaged demographic within a wider audience base suggests the development of certain skill sets for experiencing immersive theatre—a large community of Punchdrunk fans compare stories of repeated visits, one-on-ones and strategy, as well as jointly compiling technical and logistical specifications of the shows and producing increasingly sophisticated readings of a show's world, story(s) and characters. Fan activity can lead to creativity and engagement, but the "tiered" system of spectatorship that emerges can be a troubling one. Alston (2016a) suggests the idea of the "skilled" immersive theatre spectator leads to the creation of—and the encouragement or celebration of—an entrepreneurial instinct for experiencing immersive work that is worryingly in line with the creation and celebration of neoliberal value; Goode describes "immersive choose-your-own-adventures shows that penalise those with less confidence or less mobility or who simply aren't accustomed to a sense of access-all-areas entitlement" (2015: 283).

A valuable approach to interviewing individual audience members is the process described in Barker and Mathijis's *Watching the Lord of the Rings* (2007), based on data collected from nearly 25,000 questionnaires across twenty countries since 2001 (the year the first film in the trilogy was released). Barker and Mathijis write at length about the challenges of designing a questionnaire that would reveal what they wanted to know (the question of what exactly they wanted to know, of course, requiring research in itself). Larger concepts such as the audience's relationship to Tolkien, or the relationship between the books, film and the fantasy genre, were brought out by smaller, more direct questions. From these answers it became possible to identify patterns or common assumptions running across the data. Apart from the sheer numbers of people in the study, this approach to the data protected against the temptation to apply the reaction of an individual to a whole group, or to place too much importance on a single piece of evidence.

Bishop's *Artificial Hells* (2011) considers participatory art in the United States and gives an historical overview of socially engaged practice over the second half of the twentieth century. Its focus is on "art that uses people as its medium" (39), drawing on theatre and performance to consider the political and social implications of spectating in art galleries. Bishop notes the "unhelpful binary" of active/passive spectatorship that has developed regarding participatory artwork; she also notes a more recent development of a further binary—"the false polarity of 'bad' singular authorship and 'good' collective authorship" (8). This book is interested in troubling the binaries of immersive/not-immersive experience and passivity/activity within immersive environments. Bishop also describes the relationship between participatory performance and spectacle: "Far from being oppositional to spectacle, participation has now entirely merged with it" (277). This idea has similarities to the suggestion that audience members in an immersive production contribute towards creating the spectacle themselves: that "they become part of the scenography" (Barrett in Machon 2013: 160). Studies of spectatorship in immersive/participatory theatre must include responses to the other spectators, participants or performers who are in the room.

A useful model of the audience member/performer relationship can be developed from Chatman's influential study of *Narrative Structure in Fiction and Film*. Rather than a binary of writer/reader or narrator/narratee, Chatman suggests a continuum: real author; implied author; narrator; real reader; implied reader; narratee (1978: 147). Considering the "real" reader as an agent who is possibly overlapping but fundamentally separate from the "implied" reader enables a more nuanced discussion of the aims and achievements of any given text. The "absent idealised spectator" of a theatrical performance fulfils the same function as the "implied reader" of a text. A production—as a text—creates its own implied reader/idealised spectator. The *real* reader/spectator then enters and forms their own relationship with and response to the work. Tension may occur when the reader/spectator senses a gap between what is implied by, what appears to be required by, the work and what the real reader/spectator is actually able or willing to offer. A thread of enquiry running throughout this book is whether a certain kind of ideal spectator is implicitly prioritised by immersive performance (a spectator who is empowered, free, totally engaged) and whether this idealised spectator might be at odds with another kind of spectator that is actually preferred by the work (one who willingly follows its many unspoken rules).

The idealised spectator model is useful for identifying a production's implicit aims, and contrast with real audience experience is helpful. Postlewait's "twelve cruxes" (2009: 225) for theatre historians serve as a reminder of potential problems when attempting to reconstruct or describe a performance that happened in the past. Postlewait draws on Sauter's study of *The Theatrical Event* (2000), emphasising the importance of spectator response: "All too often, when we reconstruct performance events, we ignore the ways that various spectators respond to theatrical events" (Postlewait 2009: 227). It is also important to consider the political nature of documented performance, which will privilege certain sources over others. Any reviewer brings an ideological background as well as an artistic perspective to an analysis; and certain historical processes may result in identifying one viewpoint as definitive over others that come to be considered less informed or reliable. Regarding the politics of considering spectator response, Postlewait states:

> we must not only analyse the sources and establish the facts but also reflect upon the assumptions and methods that lead us to set up certain kinds of evidence to support our arguments. [...] For theatre events we need to investigate the agents, the world, the artistic heritage, and the receptions. We need to move beyond basic binaries in order to see how an event is triangulated among these four contributing factors. (2009: 268)

Sauter also argues for performance to be understood as a reciprocal exchange between performer and spectator:

> If the spectator is not reduced to a consumer of theatrical productions, but is seen as an active participant in a theatrical event, then the relationship between the agent on stage and the beholder in the auditorium can be understood to be reciprocal. (2012: 173)

In the context of immersive theatre, it is all too possible to describe only the idealised spectator implied by the work, resulting in either an uncritically celebratory reading of the form and its potentials or an equally uncritical damnation of its perceived limitations or flaws. A purely hypothetical audience member becomes the passive recipient of a series of assumptions about what immersion is like. Immersive experience is not guaranteed by certain performance types or atmospheres and an audience member is not automatically active and empowered as soon as they step into an immersive space. Immersive experience is a series of graded states that an audience member may well remain in control of: the potentially problematic consequences of the balance of power tipping too much in the favour of a theatremaker or performer are another reason to theorise the relationship as reciprocal.

Immersive was initially used primarily in the context of developments in technology, and in particular to VR environments where the spectator is instantly "immersed" in a virtual/fictional world (McKenzie 1994; Moser and McLeod 1996). Later the term was used in the context of museums (Lorentz 2007; Griffiths 2008), and this usage begins to reflect what is meant in many contemporary references to *immersive*-shaped theatre: Griffiths describes how "one feels enveloped in immersive spaces and strangely affected by a strong sense of the otherness of the virtual world one has entered, *neither fully lost in the experience nor completely in the here and now*" (3; my emphasis). Kershaw uses *immersive* to refer to the aesthetics of contemporary performance, in particular tracing a historical antecedent of "immersive participation created by the post-war, international avant-garde" (1999: 24). Fischer-Lichte describes a long history of immersive practice, arguing that current conceptions of audiences do not sit well with a passive/active model for spectatorship: "From today's vantage point there is no such thing as a passive spectator" (2016: 177). In contemporary usage, *immersive* can be used to refer to digital/VR technologies in performance (Dixon 2007) or as an aural phenomenon (Dyson 2009), in both of these contexts closely related to the concept of *presence*. However as a broader term, *immersive* is generally used in the sense Griffiths describes previously, to refer to a form or genre of theatrical work characterised by audience movement within a structural geography that resembles a combination of promenade performance and art installation (Nield 2008; Machon 2007, 2013; Shaughnessy 2012; White 2009, 2013; Purcell 2013). *Immersive* also refers to the possible sensations—visceral, emotional—of experiencing this kind of theatre:

> Anxiety and apprehension are central to many of the effects and affects evoked by participatory performance [...] For example, the large-scale installations organized by Punchdrunk are designed to test the audience's nerves. (Freshwater 2009: 65)

White recognises the term *immersive* has implications for both the setup of a physical space and the experience of a visceral sensation:

> the suggestion of being inside that comes with the idea of the immersive has resonances with the experience of being able to take action within the work, and with the changed point of view that is gained through the experience that I suggest are the special characteristics of audience participation. To be inside the work, not just inside its physical and temporal space but inside it as an aesthetic, affective, phenomenological entity gives a different aspect to the idea of a point of view, and of action. (2013: 16–17)

It is helpful to maintain the distinction between a form of theatre and the experience that may be facilitated by that form of theatre.

As briefly mentioned previously, the concept of *presence* is often used alongside *immersion*. I propose a distinction between *immersive experience* and *presence* in order to focus on the former. *Presence* (as used in Giannachi and Kaye 2011; Giannachi et al. 2012) is a particularly useful concept when considering VR experience (Spagnolli and Gamberini 2002) and multimedia/hybrid environments (Klich and Scheer 2012). Experiences of presence are "closely tied to a state of liminality, and so to relationships and acts between the live, the mediated and the simulated" (Giannachi and Kaye, *Performing Presence* 2011: 25). Birringer (2006) differentiates between interactive and immersive environments on the basis of the relationship between physical spectator/participant/artist and use of digital media: interactive environments are "based on sensors and motion tracking, and an evolving dialectic between artificial ecosystem and human agents"; immersive environments are "Virtual Reality based, e.g. the 'Cave' or panoramic installations that integrate the body, via stereoscopic devices, into the polysensual illusion of moving through space" (in Giannachi and Stewart 2006: 307). *Immersion* in the context of VR/hybrid environment implies the sensation of being physically surrounded, although not (necessarily) the sensation of being mentally/emotionally engaged. An explanation of the difference between presence and immersion in computer games (where the player is not physically surrounded, as they are in VR) offers a useful distinction.

Presence is relatively easy to achieve in VR/immersive theatre: the player/spectator is surrounded by the environment as soon as the technology is enabled/they enter the space. Immersive *experience* is harder to achieve, and trickier to define. A feeling of "being there," of "feeling/

reacting *as if you are there*," is characteristic of being highly immersed in a computer game: as the player is physically distant from the screen, such responses indicate high levels of engagement. That is why, in the context of computer games, the two concepts can be totally conflated: "total immersion is presence" (Brown and Cairns 2004: 3; McMahan 2003). However, Fischer-Lichte notes that the sensation of "being there" is characteristic only of a *weak* level of presence in the context of performance, where "being here" is a relatively easy state to achieve. The spectator and performer share the same space; presence is merely the act of being present for the gaze of another. *Strong* presence in this context describes what this book takes to be a key aspect of immersive experience: strong presence is "the actor's ability to occupy and command space and to attract the spectators' undivided attention. [...] The spectators sense that the actor is present in an unusually intense way, granting them, in turn, the intense sensation of themselves as present. To them, *presence occurs as an intense experience of presentness*" (Fischer-Lichte in Giannachi, Kaye and Shanks 2012: 108–109; my emphasis). *Presence* here begins to overlap with *stage presence*, and certainly, hidden moments of intimacy with a highly charismatic performer might employ this as a source of power to create immersive experience (see Gordon 2013 for intimacy in Punchdrunk; Goodall 2008 for stage presence and charisma in performance history.) An "intense experience of presentness" may describe immersive experience, and immersion and presence are closely related concepts: however, immersive experience is not the automatic result of presence—"being there" may result in a weak sensation of presence but not necessarily a highly engaged and energised sensation of visceral connection to the work.

Approaches to Audience: Punchdrunk and Immersive Theatre

Shaughnessy proposes that "the legacy of immersive performance extends back to the communal interactive experimentation of the 1960s avant-garde" (2012: n.p.), a similar context to Kershaw's use of the term (1999: 195–199). This book draws on lineage identified by Griffiths (2008) and Aronson (2012) who trace a longer history to immersion as a practice. Machon proposes a definition of immersive theatres as a range of work that "prioritises human contact" (2013: xvi), and excludes virtual art and games studies (a field which encompasses pervasive gaming as well as computer games). While I agree that virtual art's use of concepts such as *presence* can complicate a discussion of immersive experience as a visceral feeling, the possibility for reading immersive productions as games and drawing on developments in the study of games allows for *immersion* to be considered as both a sensation experienced by spectators and something crafted and facilitated by makers.

Punchdrunk's convention of masking audience members is a useful focus for illustrating current critical approaches to the company. They are tools of anonymity (White 2009) or visual design (Machon [2007] suggests there is a sculptural element to their visual and physical presence in the space). Freshwater suggests the masks have a threefold effect: they "distinguish [audience members] from the performers, hide their responses, and give them a ghostly anonymity" (2009: 66). Nield (2008) interrogates the idea of freedom assumed to be provided by the mask, asking whether the "enforced anonymity" created by the mask might "perhaps not be merely to give the audience the illusion of freedom? Does it not also continue to protect the theatre from having to see us seeing it?" (534). Citing Ridout's discussion of spectator embarrassment (2006), Nield concludes that "without the protective apparatus of characterisation, rehearsal, fictive otherness, perhaps we [the character named Spectator] risk staring into the black hole of the theatre itself, mute, stage-affrighted, awaking to the actor's nightmare of being on the stage, and not knowing the play" (535). The apparent freedoms in the interplay between audience presence and anonymity in immersive space come with a risk of embarrassment or awkwardness for audience members who find themselves uncomfortable, unwilling or otherwise unable to "play along." White's study of anonymity (2005) combines primary data (descriptions of individual experience and interviews with others) with theoretical considerations of voyeurism and freedom. As the masking of audience members has already been given considerable critical attention, this book is broadly concerned with other constructions of immersive experience; remaining highly relevant is the risk of embarrassment or awkwardness, and the role or consequences of anonymity.

Gordon (2013) questions assumptions about the masked spectator as a means towards audience emancipation in her consideration of intimacy and voyeurism in Punchdrunk's *Sleep No More* by drawing a comparison to sex shows. Both are sites of performance where rules of intimacy might be negotiated between the players. The spectator-performer dynamic in *Sleep No More* is informed by policed spectator behaviour (the audiences are told the rules upon entry, with certain behaviours/

actions clearly banned) and promises of further intimacy (one-on-ones with the performers) that reward the "right" behaviour. This dynamic invites comparison to gentlemen's clubs, and Gordon argues that *Sleep No More* creates a form of interactivity that emphasises spectator "neediness" that demands performer attention over any notions of an emancipated journey through the production space. Gordon points to the constantly sexual nature of the dancers' choreography and the way one-on-ones invariably include a kiss or other contact. The masks, far from freeing a spectator, serve to make the (strict, non-negotiable) rules of engagement with the performers more obvious. To Gordon, the mask is a mobile fourth wall that results in a clearly delineated spectator's gaze, likely to be compromised by voyeurism or discomfort. While for White and Machon the mask is a fundamentally emancipatory innovation, to Gordon the mask perpetuates oppressive frameworks by facilitating a patriarchal gaze above all others. Like Gordon, Maples (2016) found the seduction of *The Drowned Man* performative: Punchdrunk failed to provide the promised interconnectedness and intimacy by placing the spectator in a position as an "erotic voyeur," and by facilitating a sense of competition by the rarity and metaphor of "reward" provided by the one-on-ones. For Zaiontz (2014), the consumptive gaze of one-on-ones in *The Drowned Man* resulted in a competitive, self-entitled or narcissistic form of spectatorship.

The previously mentioned examples of varying approaches to the masked spectator demonstrate how any given aspect of a Punchdrunk production can be seen as either facilitating or troubling conventional assumptions about immersive experience. A strand of enquiry throughout this book is interested in the claims made for immersive experience and how it might be constituted. That there might be a gap between what is claimed for immersive experience and what might actually occur.

Histories of immersive theatre often consider the political implications of the form. White places contemporary interactive/one-to-one performance alongside social and applied theatres, citing theatre-in-education and pantomime as less controversial modes that also use audience participation (2013). While Punchdrunk Enrichment's socially engaged projects might be considered from the perspectives of imagination and education (the children's shows) or empowerment and engagement (the community shows), the definition of immersive experience running through their larger productions might seem entirely oppositional to the aware, distanced, critical and decisive mindset behind the engagement of, for example, a Theatre of the Oppressed spect-actor. The wider political consequences of what Kershaw calls "submission to sensory deprivation" in immersive participatory performance: "a grasp of virtual community that radically engages with the growth of global risk in the contemporary world" (1999: 24), is not, broadly speaking, a part of current conceptions of immersive theatre, which are concerned more with the individual. Purcell describes the "unashamedly escapist ends" of Punchdrunk's immersive environments (2013: 135), and Alston (2016a) draws parallels with the values of capitalist neoliberalism in this individualist ethos. The effect(s) of immersion, when related to empowerment or freedom, are almost always defined in the context of the individual: "you'll have a better time when you're fighting for yourself" (Barrett 2014). Due to the scope required for such a wider study, this book is unable to directly engage with theatrical forms that use conventions of interactivity and participation for more explicitly political ends, such as a participant in a Boal workshop or a reader of Brechtian Gestus, but this trajectory of enquiry I hope will continue elsewhere.

Drawing on the influential feminist film reading of Ubersfeld (1982), who notes that a spectator cannot touch the object of desire in film and the pleasure of spectatorship is therefore characterised by an interplay of desire and frustration, Bennett proposes that "The spectator cannot experience pleasure without experiencing its limits" (1997: 73). This conception of the spectator-performer/performance relationship provides a useful framework for considering any theatrical experience as a state with rigidly defined boundaries. The intensity of immersive experience is connected to its ephemerality: these boundaries in Ubersfeld and Bennett are linked to gender, desire and patriarchal power in ways that allow for a more explicitly feminist reading of the spectator-performer relationship. Boundaries are also connected to form. Rigidly defined temporal and spatial boundaries of theatre and film allow for an experience to be both intense and temporary. Immersive experience is an intense state defined by a somewhat paradoxical awareness of the finite nature of that state.

The following section considers approaches to *immersion* in fields outside of theatre and performance—namely cognitive science, philosophical aesthetics (the sublime and the "revered gaze") and computer games—to build a working definition of immersive experience that will be used throughout the book. Computer game studies in particular has seen a great amount of research into characteristics of immersion, providing a number of concepts that allow for a more nuanced definition of immersion than the felt/not-felt binary of VR worlds or the conflation of space and sensation—the conflation of form and effect—that potentially limits a characterisation of the processes and potentials of immersive theatre.

APPROACHES TO IMMERSIVE EXPERIENCE

> Immersion *noun* [mass noun] (1) the action of immersing someone or something in a liquid: *his back was still raw from* **immersion** *in the icy Atlantic sea*; baptism by immersing a person bodily (but not necessarily completely in water. (2) deep mental involvement in something: *a week's* ***immersion*** *in the culinary heritage of Puglia*; a method of teaching a foreign language by the exclusive use of that language: *as a teacher she advocates learning by immersion*. [as modifier]: an immersion school. (Origin: late 15th century: from late Latin immersion (n-), from immergere "dip into" [*Oxford English Dictionary*])

The definitions in this list fit with a common understanding of what it is to experience immersive theatre: audience members inhabiting—being physically surrounded by—the space of performance; and the suggestion of an overwhelming or total sensation of being enclosed. But this section begins with the dictionary because the word's etymology might also suggest *why* the experience is described as being potentially so overwhelming, or considered particularly special or desirable.

Immersion is rooted in the ritual of baptism, referring to being bodily put into water. It is a process that results in a change to the person being immersed: the obvious physical change of becoming wetter than you were before but also, and primarily, a symbolic social transformation—the reason the ritual is conducted. Immersion is an intense, temporary experience, with spatial and temporal boundaries that are strongly defined and must be adhered to. Immersive experience is both physically and mentally all-encompassing, but its temporary state is also a vital part of its defining quality. Leaving a state of immersion is as distinct and deliberate as going in. You go in; and you come out, *changed*.

In educational studies *immersion* is a successful pedagogical approach to learning new languages, characterised by efficiency and effectiveness (Bernhardt 1992; Mougeon et al. 2010; Tedick et al. 2011; Muhammad 2014 promises to teach readers *How to Get Fluent in Any Language with Immersion*). Immersive experience can be characterised as initially disorientating, and in the baptism context remains disorientating due to its brevity. However, in the immersive classroom context, once the disorientation has passed and the rules of the new environment begin to be mastered, the experience is stronger and more effective than non-immersive learning, and the after-effects are visible and long-lasting.

These two contexts—the baptism and the classroom—are useful to outline at the outset of this section as they suggest a general physical relationship between the participant and the space of the experience (suddenly surrounded by) as well as hinting at the sensation of the experience itself (overwhelming and disorientating—either continually or only initially, either way resulting in a new and rewarding sense of change or achievement over challenge). The importance of boundaries to immersive experience is also important in these contexts and is worth bearing in mind throughout a discussion of immersion in theatre. Its potential visceral impact is affected by this quality of its occurring in finite space and time. Numbering the previously outlined steps: (1) *you go in*; (2) *you come out*; (3) *changed*, theatre might be called immersive in shape if it is step (1) followed by (2). Immersive *experience* is what happens between steps (1) and (2) that results in step (3). Unpicking what exactly that is, and how it might be facilitated, framed and constituted—and the potential consequences for both audience members and makers—is the focus of this book. Although *immersion* can be used to describe a physical situation, immersive(-shaped) theatre and immersive experience are (related, but) different aspects of theatrical experience that do not guarantee each other. This discussion of existing uses of *immersion* emphasises the phenomenon as a psychological state. In particular, I am interested in how peak experience manifests in behaviour, rather than a purely cognitive perspective of how the brain responds to stimulus.

Approaches to Immersive Experience: Immersion and Cognition

The psychologist Mihaly Csikszentmihalyi uses peak experience or "flow" to describe optimal experience in psychology (1988, 1990) and aesthetics (Csikszentmihalyi and Robinson 1990), discussing how it can be developed for greater happiness and creativity (1990, 1996). Being mentally absorbed in an activity is a defining feature of the state.

Also called "optimal performance" or "peak experience," *flow* is a situation, experience or activity which is enjoyable and challenging: enjoyable *because* challenging. When in flow, the challenge of an activity is equal to a person's (sense of their) skill to match it. Constant feedback and a feeling of control are central to the experience. A sense of clear, attainable goals is also important, but in true flow these goals (the completed canvas, for example, or reaching the top of the mountain) are only excuses to engage in the activity for its own sake. Activities that create flow are undertaken primarily because they provide pleasure in and of themselves. When an experience is optimal:

1. there are clear goals every step of the way
2. there is immediate feedback for one's actions
3. there is a balance between challenge and skills
4. action and awareness are merged
5. distractions are excluded from consciousness
6. there is no worry of failure
7. self-consciousness disappears
8. the sense of time becomes distorted
9. the activity becomes autotelic i.e. performed for its own sake
  (Csikszentmihalyi 1996: 110–3)

Logan suggests this list could be reduced to three: getting caught up in what one is doing; controlling what is happening; and creating variety and stimulation so as to make the activity novel and challenging enough to stay caught up in it (in Csikszentmihalyi 1988: 172). Another important distinction to make about flow is that it does not necessarily mean enjoyment. Rather, the experience is so fulfilling enjoyment does not figure, just as failure does not: satisfaction is felt afterwards, as one reflects retrospectively on the creative experience of being "in the flow." Peak psychological experience is all about being fully in the moment; becoming so immersed in an experience or an activity, other concerns become less important than the task at hand or even seem to disappear completely.

Aesthetic experience itself can also be coded as a "skill" that can be acquired and developed in complexity over time (Csikszentmihalyi and Robinson 1990) and appreciation of art can be developed and refined by those who enjoy the activity. This concept of experience as "skill" is a useful model to consider in regard to immersive theatre. The idea that there is no "wrong way" to experience a production becomes problematic if there is also an implicit need to work towards experiencing aesthetic "flow" by being able to match a challenge or work towards a clearly defined goal. An immersive production's (unspoken or implied) rules might become hypervisible for audience members who sense these rules need to be discovered and followed to have the better experience, while frequent attendees become "experts" of immersive theatre. This has consequences for theatremakers and other audience members who by default must be missing out by lacking the time/ability/motivation to master the necessary "skills" to follow the rules of engagement. What these rules are taken to be in turn suggests what is being *valued* in a piece of immersive theatre.

Drawing on Varela et al. (1993), Lakoff and Johnson (1999) apply cognitive psychology to creativity to argue that metaphors have structured thought and philosophy throughout history. Our understanding of the world comes from an "embodied realism" (1999: 74); our mental concepts of the world are necessarily linked to how our bodies have evolved. Cognitive psychology and philosophy demonstrate the link between physical and mental immersive states. The two can be considered separately while they also inform each other and each might be crafted to facilitate the other.

McConachie and Hart (2006) identify *conceptual blending* as a cognitive concept of particular relevance to theatre and performance. The theory is first put forward in Turner and Fauconnier (2003), who use theatrical production as an example to describe mental processing. Conceptual blending is a contemporary refinement of Coleridge's *willing suspension of disbelief*, and it provides a way of understanding that inherent doubleness of theatrical representation: a fictional world existing alongside the real one. McConachie offers a helpful definition: "to describe this process at its most fundamental level, when an actor plays a character, she is able to blend a concept of herself with a concept of the character to be played" (2013: 20). Citing Eversmann's finding that theatregoers enjoyed "losing oneself in the world of the stage, of forgetting everyday reality" (2004: 155), McConachie suggests that "from a cognitive point of view, 'losing oneself' in the fiction of a play is impossible without blending and empathising" (2013: 55).

The theory of conceptual blending also questions the idea of a spectator's *willingness* in the process of suspending their disbelief. A spectator consciously deciding to allow themselves to believe in the fictional dynamics of a theatrical production contradicts that very belief, by their having to acknowledge the "outside" in order to think it away.

Conceptual blending is the creation of an extra, additional space that actors and audience share. Productions that are especially playful with the actor-character relationship benefit from the theory of conceptual blending (McConachie 2008). The concept also complicates the idea of a distinction between the active and the passive audience member (McConachie and Hart 2006). This doubled metaphorical-and-bodily engagement can be a helpful approach to immersive theatre, emphasising the relationship between a spectator's physical presence within the work and the mental/emotional effects of experiencing that work. Conceptual blending offers a theory for how immersive experience might manifest as a "blend" of the real world (the audience members, the working performers, the set as the product of designers and craftspeople, the logistical rules of navigating the space) and the fictional environment of the production (i.e. reading the masked audience members as ghosts or voyeurs, following the relationships between characters).

Given that cognitive studies have implications for the study of how audiences engage with performance, it is interesting to return to Csikzentmihalyi's summary of optimal flow experience as being ultimately built around the active production of art. He suggests that the creative process is superior to the consumption of finished works: "It is exhilarating to build culture—to be an artist, a scientist, a thinker, or a doer. All too often, however, the joy of discovery fails to be communicated to young people, who turn instead to passive entertainment. But consuming culture is never as rewarding as producing it" (1996: 342). The return to this conservative (and somewhat ageist) binary of active production versus passive consumption contradicts Csikzentmihalyi's other suggestion that aesthetic experience can be a highly nuanced experience that builds in complexity over time (1990). The theory of conceptual blending troubles that binary by suggesting the experience of watching and responding to performance is a highly creative act, not just in terms of neural activity (although neuroscience could attest to this) but also in terms of the potential for emotional fulfilment and excitement. The sense of intense engagement experienced in a state of flow can be applied to the sensation of experiencing a piece of immersive theatre—however, to further trouble the active production/passive consumption binary, immersive experience is not an automatic sensation that occurs as soon as one steps into the performance space, but is instead a more nuanced and graded state that requires overcoming barriers to become fully engaged.

If immersive experience is a state of intense psychological engagement, immersive theatre is also, generally, concerned with the creation of a (usually large-scale) space that a spectator enters, one that is often scenographically rich and multisensory and emphasises the difference between the real world outside and the fictional world that has been painstakingly built within its walls. Rather than optimal psychological flow that emphasises engagement, challenge and skill, approaches to *immersion* from philosophical aesthetics incorporate the overwhelming, visceral sensation of sublime experience which might be characteristic of entering large-scale immersive theatrical environments.

Immersion and Philosophical Aesthetics: The Sublime and the "Revered Gaze"

The relationship between a reader and a written text is a site of immersive experience in Nell's study of the psychology of reading for pleasure (1988). Griffiths' *Shivers Down Your Spine* (2008) traces a history of the human compulsion to seek out immersive experience. Other studies proposing a long history of immersive experience include Smith's *The Total Work of Art: From Bayreuth to Cyberspace* (2007) and Grau's *Virtual Art: From Illusion to Immersion* (2003). These studies consider the immersive capabilities of art, providing the historical groundwork for a consideration of contemporary immersive aesthetics. Ryan provides a history of the relationship between visual art and immersion:

> The history of Western art has seen the rise and fall of immersive ideals, and their displacement, in the twentieth century, by an aesthetics of play and self-reflexivity that eventually produced the ideal of an active participation of the appreciator – reader, spectator, user – in the production of the text. This scenario affects both visual and literary art, though the immersive wave peaked earlier in painting than in literature. (2001: 2)

Grau considers immersion to be synonymous with presence, defining both as "an impression suggestive of 'being there'" (2003: 7) while recognising that immersion is not a felt/not-felt binary but a sensation existing as movement between states of varying intensity. Grau also acknowledges that, although critical distance is not mutually exclusive from emotional involvement, immersive work generally tends to suggest that it is—there is a trajectory in immersive work towards diminishing the desire/ability to adopt a critical distance, instead moving towards increasing a participant's psychological involvement:

> there is not a simple relationship of "either-or" between critical distance and immersion; the relations are multi-faceted, closely intertwined, dialectical, in part contradictory, and certainly highly dependent on the disposition of the observer. Immersion can be an intellectually stimulating process; however, in the present as in the past, in most cases immersion is mentally absorbing and a process, a change, a passage from one mental state to another. It is characterised by diminishing critical distance to what is shown and increasing emotional involvement in what is happening. (2003: 13)

Punchdrunk's theatrical environments self-describe as having a "cinematic level of detail," and long histories of immersion in art provide a useful way of historicising this claim, and its implied relationship to immersive experience. The level of detail in any immersive environment facilitates, but does not guarantee, immersive experience. Griffiths addresses the current ahistoricism of much new media scholarship by showing that "new" ideas of immersion and interactivity have historical precedents. Immersive work, *immersive* referring to both the shape and the sensation of experiencing that work, can be traced historically to nineteenth-century fine art panoramas, galleries and modern museum spaces (Grau 2003; Griffiths 2008), and finds contemporary parallels in the total (multisensory) immersion of a twentieth-century *Gesamtkunstwerk* or VR environment created by and/or experienced in cyberspace or a theme park (Smith 2007: 157–86). Griffiths' definition of immersive experience demonstrates how space and sensation have a reciprocal relationship while also being separate aspects. Reciprocity is also central to Sauter's conceptualisation of the theatrical event: "theatre manifests itself as an event which includes both the presentation of actions and the reactions of the spectators, who are present at the very moment of the creation. Together the actions and reactions constitute the theatrical event" (2000: 11). The interplay between space, sensation and spectator facilitates the lowering of barriers to immersive experience in a performance event.

Griffiths uses the term *immersive* to refer to "the sensation of entering a space that immediately identifies itself as somehow separate from the world and that eschews conventional modes of spectatorship in favour of a more bodily participation in the experience" (2008: 2). Immersive environments are characterised by "audience mobility around the viewing space" (1). The "revered gaze" is an effect brought about by immersive experience and results in physical change: head up and eyes and mouth open, as if the human body is overwhelmed by the attempt to take everything in.

Like Griffiths, Ryan (2001) is sceptical of ahistorical claims made by and about new media. The high realism of the nineteenth-century novel made for an immersive quality that interested readers of the time: they became emotionally invested in the fate of the characters and held in suspense by plot developments. Then, "as happened in the visual arts, immersion was brought down by a playful attitude towards the medium [...] Meaning came to be described as unstable, decentered, multiple, fluid, emergent—all concepts that have become hallmarks of postmodern thought" (Ryan 2001: 5). For Ryan, the interactive nature of virtual texts allows for a postmodern making of stories or meanings: for example hypertexts allow for non-chronological readings. Ryan is rightly sceptical about the notion of hypertextual navigation equalling an accession of the role of the reader to that of something approaching authorship, stating that "aesthetic pleasure, like political harmony, is a matter not of unbridled license but of controlled freedom" (9). This "controlled freedom" is similar to the "revered gaze" in that it implies an asymmetrical relationship between the level of agency and power in a spectator and in the maker or author of an immersive and/or interactive work. The tension between claims of audience empowerment, and the organisation and clear sense of authorship encoded in a production's own structural and logistical rules is where immersive experience is negotiated. Becoming "lost" or "immersed," in the context of the "revered gaze," means surrendering authority to a higher power.

Immersion, when described in these terms, is characterised by a diminishing of the spectator's ability to (or their desire to attempt to) form a distanced, critical response to something in favour of a more immediate, emotional, visceral reaction to the work. Such a response might seem ideal for a theatrical form which places an emphasis upon audience effect or experience. Overwhelming awe or other-worldliness that results in the revered gaze might be a suitable description of what much immersive theatre aims to achieve. There is, therefore, a tension between this effect and the idea of audience empowerment. If the central effect of sublime experience is the confounding of the senses, or, to go back to Griffiths' early example of the Gothic cathedral, to create "reverence" in the spectator in something bigger/higher/better than themselves—the revered gaze begins to sound like coercion or control rather than empowerment. How interactive an experience feels and how interactive it really is may be two very different things.

One approach to examining the tension between audience empowerment and the revered gaze is go back to the origins of the sublime in philosophical aesthetics. A definition of the term might appear self-defeating, for the best way the sublime can be described is indescribable. It is a sensation that resists attempts to put it into words: its power is to leave its describers unable to articulate. An object in nature is often the source, such as a mountain or the expanse of the ocean; the word might also refer to an ungraspable idea such as the number of stars in the universe, or an extreme of emotion like grief. The sublime occurs where something's greatness (in size or quality) defeats any attempt to describe it: the paradox being that this very inability to articulate the sensation manages, like a photographic negative, to express it:

> The sublime marks the limits of reason and expression *together with a sense of what might lie beyond these limits* … descriptive failure raises a negative, even painful, presentation of the ineffable. Sublimity … refers to the moment when the ability to apprehend, to know, and to express a thought or sensation is defeated. Yet through this very defeat, the mind gets a feeling for that which lies beyond thought and language. (Shaw 2006: 2–3; my emphasis)

The way the sublime takes away the ability to express it does, in a roundabout way, describe the experience. A person left speechless after an experience does manage to articulate a sense of the magnitude of what they are (not) talking about. Grau suggests that "Immersion arises when artwork and technologically advanced apparatus, message and medium, are perceived to merge inseparably" (2003: 339). Immersive experience may be a response to this merging of content and form into a "total" whole.

Two major philosophical works in relation to the sublime are Burke's *A Philosophical Enquiry into the Origin of Our Ideas of the Sublime and Beautiful* (published 1757) and Kant's "Analytic of the Sublime" in *Critique of Judgement* (published 1790). Both define the sublime as in opposition to the beautiful. A central concept to Burke's *Enquiry* is the connection he makes between sublimity and terror. Burke's focus on the psychological effect of fear in those who experience the sublime emphasises the cognitive (and emotional) aspect of the experience. He argues that language's (in)ability to adequately capture the sublime shows its superiority in conveying the idea of the sensation—as opposed to, for example, painting, which could depict something we have seen before but lacks the indistinctness of language to convey something beyond imagining.

Like Burke, Kant identifies a distinction between the sublime and the beautiful, and the former again dominates: the beautiful is self-contained and serves little purpose other than itself, while the sublime is an experience that allows for a transcendence of the human mind. I have said that the defining quality of the sublime is its inherent indescribable quality, which does, in negative, manage to convey something of its quality, its magnitude and its effect. Kant saw the effect of the sublime as (ultimately) a triumph of reason—demonstrating, in negative, that the mind can grasp the rational idea of such totality. Then there is the question of cause: does the sensation originate in the objects of nature which inspire it, or the minds of those who experience it? For Burke, due to his emphasis on the emotion of terror, the source of the sublime moves away from nature and into the mind of the spectator. Kant takes this further. Not only does the sublime occur in the mind of the spectator, but this can be taken to represent a triumph of that mind. The temporary confounding of the mind is ultimately an expression of its capabilities: "*The sublime is that, the mere ability to think which, shows a faculty of the mind surpassing every standard of Sense*" (Kant [trans. 2005]: 66; original emphasis). Both Burke and Kant propose that there is ultimately something to be gained from the temporary loss of the self or the self's rational faculties during an encounter with the sublime.

Sublime experience and immersion might be construed as empowerment or disempowerment. On the one hand, the confounding, overpowering sensation of sublime experience that affects someone so much on an emotional or a visceral level feels inherently contradictory to the idea of empowerment; they are stunned into paralysis, made acutely aware of the scale or power of the work. On the other hand, if the sublime does not occur all the way through a work but only at particular moments—for example during a visually spectacular finale—the fact they occur at the end of the experience may create a sublime sensation that is precisely what empowers a spectator—in the context of psychological flow, if an audience member feels (whether it is an illusion or not) that they have somehow played an important part in reaching that point, sublime experience might be coded as a reward for skill demonstrated, rather than a display of asymmetrical power relations. Both of these interpretations regarding audience dis/empowerment exist for immersive theatre: best illustrated in the existence of two articles about Punchdrunk's *Sleep No More* with very similar titles: Green's "Immersive Theatre and the Freedom of Choice" (2013) and Burton's "Immersive Theatre and the Anxiety of Choice" (2013). The relationship between immersive experience and the idea of choice is particularly relevant to the question of interactivity.

In his history of the sublime Shaw laments that an "instinctive feeling for the transcendental is rare these days. As a result of secularism, together with increasing global awareness and media sophistication, we seem less inclined to regard the breakdown of reason and expression as indicators of a higher or spiritual realm" (2006: 3). Griffiths rejects such a fatalist approach to new media, suggesting that an ingrained human compulsion to enter immersive spaces, to seek out sublime or overwhelming environments, will survive any such threats as increased levels of media sophistication and the rise of secularism. Burke and Kant's historical sublime has its roots in nature, and is not an experience that can be created or controlled—certainly not imagined, designed and built—by human agency. Griffiths' examples of immersive spaces demonstrate successful, and long-running, human attempts to recreate the natural experience of the sublime.

Philosophical aesthetics and cognitive psychology give some useful frameworks for thinking about immersive experience in theatre. The tension between immersive experience, the revered gaze and the notion of individual political agency becomes particularly acute in the context of claims for the empowerment of audiences. Optimum experience or peak psychological "flow" is one description of how immersive experience manifests: losing track of time; feeling fully engaged and interested; encountering challenges for which your skills are matched; feeling fulfilled and satisfied afterwards. This state can occur in the context of producing art as well as consuming it: peak experience manifesting in the creation of alternate worlds for audiences to get lost in, as well as the sensation felt in a spectator when lost in those worlds. The revered gaze is also highly useful as a description of how immersive experience might manifest; however, it is also necessary to build a more nuanced definition of immersive experience to consider how it is created and claimed beyond overwhelming totality. Studies of computer games have undertaken much work in this area; immersive experience has been repeatedly analysed and defined with many perspectives on what immersion is and how it manifests. The amount of research in this field may have roots in anxieties around possible (anti-)social side-effects of becoming too engaged (for example Seah and Cairns [2008] on immersion and addiction). Immersion in gaming research provides the conceptualisation of immersion as a non-binary state; barriers to immersion; Real World Disassociation (RWD); and the relationship to distractions, all extremely useful for thinking about how immersion might be facilitated and crafted by theatremakers, and how it might be experienced by its audiences.

Approaches to Immersive Experience: Immersion and Computer Games

Although *immersion* is a prevalent and powerful experience of gaming, it is slippery to define and often used inconsistently. Put generally immersion occurs when a player's thoughts, attention and goals are centred on the game they are playing. The specifics can differ, but this general definition is in itself quite helpful as it is inclusive of several questions: whether immersion is a graded experience, and how those grades are defined; how fleeting it may be; its relationship to presence; how much of the outside world a gamer notices; what a gamer is actually immersed *in*; and how and why that happens. All these aspects are useful for approaching immersive experience in theatre.

Brown and Cairns (2004) establish a definition of *immersion* based on the qualitative experience of gamers, defining it in terms of gaming itself—differentiating it from immersion in VR, interface design or information technology more generally (as in Agarwal and Karahanna [2000], a study of cognitive absorption in IT). Using questionnaires and semi-structured interviews, the study uses the grounded theory method to build a definition of immersion. (As *immersion* is often coded as an individual, personal phenomenon, many studies seeking to define its qualities are built around interviews. The subjectivity of such a qualitative has led to attempts to build a more objective measure of immersion, such as eye-movement tracking [Tijs 2006; Cox et al. 2006; Jennett et al. 2008]. Such studies tend to find a positive correlation between subjective and objective methods of measuring gameplay experience, suggesting that both are useful for defining and measuring immersion in games.)

Brown and Cairns (2004) suggest that immersive experience is not a felt/not-felt binary but can instead be graded into three states: engagement, engrossment and total immersion. They identify barriers to all three levels of immersion, with each barrier having to be overcome for the player to reach the next level. They also stress that the removal of these barriers does not guarantee immersion, but merely allows for it. This has implications for makers, who cannot forcibly control a player's becoming immersed in their product but can design work that has its barriers to immersion lowered as much as possible.

At a level of *engagement*, a player has invested enough time and attention to have learned the controls and be interested in continuing to play. From the perspective of the computer system, the barrier to this level is accessibility. The player has to be able and willing to learn the arbitrary relationship between the game and its controls; once these are learned, they effectively disappear. The importance of the "disappearance" of controls has been noted earlier by Laurel (1991) and Newman (2002), who suggests that "many a great game has poor visuals—but there are few good games with bad controls" (n.p.). An experienced gamer might learn the controls of a new game with relative ease using a combination of existing knowledge and informed guesswork, and have less trouble reaching the state of engagement since they are accustomed to overcoming these initial barriers.

Engrossment occurs when a player's emotions are directly affected by the game. The barrier to this level is the actual game construction—here, the designer is concerned less with the controls or the interface, and more on creating interesting tasks for the player to perform, or a plot, world and/or characters it is possible to care about. *Total immersion* occurs when attention and emotional investment is such that it feels as if the game is all that matters, or that the game is all that there is. Describing this level of immersion, gamers used phrases such as feeling "in the game" or "you feel like you're there." The game has such impact a player feels they are part of it. The barrier to this level of engagement is an extension of those required for engrossment; players go beyond interest to empathy, and the role of atmosphere in the game becomes very important (Brown and Cairns 2004).

Cheng and Cairns (2005) extend the study of barriers to immersion. By manipulating the graphics of a game in order to make gameplay incoherent (i.e. deliberately creating a barrier), they attempted to deliberately disrupt players' immersion. The results were surprising: players could be so immersed in a gaming environment, even a relatively simple one, that significant changes in the game's behaviour had little effect on their levels of immersion. Incoherence is initially a barrier to immersion, but once immersion had been achieved, newly introduced incoherence went relatively unnoticed, or at any rate did not seem to affect the players' levels of enjoyment. Jennett, Cox and Cairns's study of a concept they term Real World Disassociation or RWD (2008)—describing a state where gamers are so immersed in the game world they become unaware of the real world—further refines ideas around barriers to, and disruption of, gaming immersion and raises interesting questions around how aware a player is of the real world. And how conscious that (un)awareness is: a player can notice the existence of potential distractions (barriers to immersion) and choose to ignore them. Gamers played both low- and high-immersion games while being subjected to a series of distractions. Players were not only less aware of their real environment while playing the more immersive game but were also able to be less aware of *certain aspects* of their real environment, depending on how relevant these aspects were to them. For example a switched-on television while the game is played could be ignored or "tuned out" with relative ease; someone saying the player's name (a more relevant distraction) affected immersion more. However, this in turn revealed another finding, as gamers were potentially able to choose not to respond, to hear/be aware of their name being called, but ignore it: that is, making a deliberate choice to stay immersed. Pace (2008) also finds irrelevant factors disappear from a player's consciousness during a state of immersion or flow. This is a defining aspect of RWD: "at that moment in time, the game is simply viewed as more important than reality" (Jennett et al. 2008: 3).

Jennett et al. (2008) build on the three graded levels. *Presence* is the term used by Brown and Cairns (2004) as the defining feature of total immersion—feeling "in the game," feeling as though one is actually one of the characters, or actually present in the game world: "total immersion is presence" (3). However, at the highest level of immersion not every player necessarily experiences this kind of presence (Jennett et al. 2008). Some gamers used the phrase "in the game" or "immersed" to mean only that they fully believed in the game's world or the story: they did not feel they *were* the character, or have a strong emotional investment in the game's outcome as if the game were real. As one might when watching a play or film, they were able to suspend their disbelief about the world, or its characters or its story, without actually making the leap to feeling as if they were really (physically) present *in* that world. It is the difference between thinking, in the heat of the trigger-pulling moment, "that character shot that character" rather than "he shot me!" Both might be said by a person experiencing a state of immersion, but only the latter indicates a momentary sensation of *presence*. (See also: "he hit me!" when the speaker really means "his car hit my car." Immersive experience here begins to resemble Heidegger's *ready-to-hand*, consciousness of a tool occurring as it becomes unable to fulfil its function).

The study of immersion in gaming has developed as further research builds on and modifies the earlier definition of three grades by adding more levels and suggesting that travel between them is fluid and fleeting. What remains constant is the idea that empathy only occurs at the highest level of immersion. Books on game design such as Freeman's *Creating Emotion in Games: The Craft and Art of Emotioneering* (2004) imply in their title that narrative/character empathy is not an automatic aspect of gaming but a feat that can be aimed for in the making: and that a game will be better off (and might even stand a chance of being considered a work of art) for including and achieving it successfully.

Emotion, empathy, caring about a narrative or the outcome of a character: that these are what immerses a player might at first seem the most applicable aspect of gaming immersion to theatre. But another perspective within gaming studies is that this is not necessarily what immerses a player at all. An alternative argument runs that the immersive potential of a game stems from its gaming mechanics, not from its storyline or world design. Jørgensen (2003) defines the basic activity of a gameplayer as problem-solving; Pace (2008) argues that immersion depends upon a suitable balance between the challenge of the game and the skill of the player: the problems to be solved and the skills and desire to solve them (Pace's definition of immersion is drawn from Csikszentmihalyi's *flow*). Frome (2007) provides a model for how games generate emotion within a player, making a distinction between character/narrative games and puzzle games. Frome argues the emotions games can generate within a player depend upon the type of game being played, and the player's relationship to the game and role within it.

Following Frome's distinction between narrative games and puzzle games, it is possible make a distinction between narrative immersion and puzzle immersion (immersion in the gaming mechanics). Rather than attempting to definitively categorise what kind of immersion occurs in different games, the key point is that it is not necessarily games with characters and a narrative that are the more immersive. Tetris is an example Salen and Zimmerman (2004) use to debunk what they term "the immersive fallacy"—that is the idea that immersion occurs when a player is transported to an illusory reality. Tetris can definitely be called an immersive time-bin but it has no character to become or empathise with, no world to enter. Immersion occurs through engagement with the action of play itself, not because the player might come to find the game's environment indistinguishable from the real world.

Seeing narrative and gameplay as separate aspects that facilitate immersive experience is useful, for gaming mechanics (including aspects such as problem-solving or rewards for exploration), are a useful way to think about a piece of immersive theatre where both aspects are at work. This division does not mean narrative and gaming mechanics are mutually exclusive: a puzzle solution that takes the story forwards would be a way of achieving satisfaction in both. In 1989 the game designer Ron Gilbert wrote an influential and brilliantly irreverent polemic called "Why Adventure Games Suck (And What We Can Do About It)." In it, he proposed that adventure games are better off without redundant puzzles. When arbitrary quests are only included for the sake of making the game longer and do not take it forwards in terms of narrative or gameplay they slow it down needlessly, detracting from the potential of a game to otherwise provide an immersive "intense ride":

> If I could have my way, I'd design games that were meant to be played in four to five hours. The games would be of the same scope that I currently design, I'd just remove the silly time-wasting puzzles and take the player for an intense ride. The experience they would leave with would be much more entertaining and a lot less frustrating. The games would still be challenging, but not at the expense of the player's patience. (1989: 7)

The relationship between gameplay and story in immersive theatre is considered more fully in Chap. 7.

Having made a distinction between immersion in story/character, and immersion in gameplay and puzzle-solving, the latter has been further sub-divided. Pace (2008) separates immersion into two components—immersion in the gameplay (diegetic immersion) and immersion in the game's representational space (situated immersion, or presence). McMahan also breaks immersion into two categories:

… immersion means the player is caught up in the world of the game's story (the diegetic level) but it also refers to the player's love of the game and the strategy that goes into it (the nondiegetic level). It seems clear that if we are talking about immersion in video games at the diegetic level and immersion at the nondiegetic level, then we are talking about two different things, with possibly conflicting sets of aesthetic conventions. Narrative and narrative genres are often used as a way of defining the conventions of a world and to help the user align their expectations with the logic of the world. (2003: 68–69)

Narrative can help define the conventions of a world, but is only one way of doing so. A player encountering conventions of narrative they are familiar with (protagonist, conflict, climax) are a way of getting into the world of a game, understanding its power dynamics, the landscape. The "immersive fallacy," however, suggests it is not the world that matters the most, but the gameplay. The argument put forward by McMahan, that narrative can be an important means *of gameplay* to draw a player into a world, suggests the two aspects have a reciprocal relationship. Newman suggests a player doesn't empathise or relate to a specific character, but that "character is conceived as capacity—as a set of characteristics. […] The primary-player may not see themselves as any one particular character on the screen, but rather as the sum of every force and influence that comprises the game" (2002: n.p.). The characters of a game are intrinsically bound up in the world of the game, and how a player engages with that world; a player might see a character as the means/capacity to undertake certain actions within the game's world. This relationship between character and game world is what a player empathises with, and for perhaps a few intense moments feels to really *be*. This point might seem to run counter to the idea that emotion and empathy must be generated by games with gripping storylines, exciting plot twists and strong, compelling characters; and there are many games that have well-written storylines, genuine dramatic tension and characters who are not empty vessels for the gamer to fill. The larger point is that characters are only one way in which a gamer might enter the world of the game: the gamer's capacity for action with the game's world is an important component of what constitutes immersive experience.

Newman (2002) acknowledges that many games are sold on the quality of their visuals, and it may seem counter-intuitive to suggest that these might not actually be what facilitates immersion. The brilliance of a game's graphics might instead facilitate social interaction, benefiting those who are playing alongside the gamer but not actually holding the controls themselves: secondary players who are not able to become immersed in the mechanics of gameplay in the same way as the primary player but might get involved in the task or the story, offering tips of varying helpfulness. However, Pace (2008) suggests 3D graphics are an important part of creating an immersive experience and may even be a prerequisite for it. This apparent contradiction can be resolved by separating the concepts of immersion and presence. As discussed earlier, *presence* is a concept often used in the context of VR. Presence in gaming may be increased by 3D graphics, but presence is different from immersion.

Describing the highest state of immersion in gaming, Brown and Cairns state that "total immersion is presence" (2004: 3). Presence is the feeling of "being there," of feeling at one with the work. This relationship is complicated in Jennett, Cox and Cairns (2008), who find that these feelings of being in the game may be fleeting or, even in a state of immersion that is otherwise high, not occur at all. As immersion is defined primarily as occurring within the mind of the gamer— their thoughts, feelings, and so on—many studies define immersion as a cognitive process. Presence in relation to VR (as in Spagnolli and Gamberini 2002) means something different from immersion. In VR a player is immediately "present," for they can instantly see the virtual environment all around them; in gaming it takes the highest level of immersion for such an effect to be felt, if it is felt at all. It is possible to feel presence but not to be immersed, such as by being in a VR environment and doing a boring task. Similarly, a computer game with excellent 3D graphics on a huge screen might make a gamer feel something approaching presence, but a boring storyline or a glitch in the gameplay then prevents their feeling immersed; just as a theatregoer might stand in a room that has been painstakingly and intricately decorated and feel vaguely bored. Immersion is different from presence, because in the context of VR (and immersive *theatre*) presence is (relatively) easy, physical and instant; whereas immersion in gaming (immersive *experience*) is more gradual, fleeting and connected to more cognitive/emotional responses. Feeling "as if you are really there" is nothing particularly special if "there" is quite dull.

The argument that feeling physically present in the world may not be the defining aspect of immersive experience is a long way from the "total immersion is presence" definition. The feeling that one is present or was for a few fleeting moments "there" may be a defining aspect of immersion (in the category of McMahan's diegetic immersion), but is not the only one. In Jennett, Cox and Cairns (2008) gamers used the phrase "feeling in the game" variously to mean they believed in the fictional world, felt an emotional attachment to the story or a character, or simply got interested in the puzzle or the challenge (the gaming mechanics). These are all viable definitions of being immersed in a game, and it is useful to separate immersive experience into components this way. It helps us to consider what a player might be immersed *in*, or what they might expect to be immersed in, and therefore what is *valued* in a game—or any other experience. But, as ever, barriers can be lowered but immersion can never be fully guaranteed. After many attempts to define immersive experience, the graded and barriered and individual nature of the phenomenon might mean one person's highly engrossed experience is another's indifference on seeing what all the fuss is about.

A further difference between VR experience and gameplay concerns the relationship between body and mind. Immersion in computer games is a cognitive or psychological state, since the gamer is physically separated from the screen. Spagnolli and Gamberini (2002) find that in VR the mind of the player is able to spread across the dual environments: it is possible for a player in VR to pick up or interact with a virtual object, while maintaining a conversation with the real-life researcher. The mind's ability to exist between and across the hybrid environment(s) of VR world and real world may be an enrichment of a player's VR experience. This result is somewhat contradicted by Young (2005) in his study of the mind/body split in computer games, particularly first-person shooters. Rather than allowing a mind to stretch across multiple environments, computer games disembody the player: first by removing awareness of the player's own body by creating a new, virtual one; then by removing the player's awareness of that second body (the persona or avatar) to leave finally only the mind. The suggestion that it might enrich a player's experience to have their mind exist in the real world as well as the game world might seem to go against the general definition of immersion in gaming: that an immersed player is unaware of the world around them and feels the game is more important than reality, ignoring the real world should distractions occur. But both Pace (2008) and Jennett et al. (2008) note instances where gamers *choose* to stay immersed—they hear someone saying their name, and they ignore it. The idea that consciousness can exist across hybrid environments is applicable to an immersive theatre experience, where an awareness of the existence of the show's rules (its gaming mechanics) might enhance an audience member's experience, rather than automatically troubling it by jolting them out of the fiction.

A final observation from game studies brings up an interesting point about wider social perceptions of immersion. Jennett et al. (2008) note that the distinction they uncover between immersion and presence may be explained by social pressures, as some responses in interviews might stem from a player wishing to avoid the stigma attached to becoming too immersed, talking down how much it really happened. Brown and Cairns (2004) also note that in their interviews, "No one described an experience of immersion that they did not enjoy. However, this was moderated by guilt from a sense of wasting time on a game" (5). Concerns about the anti-social effects of too much immersion in games is an ongoing cultural anxiety—see Seah and Cairns (2008) on whether addiction is linked to immersion—and although immersive theatre does not at the time of writing suffer under a similar social prejudice, an awareness of this wider landscape may affect how immersive experience is described, marketed or claimed to occur in interviews.

The overlapping use of *immersive* to refer variously to space, experience, genre, form and effect resembles the complex relationship visitors have to the wondrous Barnum Museum in Stephen Millhauser's short story of the same name:

> For some, the moment of highest pleasure is the entrance into the museum: the sudden plunge into a world of delights, the call of the far doorways. For others, it is the gradual losing of the way: the sense, as we wander from hall to hall, that we can no longer find our way back. This, to be sure, is a carefully contrived pleasure, for although the museum is constructed so as to help us lose our way, we know perfectly well that at any moment we may ask a guard to lead us to an exit. For still others, what pierces the heart is the stepping forth: the sudden opening of the door, the brilliant sunlight, the dazzling shop windows, the momentary confusion on the upper stair. (*The Barnum Museum* 1990: 90)

Entrance, exploration, exit; getting lost, finding your way; the suddenness of boundaries or their porousness: all valid sites for immersion. This book's discussion of immersive experience aims for an untangling of these various types. Structured across three main areas of enquiry, my discussion seeks to explore audience experience in immersive theatre within a flexible definition drawn from the previous discussion, one that allows for detailed exploration of a genre of theatrical work characterised by particular audience dynamics.

Describing peak experience in performance, McConachie suggests that:

> "flow" does not occur throughout a performance. Audience attention at the theatre may be momentarily interrupted, or spectators may choose to stop the "flow" of a performance by un-blending actor/characters to momentarily think about the work of such singular agents as actors, directors, and playwrights. But usually not for long. The pleasurable effects of "flow" generally pull spectators back into the cognitive activities of blending and empathizing. […] we enjoy immersing ourselves in the fictional world of the play, and blending and empathizing are the (mostly unconscious) cognitive operations that get us there. (2013: 56)

Even in the context of cognitive activity, a feeling of interplay and *movement*—a sense of being emotionally or mentally in motion, even if sitting still—is key to immersive experience.

Immersive experience is not a felt/not-felt binary, but exists as a series of graded states. It is a necessarily temporary state that makers can do their best to construct/allow for in advance but can never guarantee. Its intensity in the performance moment is linked to its temporary nature, and also key is the idea of barriers to immersion and a spectator's being able to differentiate between the relevance of various distractions.

The relationship between challenge, skill and feedback is an important part of how game designers work towards getting their players immersed in the mechanics of play. This could be considered a separate concern from the creation of atmosphere and the writing of characters and storylines. A more reciprocal model would have it that engaging with story can be what creates that challenge/skill/feedback relationship. It is useful to separate these components while not thinking of them as a binary: interplay between content and form, and the ways each may facilitate immersion, is key to this book's approach to audience experience in immersive theatre. I am interested in a graded definition of immersion and how it might be facilitated, manipulated, troubled or blocked by interactivity, story and space.

Outline of the Book

This book considers immersive experience along three strands of enquiry—interactivity, narrative and environment. Each chapter outlines some theoretical groundwork, then considers how each area enriches discussion of immersive theatre, using one or more Punchdrunk productions as its examples.

Chapters 2–4 consider interactivity and immersion. Chapter 2 asks what is meant by interactivity, considering how approaches from computer games, pervasive gaming in theatre, VR and interactive performance enable analysis of immersive theatre, finally arguing for a multivalent model drawn from game design. The chapter explores various ways interactivity can manifest in immersive theatre and the relationship(s) between these claims for interactivity and immersive experience.

Chapter 3 considers the relationship between interactivity and immersion in more detail, using Punchdrunk's *The Drowned Man* as a case study. From the model proposed in the previous chapter, I argue that interactivity occurs in multiple forms, and a flexible definition allows audience experience to be considered in the wider contexts of production design, structure, exploration and the empty room—as well as in more explicitly interactive moments such as one-to-one scenes with individual performers. I argue for a definition of interactivity that is not limited to outcomes and ideas of "choice," "freedom" or "empowerment," but that exists in the interplay between an audience member's understanding of "immersive" and "interactive" and how they might approach a performance with this understanding in mind.

I discuss *The Drowned Man* and interactivity from the position of being inside the walls of the performance space. Chapter 4 moves outside the production itself to consider *interactivity* as a wider social practice. I argue for a mode of analysis that lasts beyond the moment of theatrical encounter, a model that is inclusive of how interactivity manifests in memory and communication after the event. Drawing on access to Punchdrunk's fan mail archive, the chapter considers audience communication during their earlier shows *Faust* and *The Masque of the Red Death*, and the development of fan communities around the later productions *Sleep No More* and *The Drowned Man*, to situate immersive experience within a wider type of interactivity: considering discourses with the show itself (i.e. through repeat attendance) or with the company as a whole. The chapter also questions the formulation of immersive experience as being inherently individual.

Chapters 5–7 consider narrative and immersion. The role of "story" in immersive theatre is one of continual interest. Chapter 5 introduces concepts from narrative theory, outlining models of the relationship(s) between discourse, plot, story, character and causality. The chapter then proposes a means to apply these concepts to a discussion of immersive experience in theatre. Drawing on my own presence at rehearsals for Punchdrunk's *The Crash of the Elysium*, the chapter considers how immersive experience is formulated and crafted in process, arguing that theatrical form and story structure have a reciprocal relationship in facilitating audience immersion.

Chapter 6 considers the relationship between immersive experience and story in relation to chronology, structure and time: making particular reference to the technique common to Punchdrunk's larger productions of spreading scenes throughout large buildings for audiences to seek out and discover. The chapter explores how this technique affects immersive experience, drawing on theoretical approaches to narrative and time by Genette and Ricoeur. I argue that a sense of "rules of engagement" with a piece of immersive theatre—whether these rules are implied, explicitly stated or folded into assumptions made by audience members—affects what is meant by *story* and whether there is a "correct" way to engage with it. To consider narrative events and theatrical structure, I analyse the endings of two Punchdrunk shows from the same year, *It Felt Like A Kiss* and *The Duchess of Malfi*, one successful and one unsuccessful in dovetailing form and story.

The field of game study and design runs through much of this book: it informs my definition of immersive experience and provides useful models to theorise interactivity. In Chap. 7 the link with this field is made explicit. The similarities between immersive theatre and gaming have been noticed elsewhere, in scholarship (Green 2013; Kilch in Frieze 2017) and the work of other artists. This chapter asks how this overlap might help us to talk about immersive experience, introducing a model from game studies: the (so-called) "debate" between narrative and ludology, two approaches to studying the role of story in games. This model is highly applicable to immersive performance, looking as it does at the relationship between game mechanics, structure and story events, and what it means to be immersed in each of these aspects. The usefulness of this model is emphasised with an analysis of Punchdrunk's *Sleep No*

More and the show's additional partnership with MIT Media Lab in 2012 on a project exploring "long distance-real world theatrical immersion" (Higgin 2012) that connected—via gaming mechanics—the theatrical production in New York and a remote audience member/player who could be anywhere else in the world. The chapter concludes by emphasising the overlap between immersive theatre and games by demonstrating the extent of current interest in this area, citing game designers influenced by Punchdrunk and theatremakers influenced by games.

Chapter 8 focuses on immersion and environment, considering what happens in the space of an immersive performance and how environments (both the original "found" space and a production's added design elements) affect immersive experience. The word *immersive* is frequently used to refer to the manipulation of performance space or audience configurations. Thinking of immersive theatre and immersive experience separately enables further analysis of *how* Punchdrunk's use of space affects audiences. My discussion looks at *The Drowned Man* to consider environment and immersive experience in a more typically "immersive" mode, in which audience members and performers shared a space rigidly defined by the walls of a building. This is contrasted with *The Borough*, a production which, unusually for Punchdrunk, occurred mostly outside. Immersion and environment in both these shows demonstrate that space and site work together with structure to achieve immersive effects. By considering *The Borough*, this chapter also anticipates questions about the consequences for understanding immersion and space when *immersive* (typically indoor) and *pervasive* (typically outdoor) genres of making overlap. In the concluding chapter, I return to my findings regarding immersive experience, the relationship between immersive experience and immersive theatre, and the intersection(s) of narrative, environment and interactivity with immersion: and invite further exploration.

References

Abercrombie, Nicholas, and Brian Longhurst. 1998. *Audiences: A Sociological Theory of Performance and Imagination.* London: Sage.

Agarwal, Ritu, and Elena Karahanna. 2000. Time Flies When You're Having Fun: Cognitive Absorption and Beliefs about its Usage. *MIS Quarterly* 24 (4): 665–694.

Alston, Adam. 2013. Audience Participation and Neoliberal Value: Risk, Agency and Responsibility in Immersive Theatre. *On Value Edition. Taylor & Francis Performance Research* 18 (2): 128–138.

Alston, Adam. 2016a. *Beyond Immersive Theatre: Aesthetics, Politics and Productive Participation*. London: Palgrave Macmillan.
Alston, Adam. 2016b. Making Mistakes in Immersive Theatre: Spectatorship and Errant Immersion. *Journal of Contemporary Drama in English* 4 (1): 61–73.
Ang, Ien. 1991. *Desperately Seeking the Audience*. London: Routledge.
Arnott, Jack. 2011. Punchdrunk? Try Petrified—Gaming Gets the Immersive Theatre Treatment. *Guardian*, September Friday 2. Accessed April 2012.
Aronson, Arnold. 2012. Environmental Theatre. In *The Oxford Companion to Theatre and Performance*, ed. Dennis Kennedy. Oxford: Oxford University Press.
Auslander, Philip. 1999. *Liveness: Performance in a Mediatized Culture*. London: Routledge.
Babbage, Frances. 2009. Heavy Bodies, Fragile Texts: Stage Adaptation and the Problem of Presence. In *Adaptation and Contemporary Culture: Textual Infidelities*, ed. Rachel Carroll, 11–22. London: Continuum.
Barker, Martin. 2003. *Crash*, Theatre Audiences, and the Idea of 'Liveness'. *Studies in Theatre and Performance* 23 (1): 21–39.
Barker, Martin, and Ernest Mathijis. 2007. *Watching the Lord Of The Rings: Tolkien's World Audiences*. New York: Peter Lang.
Barrett, Felix. 2013. Burn the Seats: Audience Immersion in Interactive Theatre. Promotional video for Future of StoryTelling Summit, New York, 2–3 October.
Barrett, Felix. 2014. Felix Barrett, Artistic Director, Punchdrunk. Speaking at Remix Summit: *Experience Economy: Creating Extraordinary Moments and Stories that Get People Talking*. https://www.youtube.com/watch?v=xCRcuHiDEYs. Accessed Mar 2014.
Bennett, Susan. [1990] 1997. *Theatre Audiences: A Theory of Production and Reception*. London: Routledge.
Bennett, Susan. 2006. Theatre Audiences, Redux. *Theatre Survey* 47 (2): 225–230.
Bernhardt, Elizabeth B. (ed.). 1992. *Life in Language Immersion Classrooms*. Clevedon: Multilingual Matters.
Billington, Michael. 2010. The Duchess of Malfi. *Guardian*, July 14 2010. http://www.guardian.co.uk/stage/2010/jul/14/duchess-of-malfi-review. Accessed Jan 2013.
Birringer, Johannes. 2006. Environments for Interactive Dance. In *Performing Nature: Explorations in Ecology and the Arts*, ed. Gabriella Giannachi and Nigel Stewart, 303–325. Oxford: Peter Lang.
Bishop, Claire. (ed.). 2006. *Participation*. London: MIT Press.
Bishop, Claire. 2011. *Artificial Hells: Participatory Art and the Politics of Spectatorship*. London: Verso.
Brook, Peter. 1968. *The Empty Space*. London: Penguin.

Brooker, Will, and Deborah Jermyn (eds.). 2003. *The Audience Studies Reader*. London: Routledge.

Brown, Emily, and Paul Cairns. 2004. A Grounded Investigation of Game Immersion. CHI 2004 Extended Abstracts on Human Factors in Computing Systems, 1279–1300.

Burke, Edmund. [1757] 1958. *A Philosophical Enquiry into the Origin of Our Ideas of the Sublime and the Beautiful*, ed. J.T. Boulton. London: Routledge.

Burton, Tara Isabella. 2013. Immersive Theatre and the Anxiety of Choice. *New Statesman*. Accessed 16 Mar 2013.

Butsch, Richard. 2000. *The Making of American Audiences: From Stage to Television, 1750–1990*. Cambridge: Cambridge University Press.

Carlson, Marvin. 1989. Theatre Audiences and the Reading of Performance. In *Interpreting the Theatrical Past*, ed. Thomas Postlewait, and Bruce McConachie, 82–98. Iowa City: University of Iowa Press.

Chatman, Seymour. 1978. *Story and Discourse: Narrative Structure in Fiction and Film*. Ithaca: Cornell University Press.

Cheng, K., and Cairns, P. 2005. Behaviour, Realism and Immersion in Games. ACM Conference on Human Factors in Computing Systems, CHI 2005, ACM Press, 1272–1275.

Colette, Gordon. 2012. Pedestrian Shakespeare and Punchdrunk's Immersive Theatre. Cashiers Elizabethains, Autumn 2012, 43–50.

Cox, A.L., P.A. Cairns, N. Berthouze, and C. Jennett. 2006. The Use of Eyetracking for Measuring Immersion. UCL Interaction Centre, Department of Psychology. https://www-users.cs.york.ac.uk/~pcairns/papers/CoxEyetracking.pdf. Accessed Dec 2010.

Csikszentmihalyi, Mihaly. 1988. *Optimal Experience: Psychological Studies of Flow in Consciousness*. Cambridge: Cambridge University Press.

Csikszentmihalyi, Mihaly. 1990. *Flow: The Psychology of Optimal Experience*. New York: Harper & Row.

Csikszentmihalyi, Mihaly. 1996. *Creativity: Flow and the Psychology of Discovery and Invention*. New York: Harper Collins.

Csikszentmihalyi, Mihaly, and Rick E. Robinson. 1990. *The Art of Seeing: An Interpretation of the Aesthetic Encounter*. The J. Paul Getty Museum and The Getty Education Institute for the Arts.

Dinesh, Nandita. 2016. *Memos From a Theatre Lad: Exploring What Immersive Theatre "Does"*. London: Routledge.

Dixon, Steve. 2007. *Digital Performance: A History of New Media in Theatre, Dance, Performance Art and Installation*. Cambridge, MI: MIT Press.

Dusinberre, Juliet (ed.). 2006. *As You Like It*. London: Arden Shakespeare.

Dyson, Frances. 2009. *Sounding New Media: Immersion and Embodiment in the Arts and Culture*. Berkeley: University of California Press.

Eglinton, Andrew. 2010. Reflections on a Decade of Punchdrunk Theatre. *TheatreForum*, Issue 37, 46–56.

Eversmann, Peter. 2004. The Experience of the Theatrical Event. In *Theatrical Events: Borders, Dynamics, Frames*, ed. Vicky Ann Cremona, Peter Eversmann, Hans van Maanen, Willmar Sauter, and John Tulloch, 139–174. New York: Rodopi.
Fischer-Lichte, Erika. 2016. The Art of Spectatorship. *Journal of Contemporary Drama in English* 4 (1): 164–179.
Freeman, David E. 2004. *Creating Emotion in Games: The Craft and Art of Emotioneering*. Indianapolis, IN: New Riders.
Freshwater, Helen. 2009. *Theatre & Audience*. Basingstoke: Palgrave Macmillan.
Frieze, James. 2017. *Reframing Immersive Theatre: The Politics and Pragmatics of Participatory Performance*. London: Palgrave Macmillan.
Frome, Jonathan. 2007. Eight Ways Videogames Generate Emotion, Situated Play. Proceedings of DiGRA 2007 Conference. Accessed Nov 2010.
Gardner, Lyn. 2006a. An Offer They can't Refuse: Lyn Gardner on Why Theatre Companies are Taking the Corporate Shilling. *Guardian*, 20 June.
Gardner, Lyn. 2006b. Faust. *Guardian*, October 19.
Gardner, Lyn. 2007a. We Make Our Own Ghosts Here. *Guardian*, September 12.
Gardner, Lyn. 2007b. The Masque of the Red Death left me Punchdrunk. *Guardian*, October 4.
Gardner, Lyn. 2012. Interactive Theatre: With Power Comes Responsibility. *Guardian Theatre Blog*. Accessed 12 July 2012.
Gardner, Lyn. 2012. Lyn Gardner's Theatre Roundup: Advice for Playwrights. *Guardian Theatre Blog*, 30 April 2012. Accessed May 2014.
Gardner, Lyn. 2014. Venice Preserv'd review—Immersive Drama That's More of an Aimless Wander. *Guardian*, May 1 2014.
Giannachi, Gabriella, and Nigel Stewart (eds.). 2006. *Performing Nature: Explorations in Ecology and the Arts*. Oxford: Peter Lang.
Giannachi, Gabriella, and Kaye Nick. 2011. *Performing Presence: Between the Live and the Simulated*. Manchester: Manchester University Press.
Giannachi, Gabriella, Nick Kaye, and Michael Shanks (eds.). 2012. *Archaeologies of Presence: Art, Performance and the Persistence of Being*. London: Routledge.
Gilbert, Ron. 1989. Why Adventure Games Suck (and What We Can Do About it). *The Journal of Computer Game Design* 2 (2): 4–7.
Gillinson, Miriam. 2012. Punchdrunk's Sleep No More: Is This a sell-out Which I see Before me? *Guardian Theatre Blog*, Feb 6 2012.
Godbout, Jenn. 2012. Felix Barrett: On Pushing the Limits of Curiosity and Comfort Zones. 99u, 23 August 2012.
Goodall, Jane. 2008. *Stage Presence: The Actor as Mesmerist*. London: Routledge.
Goode, Chris. 2015. *The Forest and the Field: Changing Theatre in a Changing World*. London: Oberon.
Gordon, Colette. 2013. Touching the Spectator: Intimacy, Immersion and the Theater of the Velvet Rope. *Borrowers and Lenders*. Accessed November 2013.

Gorton, Kristyn. 2009. *Media Audiences: Television, Meaning and Emotion*. Edinburgh: Edinburgh University Press.

Grau, Oliver. 2003. *Virtual Art: From Illusion to Immersion*. Cambridge, Mass.: MIT Press.

Green, Adam. 2013. Immersive Theatre and the Freedom of Choice. TGC Circle.

Griffiths, Alison. 2008. *Shivers Down Your Spine: Cinema, Museums and the Immersive View*. New York: Columbia University Press.

Heddon, D., H. Iball, and R. Zerihan. 2012. Come Closer: Confessions of Intimate Spectators in One to One Performance. *Contemporary Theatre Review* 22 (1): 120–133.

Hemley, Matthew. 2016. Punchdrunk's Sleep No More to be staged in Shanghai. *The Stage*, July 13 2016.

Higgin, Peter. 2012. Innovation in Arts and Culture #4: Punchdrunk—Sleep No More. *Guardian Culture Professionals Network*, 5 May 2012.

Higgins, Charlotte. 2009. Immersive Theatre: Tired and Hackneyed Already? *Guardian Theatre Blog*, December 7.

Higgins, Charlotte. 2011. Arts Council England Funding Cuts—The Great Axe Falls. *Guardian Theatre Blog*, March 30.

Hoggard, Liz. 2013. Felix Barrett: The Visionary Who Reinvented Theatre. *Guardian*. Accessed 14 July 2014.

Hurley, Erin. 2010. *Theatre & Feeling*. London: Palgrave Macmillan.

Jancovich, Mark, Lucy Faire, and Sarah Stubbings. 2003. *The Place of the Audience: Cultural Geographies of Film Consumption*. London: BFI Publishing.

Jenkins, Henry. 2008. *Convergence Culture: Where Old and New Media Collide*. New York: New York University.

Jenkins, Henry. [1992] 2012. *Textual Poachers: Television Fans and Participatory Culture*. London: Routledge.

Jenkins, Henry, and Tulloch John. 1995. *Science Fiction Audiences: Watching 'Star Trek' and 'Doctor Who'*. London: Routledge.

Jennett, Charlene, Anna L. Cox, Paul Cairns, Samira Dhoparee, Andrew Epps, Tim Tijs, and Alison Walton. 2008. Measuring and Defining the Experience of Immersion in Games. *International Journal of Human Computer Studies* 66 (9) (September): 641–661. Accessed Nov 2010.

Kant, Immanuel. [1790] 2005. *The Critique Of Judgement*, ed. J.H. Bernard. New York: Dover.

Kershaw, Baz. 1999. *The Radical in Performance: Between Brecht and Baudrillard*. London: Routledge.

Klich, Rosemary, and Edward Scheer. 2012. *Multimedia Performance*. London: Palgrave Macmillan.

Knowles, Richard Paul. 2004. *Reading The Material Theatre*. Cambridge: Cambridge University Press.

Krasner, David. 2006. Empathy and Theatre. In *Staging Philosophy: Intersections of Theater, Performance and Philosophy*, ed. David Krasner, and David Saltz, 255–277. Anne Arbour: Michigan University Press.
Kristine, Jorgenson. 2003. Problem Solving: The Essence of Player Action in Computer Games, Level Up. Accessed Nov 2010.
Lakoff, G., and M. Johnson. 1999. *Philosophy in the Flesh: The Embodied Mind and Its Challenge to Western Thought*. New York: Basic Books.
Laurel, Brenda. 1991. *Computers as Theatre Reading*. Boston, MA: Addison-Wesley.
Logan, Richard. 1988. Flow in Solitary Ordeals. In *Optimal Experience: Psychological Studies of Flow in Consciousness*, ed. Mihaly Csikszentmihalyi and Isabella Selega Csikszentmihalyi, 172–180. Cambridge: Cambridge University Press.
Lorentz, Diana. 2007. A Study of the Notions of Immersive Experience in Museum Based Exhibitions. Thesis (M. Design): University of Technology, Sydney.
Machon, Josephine. 2007. Space and the Senses: The (syn)aesthetics of Punchdrunk's Site-Sympathetic Work. *Body, Space & Technology* 7 (1), n.p.
Machon, Josephine. 2011. *(Syn)aesthetics: Redefining Visceral Performance*. London: Palgrave Macmillan.
Machon, Josephine. 2013. *Immersive Theatres: Intimacy and Immediacy in Contemporary Performance*. London: Palgrave Macmillan.
Machon, Josephine. 2016. Watching, Attending, *Sense*-making: Spectatorship in Immersive Theatres. *Journal of Contemporary Drama in English* 4 (1): 34–48.
Maples, Holly. 2016. The Erotic Voyeur: Sensorial Spectatorship in Punchdrunk's *The Drowned Man*. *Journal of Contemporary Drama in English* 4 (1): 119–133.
McConachie, Bruce. 2008. *Engaging Audiences: A Cognitive Approach to Spectating in the Theatre*. New York: Palgrave Macmillan.
McConachie, Bruce. 2013. *Theatre & Mind*. London: Palgrave Macmillan.
McConachie, Bruce, and F. Elizabeth Hart (eds.). 2006. *Performance and Cognition: Theatre Studies and the Cognitive Turn*. London: Routledge.
McKenzie, Jon. 1994. Virtual Reality: Performance, Immersion and the Thaw. The Drama Review, 38.4 (T144) Winter, 83–106.
McKinney, Joslin. 2012. Empathy and Exchange: Audience Experiences of Scenography. In *Kinesthetic Empathy In Creative and Cultural Practices*, ed. Reynolds and Reason, 219–235. Bristol: Intellect.
McMahan, Alison. 2003. Immersion, Engagement and Presence: A Method for Analysing 3-D Video Games. In *The Video Game Theory Reader*, ed. Mark J.P. Wolf and Bernard Perron, 67–86. London: Routledge.
Megson, Chris, and Janelle Reinelt. 2016. Performance, Experience, Transformation: What do Spectators Value in Theatre? *Journal of Contemporary Drama in English* 4 (1): 227–242.

Millhauser, Steven. 1990, 1998. *The Barnum Museum*. London: Pheonix.
Moores, Shaun. 1993. *Interpreting Audiences: The Ethnography of Media Consumption*. London: SAGE.
Moser, Mary Ann, and Douglas MacLeod. (eds.). 1996. *Immersed in Technology: Art and Virtual Environments*. Cambridge, MA: The MIT.
Mougeon, Raymond, Terry Nadasdi, and Katherine Rehner. 2010. *The Sociolinguistic Competence of Immersion Students*. Bristol: Multilingual Matters.
Muhammad, Naim. 2014. *How to Get Fluent in Any Language with Immersion*. Amazon Media.
Nell, Victor. 1988. *Lost in a Book: The Psychology of Reading for Pleasure*. New Haven, CT: Yale University Press.
Newman, James. 2002. The Myth of the Ergodic Videogame: Some Thoughts on Player-Character Relationships in Videogames. *The International Journal of Computer Game Research* 2 (1), July 2002.
Nield, Sophie. 2008. The Rise of the Character Named Spectator. *Contemporary Theatre Review* 18 (4): 531–544.
Nightingale, Virginia. 2011. *The Handbook of Media Audiences*. London: Wiley Blackwell.
Nightingale, Virginia, and Karen Ross. 2003. *Critical Readings: Media and Audiences*. Maidenhead: Open University Press.
Pace, Steven. 2008. Immersion, Flow and the Experiences of Game Players. SimTecT 2008 Simulation Conference: Simulation—Maximising Organisational Benefits (SimTecT 2008) Melbourne, Australia, May 12–15.
Postlewait, Thomas. 2009. *The Cambridge Introduction to Theatre Historiography*. Cambridge: Cambridge University.
Punchdrunk. 2008. The Masque of the Red Death: Sample Feedback to www.punchdrunk.org.uk. Punchdrunk Archives.
Purcell, Stephen. 2013. *Shakespeare & Audience in Practice*. London: Palgrave Macmillan.
Reason, Matthew. 2006. *Documentation, Disappearance and the Representation of Live Performance*. London: Palgrave Macmillan.
Reason, Matthew. 2010. *The Young Audience: Exploring and Enhancing Children's Experiences of Theatre*. Stoke on Trent: Trentham Books.
Reynolds, Dee. 2012. Kinesthetic Empathy and the Dancer's Body: From Emotion to Affect. In *Kinesthetic Empathy in Creative and Cultural Practices*, ed. Reynolds and Reason, 121–136.
Reynolds, Dee, and Matthew Reason (eds.). 2012. *Kinesthetic Empathy in Creative and Cultural Practices*. Bristol: Intellect.
Ridout, Nicholas. 2006. *Stage Fright, Animals and Other Theatrical Problems*. London: Cambridge University Press.
Rose, Frank. 2012. How Punchdrunk Theatre Reels 'em In With Immersive Storytelling. *Wired*. Accessed 12 Mar 2012.

Ruddock, Andy. 2007. *Investigating Audiences*. London: Sage.
Ryan, Marie-Laure. 2001. *Narrative as Virtual Reality: Immersion and Interactivity in Literature and Electronic Media*. Baltimore: John Hopkins University.
Salen, K., and E. Zimmerman. 2004. *Rules of Play: Game Design Fundamentals*. Cambridge, MA: MIT.
Sauter, Willmar. 2000. *The Theatrical Event: Dynamics of Performance and Perception*. Iowa City: University of Iowa.
Sauter, Willmar. 2012. The Audience. In *The Cambridge Companion to Theatre History*, ed. David Wiles and Christine Dymkowski. Cambridge: Cambridge University Press, 169–183 [Accessed via Cambridge Companions Online, April 2014].
Seah, M., and P Cairns. 2008. From Immersion to Addiction in Videogames. England, D. and Beale, R.Proc. of HCI 2008, vol 1 BCS, 55–63.
Seiter, Ellen. 1999. *Television and New Media Audiences*. Oxford: Oxford University Press.
Shaughnessy, Robert. 2012. Immersive Performance, Shakespeare's Globe, and the 'Emancipated Spectator.' *The Hare* 1 (1).
Shaw, Philip. 2006. *The Sublime*. London: Routledge.
Smith, Matthew Wilson. 2007. *The Total Work of Art: From Bayreuth to Cyberspace*. New York: Routledge.
Spagnolli, Anna, and Luciano Gamberini. 2002. Immersion/Emersion: Presence in Hybrid Environments, Presence 2002. Conference Proceedings, Accessed Dec 2010.
Spigel, Lynn. 1992. *Make Room for TV: Television and the Family in Postwar America*. Chicago: The University of Chicago Press.
Stafford, Roy. 2007. *Understanding Audiences and the Film Industry*. London: BFI Publishing.
Staiger, Janet. 2000. *Perverse Spectators: The Practices of Film Reception*. New York: New York University Press.
Tedick, Diane J., Donna Christian, and Tara Williams Fortune. 2011. *Immersion Education: Practices, Policies, Possibilities*. Bristol: Multilingual Matters.
Tijs, T.J.W. 2006. *Immersion in Games: An Eyetracking Study*. Unpublished Master's thesis. Department of Computer and Systems Science, Royal Institute of Technology, Stockholm.
Tulloch, John. 2005. *Shakespeare and Chekhov in Production and Reception: Theatrical Events and Their Audiences*. Iowa City: University of Iowa.
Turner, Mark, and Giles Fauconnier. 2003. *The Way We Think: Conceptual Blending and The Mind's Hidden Complexities*. New York: Perseus.
Ubersfeld, Anne. 1982. The Pleasure of the Spectator, trans. Pierre Bouillaguet and Charles Jose. *Modern Drama* 25 (1): 127–139.

Varela, Francisco J., et al. 1993. *The Embodied Mind: Cognitive Science and Human Experience.* Cambridge, MA: MIT.

Warren, Jason. 2017. *Creating Worlds: How to Make Immersive Theatre.* London: Nick Hern Books (forthcoming).

White, Gareth. 2009. Odd, Anonymised Needs: Punchdrunk's Masked Spectator. In *Modes of Spectating,* ed. Oddey and White, 219–229. Bristol: Intellect Books.

White, Gareth. 2012. On Immersive Theatre. *Theatre Research International* 37 (3), October: 221–235.

White, Gareth. 2013. *Audience Participation in Theatre: Aesthetics of the Invitation.* London: Palgrave Macmillan.

Worthen, W.B. 2012. The Written Troubles of the Brain: 'Sleep No More' and the Space for Character. *Theatre Journal,* 64 (1): 79–97.

Young, Bryan Mitchell. 2005. Gaming Mind, Gaming Body: The Mind/Body Split for a New Era, Changing Views. Accessed Nov 2010.

Zaiontz, Keren. 2014. Narcissistic Spectatorship in Immersive and One-on-One Performance. *Theatre Journal,* 66 (3): 405–425.

CHAPTER 2

Interactivity and Immersion: Theoretical Approaches

Interactivity is a rich and oft-contested term, and it will be helpful to outline various approaches and definitions before considering its relationship to immersive theatre and audience experience. This chapter considers interactivity from the perspective of digital and multimedia performance, the theatrical event and computer games, concluding with a working definition that provides the framework for the following chapters' analysis of interactivity and immersion in relation to Punchdrunk. Chapter 3 proposes a methodology for analysing interactivity in immersive theatre with an extended case study of Punchdrunk's *The Drowned Man*; Chap. 4 expands the discussion outside the walls of an immersive production to consider interactivity across a wider social and cultural canvas. I use a deliberately inclusive "multivalent model" of interactivity in which different, often overlapping, modes of interactivity can take place within, and with, a designed system.

Existing models of interactivity can be located in various academic contexts, adding to a longer body of work arguing for the importance of play to human experience (Huizinga 1950; McGonigal 2011). Studies of digital/computer games and analogue gaming have considered interactivity (Bramer 1983; Salen and Zimmerman 2004; Dovey and Kennedy 2006) as it is a defining feature of gaming (Crawford 2003a): but the field also contains studies that question assumptions regarding interactivity and player agency or control (Perron 2003; Newman 2004). This makes studies of interactivity in gaming particularly relevant to immersive theatre, where similar assumptions about audience agency/empowerment

© The Author(s) 2017
R. Biggin, *Immersive Theatre and Audience Experience*,
DOI 10.1007/978-3-319-62039-8_2

might be made on the basis of an audience member's ability to engage with performers (O'Grady in Pitches and Popat 2011; Broadhurst and Machon 2012; White 2013). The overlap between gaming mechanics and performance is particularly relevant to digital and multimedia performance (Dixon 2007; Montola et al. 2009; Klich and Scheer 2012; Rose 2012). Wider social contexts also provide various models of interactivity, such as the theatrical event (Schani 2004) stressing the importance of social or civic connection, or multimedia advertising campaigns that seek to involve participants in the brand of a film or other media (Rose 2012), a means of interactivity with more explicitly commercial ends. This cultural context in particular requires critical engagement regarding the relationship between immersive experience and economic pressures (Alston 2012) or ethical boundaries (Ridout 2009). Scenography and design is also an important perspective on immersion (McKinney and Butterworth 2009: 192–195), as the sensory and aesthetic elements of much immersive work influence how a production is explored and experienced in the moment. The relationship between interactivity and scenographically immersive performance is an important element to Griffiths' "revered gaze" (2008), as it includes the effect of physically stepping into an immersive (scenographically rich, multisensory, other-worldly, etc.) space. All these perspectives allow immersive experience to be theorised as something that can be deliberately aimed for by makers. This in turn allows for enquiry into any potentially problematic aspects of the relationship between interactivity and immersion, particularly when it is seen to affect notions of audience agency.

Introduction(s) to Interactivity

Digital and Multimedia Performance

Multimedia performance can be defined as a medium that includes both live and mediated elements, both the "real" and the "virtual." Klich and Scheer consider technology and aesthetics in multimedia performance, "tracking the kind of performance work that highlights the ways in which representational, largely audio-visual, media can activate new aesthetic potentials and new spectatorial experiences" (2012: 1). They define immersion as "the way multimedia creates a form of sensorial overload to exhaust the subjective experience of the object or event" (9) and propose two concepts of immersion: cognitive and sensory.

Cognitive immersion is related to brain activity. Sensory immersion is concerned with how a participant is engaged in the here and now of performance, making this the more relevant model for approaching immersive experience in theatre. Immersion and interactivity are not mutually exclusive in this context; nor do they guarantee each other. The purpose of immersion (when defined as sensory overload or exhaustion) is to place an audience member/participant within the world or the aesthetic of the work. Achieving this effect may not necessarily require them to engage with the work physically.

Packer and Jordan name five characteristics as an intrinsic part of computer-based multimedia: integration, interactivity, hypermedia, immersion and narrativity (2001: xxx). They consider interactivity "in terms of the extent to which spectators or users can *determine the structure of the work* through their own interactions with the work. This idea of a complex interactivity empowers the spectator or user not merely to experience the work in a more active way but to contribute to a re-iteration of the work in a modulated form" (2012: 8–9; my emphasis). Interactivity is associated with an audience not merely acting within the boundaries set by the work—going along with its rules—or completing the tasks a show allows or asks for, but changing the work, mattering to the completion of the work. An assumption of empowerment emerges through these considerations of interactivity and immersive experience. Technology and empowerment in embodied digital performance is further considered in Broadhurst and Machon (2006). The sensory overload described by Kilch and Scheer would seem to de-empower an audience member by overstimulation.

Dixon considers interactivity in four categories: navigation, participation, conversation and collaboration. These categories are defined by "the incremental levels of a user's creative freedom they delineate [...] and are in no way relative to an individual artwork's quality, originality, or impact" (2007: 564). *Navigation* is the simplest form of interaction, "epitomized by the single click of a mouse." Surfing the web becomes a form of navigational interactivity as a user clicks through texts, pages and links. *Conversation* is a more "meaningful" level of interactivity: "dialogue … is reciprocated and is subject to real interchange and exchange" (584). Such interaction might take place between the user and the hardware or software, or between users themselves. In conversational works "there is often a complex relationship or negotiation established between the user/audience and the work, which is reliant on such issues as trust, cooperation, and openness" (585). *Collaboration* "comes about when the interactor becomes a major author or co-author of the artwork, experience, performance or narrative" (595). Although, as Dixon rightly states, these categories cannot be used to draw conclusions about the artistic merit of an individual work, this four-stage taxonomy of interactivity remains fundamentally hierarchical. The level of interactivity is defined not only by the role an audience member is invited to play in the work, but also by the effect they have on the final work. In the fourth category, *collaboration*, the artwork will be physically different (it will look, it will read, it will *be* different) because of the input it has received. There is an implicit value judgement in this hierarchical system that focuses on the role of the user. The more an audience member is able to influence and change a work, the greater the interactive experience, and the more rewarding for the player. Dixon defines most sensory installation environments (which might, via Kilch and Scheer, also be called immersive environments) as *participatory* rather than interactive: an audience may be able to operate a series of objects (for example) but an overall feeling of direct agency is limited. A direct correlation between interactivity and empowerment again becomes prominent in this theorisation of interactivity.

Dixon's system is useful as graded and incremental means of defining interactivity. It also allows that different types of interactivity, even when separated into categories, might begin to blend into the other. A single work can exist across all four categories:

> In installations where visitors' walking or movement triggers sensors to activate planned events and programmed sequences and effects, it is arguable whether the primary interactive paradigm is, according to our continuum, navigation (the course the user takes), participation (users helping to bring to life the environment's sensory features), conversation (a dialogue between the user and the computer) or collaboration (the user and computer creating art together). (2007: 583)

Although by definition the user's input is a vital aspect of interactivity, immersive experience is something which must be accommodated or allowed for, rather than forced; it is useful to consider how interactivity might be crafted and designed as a means to lowering barriers to immersive experience, rather than implying that one "type" of interactivity is going to provide the "better" results (whatever is meant by *better*). Any one of Dixon's four types of interactivity might lead to immersive experience. Drawing on Dixon's model, O'Grady suggests that "interactivity can function as both aesthetic principle and a political ideology. [...] Often, how one can interact is given priority over the *quality* and significance of the interactions taking place" (in Pitches and Popat 2011: 146; original emphasis). Dixon's model is useful for considering the quality of interactivity in terms of defining how an audience member is able to affect the work; when considering how interactivity may lead to immersion the model becomes less useful, as the type of input an audience member has on the work will not necessarily be the aspect that opens up immersive experience.

There is a further reason to look elsewhere for a model of interactivity. Discussion of interactivity and immersive experience, particularly in reference to performance, is often related to new media and digital technology, especially performance using multimedia and/or virtual reality. Punchdrunk shows might not immediately call to mind the label multimedia, as this term generally refers to work that explicitly uses technology. With the exception of *It Felt Like A Kiss*, film does not tend to feature in Punchdrunk shows, at least as an explicit medium used as part of the work, as opposed a more general aesthetic of film genres (pulp/noir/detective/horror). In *The Crash of the Elysium*, the physically absent Doctor communicated with his audience via television screens, and Higgin has cited the difficulty of getting the televised segments to meld with the physical show in a way that would keep the audience engaged (in Machon 2013: 214–218). Digital technology is used to create technical effects, of course, and Punchdrunk shows are highly sophisticated in this sense. But the relationship between interactivity and immersion should be considered separately to the means of engagement with the technology used to create the experience. Feelings of immersion do not stem directly from the use of technology in the way virtual reality or multimedia performance seeks to create immersive experience. The goal of any technology used in a Punchdrunk production—and much immersive theatre—is to effectively disappear behind the effects this technology creates (lowering the initial barriers to immersion of accessibility), allowing for immersion in the world of the production created by technology and SFX, rather than forefronting an audience member's relationship to, or within, the technology itself.

Improvisatory Theatre and Pervasive Gaming

Izzo (1997) emphasises interactivity as a form of theatre with historical antecedents, defining *interactive* performance as a form in which the actor conducts semi-improvised in-character conversations with passers-by. He describes the mindset of an interactive performer as being fully (emotionally, cognitively, imaginatively) immersed in the work, emphasising playfulness, flexibility and fluidity in the experience. Their performance, emotional journey and individual lines will alter depending on the response they receive from other actors and non-performing audience members (this type of interactivity occurs at the levels of *conversation* and *collaboration* as defined by Dixon). The negotiation of barriers to interactivity—overcoming reluctance with certain participants, for example—is very similar to the gradual process, on the spectator's side, of reaching a state of immersion in the performance. The audience member might even temporarily forget they are in (for example) a theme park and become fully engaged with the performer (who is also having an immersive experience as they perform). Though not a book about immersive theatre per se, Izzo's study considers interactive performance from the perspective of both makers/performers and spectators as a means to generate immersive experience in engagement. There is also a wider social consideration as Izzo suggests the form is deeply personally rewarding for a performer. Social aims of interactivity are also considered by O'Grady (2011), who compares contemporary interactive performance (such the pervasive games of Blast Theory) to Boal's Forum Theatre. There are many aesthetic and political differences of course, but the two forms do, also, share some similarities: in both, the invitation to engage with the content of the performance is integral to the form (146–175). The participant becomes an active co-creator of meaning and might become extremely engaged in what is going on, having an immersive experience in the work.

The performance form of pervasive gaming enables a further distinction to be made between interactive performance and immersive theatre. Montola, Stenros and Waern (in *Pervasive Games*: 2009) consider interactivity as a defining aspect of performative games and play. Unlike spatially immersive work where the performance is contained within defined walls of a building, pervasive games have either wide boundaries—city-wide, for instance—or no defined geographical limits at all. Players may become mentally immersed in the experience of the game and must overcome barriers to become immersed, gradually becoming accustomed to the game's rules and/or losing themselves in the world or the mechanics of play. Pervasive gaming is not immersive theatre, but it may provide an immersive experience. Like urban exploration, "Seeing the backside of the city, from run-down industrial areas to shady alleys, is a physically immersive experience that conveys a strong feeling of *being there*" (85). Pervasive gaming may also have a wide or undefined temporal dimension, as well as a wide or undefined spatial one.

Some immersive theatre productions, including Punchdrunk's bigger shows, may have aspects that resemble pervasive gaming built into their structure or form, such as an emphasis on searching or exploration or the use of cryptic clues. These aspects may lead to people engaging with them as if they were pervasive games. *Emergent interaction* in pervasive gaming occurs when "playing pronoia-inducing games in public spaces ... If the game design succeeds in instilling players with a feeling that it is safe to talk to anyone to try to enlist their help, the game world comes alive socially" (Montola et al. 2009: 123). The ideal, therefore, is for the game world to become blurred with real world: this occurs when "play is not limited temporally, social, or spatially" (122) and the resulting experience resembles psychological immersion or "flow." In much immersive theatre, hierarchies within the space are strictly defined, and there may be variously explicit or implicit rules about what is and is not allowed. Immersive experience is intense, fleeting and temporary; spatially, immersive theatre takes place within a strictly defined site (three hours in this building; three minutes in this room; three seconds of eye contact). This is opposite to pervasive gaming, which aims for the real world and game world to become blurred, both in content (Is that person part of the game or not?) and in form (What if I go over here? Is *this* allowed?). Both forms of theatre manipulate notions of boundaries and rules to create interactive and immersive effects.

Popat suggests that "in interactive artworks the power given to the audience is far greater, and they are made aware of its existence" (2006: 34). This distinction—the audience's awareness of the dynamics of power—is key to considering interactivity and immersion in immersive theatre. Interactive work makes the role the audience has to play. In immersive theatre, and particularly Punchdrunk's larger productions from *Faust* through to *The Drowned Man*, the way an audience member might actually affect the work is never overtly suggested. It might be implied in the moment of performance that one-on-one scenes are dependent upon an audience member's input, and where an audience member goes will affect what they see, but they cannot actively influence anything that occurs in performance. Interactive work depends upon a negotiation of hierarchies of space and time and tends to emphasise playfulness; in immersive theatre, boundaries and rules regarding an audience's behaviour are generally non-negotiable. "For *interactive* theatre, participants are asked to bring their own experience and understanding to bear on the drama as it progresses and illusion is kept to a minimum" (O'Grady 2011: 172; my emphasis). For *immersive* theatre, participants are asked to lose themselves in the drama as it progresses and makers work towards the aim of keeping illusion to a maximum. Although it can be well made, tightly structured and carefully crafted, "Interactive performance is always incomplete" (168) relying on the input of audience members (however that input manifests) to make the experience whole. A piece of immersive theatre, while it may contain moments where types of interactivity might occur, is generally presented as a complete creation; a whole world the participant visits, or an all-encompassing scenography. Bartley's term "narrator-visitor" for members of a Punchdrunk audience (2013) emphasises the temporary nature of their experience and the power dynamics they have during it: a narrator-visitor is able to author their own experience, but only temporarily and in response to invitation.

Social Contexts of Interactivity: The Experience Economy and the Theatrical Event

Immersive experience is often framed in terms of individual journeys, but it also creates conversation and the urge to share afterwards. David Jubb described "the bar at the end of a Punchdrunk show" as the most exciting place to be during *The Masque of the Red Death*, it being a place of excitement and exchange where "everyone wants to share what happened to them" (in Gardner 2007: n.p.). A social aspect of immersive experience is brought about by a desire to compare what happened on different days or in different parts of the building. (This mode of interactivity is discussed further in Chap. 4 on fan communities.) However, one potentially problematic consequence of this social emphasis is the operationalising of immersion: the way, as suggested previously, audiences are invited to *experience* a world rather than to explicitly *interact* with it suggests a top–down power dynamic with the potential for the commodification of experience. An aspiration for the creation of immersion, from a marketing perspective, is a one-way type of "interactivity" that goes from product to person.

Frank Rose (2011) considers interactivity between audiences and media with an emphasis on how it enhances marketing, branding and engagement between a product and its audience. He proposes that a new type of narrative is emerging that is non-linear and multimedia, characterised by interactive/participatory elements. The relationship between interactivity and immersion is a straightforward one of positive correlation: immersive experience allows for empowering participations with marketing. The creation of a fully immersive experience is a key way in which to engage fans with products. The fictional world of Pandora from Cameron's *Avatar* (2009), for example, is cited as a fully immersive and detailed world that can be explored beyond the film, in games or print media. Interactivity becomes a means of enhancing engagement with a film/story/product, and multimedia is integral to this approach: interactivity is designed to occur across different media at the same time. The experience of interactivity is a social one, in that there is an emphasis on conversation between players: multiple people engaging with a product at the same time can—and should be encouraged to—communicate while doing so. Such uses of technology's potential for immersion provide a useful context of some common discourses surrounding immersive theatre and performance that plays with notions of intimacy or individual experience. Rose's emphasis on the revolutionary potential of interactive marketing campaigns risks an oversimplification of what new media can achieve. *Avatar* is cited as a major success in the art of filmmaking due to the level of detail that went into its three-dimensional worldbuilding. Its one-dimensional story and characters go unmentioned. The success of the interactive trailer/game *Why So Serious?* is defined in terms of the box office receipts for the film it advertised, *The Dark Knight* (2008). Interactivity with new media is framed as successful when it immerses players in a *product*: the creation of experiences that fans will want to talk about is the blurring of an experience into sellable content. The claims made for immersion in the context Rose celebrates require careful analysis. The ability to interact with a piece of art will not in itself make for an immersive experience, but it may not even be particularly desirable.

The marketing campaigns Rose describes were carefully crafted experiences designed to create an extension of pre-existing fictional worlds: barriers to immersion were lowered, clues were laid and rewards for them planted, and fans who put the effort into respond enjoyed a unique experience that later tied into the story of the films. The campaigns used interactivity to enable, and guide the players towards, immersive experience—with the ultimate goal of making the player (more) aware of a product or brand. The economic imperative behind the crafting of immersion in this way has drawn criticism in terms of Punchdrunk's commercial projects. Alston considers product placement and the question of sustainable arts funding in regard to Punchdrunk's *The Black Diamond*, proposing a critical approach in which "audience members might assume partial responsibility for recognising and responding to the control of art production at the institutional level" (2012: 193). This response to immersive product placement in effect requires an audience member to create their own barrier to immersive experience: the critical engagement required to be aware of wider economic and cultural contexts of product placement takes an audience member outside the world presented by the work. The relationship between interactivity and audience experience will be key to considering further issues of agency and immersive marketing. This book does not have the scope to consider interactivity in detail in these contexts, instead focusing on approaches to analyse immersion and interactivity in the moment of performance. However, overlaps between interactivity, immersive experience and commercial imperatives, when considered in the context of the kind of creative marketing Rose and Alston describe, reveal a possible interpretation of the purpose for creating experiences people will want to talk about afterwards. This is an increasingly prevalent trajectory of immersive practice that demands acknowledgement and further analysis.

The theatrical event is another lens to view the social potentials of interactivity. Schani considers what qualities constitute "eventness" in theatre, distinguishing event from performance through "the presence of concrete conditions, whose most important dimensions are time and place" (2004: 111) and interactivity between participants. The idea of reciprocity in the theatrical event provides a useful way of thinking about immersive experience and interactivity from the perspective of performer as well as audience member. It enables a reading of immersive productions that encapsulates multiple types of interactivity occurring within the walls of the building, as well as outside and beyond the moment of theatrical encounter—and the reciprocal relationship between all of these.

Schani proposes a model of dynamic interactivity that emphasises reciprocity between the moment of performance, the stage play itself and the wider cultural situation that surrounds it. The difference between performance event and theatrical event lies in these relationships between and among the people involved. The case studies in the following chapters contain various suggestions of reciprocity between participants and the shows, and (particularly in fan communities) between each other. Reading them for their "eventness" enables a further distinction to be made between the theatrical event and the marketing event, in terms of how they manipulate immersive experience, interactivity and agency.

The model of "eventness" is a continuum, not a binary: and one example of a space existing across and between social event and cultural event are Punchdrunk's "decompression" areas. *The Masque of the Red Death*, *The Duchess of Malfi*, *Sleep No More* and *The Drowned Man* all contained a room in which the atmosphere could be notably different, louder and more relaxed and sociable. There could be music or other entertainers, a working bar and, most notably, masks need not to be worn. These spaces are the immersive theatre equivalent to an interval. Unlike a conventional interval they exist in space, rather than time: audience members are free to spend as long as they like in the interval space, provided they can find it. They offer a break from the intensity of the rest of the show and allow for movement between different kinds of interactivity (with the show as an audience member, to a more sociable kind) and behaviour (silence to talking, exploring to relaxing). These spaces can also be where the performance ends, or where the audience are led after the finale and permitted to remain. These "interval" spaces can be defined in terms of their relationship to immersive experience in the rest of the show, as they provide further boundaries in both time and space. They might also be framed in terms of providing a commercial aspect to the production (the drinks aren't free); or perhaps they represent a return to the conventional rules and social dynamics of the "real" world, as opposed to the otherworldly dreamland of the show (after all, the drinks wouldn't be free anywhere else either).

COMPUTER GAMES: A MULTIVALENT MODEL

Discourses around gaming reveal a history of social anxiety regarding the antisocial consequences of too much immersion. *Interactivity* can be used to suggest a more enriching or educational experience: a euphemism employed to gloss over the negative connotations of becoming too immersed in a game. Products invoke *interactivity* to create a "veneer of respectability [...] Thus, we find certain companies preferring to consider themselves contributing to a world of 'interactive entertainment' [...] It follows that the products of an interactive entertainment industry are not games. Rather, they are 'interactive fiction' or 'interactive narratives'" (Newman 2004: 7). Interactivity is invoked as a response to the fear of too much immersion: it is immersion's socially acceptable opposite.

Newman emphasises the importance of *"player activity"* (16; original emphasis), arguing that games "may be characterised by a sense of 'being there', rather than controlling, manipulating or perhaps even 'playing a game'" (17). Immersion is linked with a sense of control, and the interactive aspects of a game are designed to create and ensure this. A visible (i.e. clear, fair) system of challenge and reward are key, and it is important that the manner in which a gamer is immersed does not feel contrived. Crafting for immersive experience in theatre has some parallels with the challenge faced by game designers, particularly in reference to interactivity. Game designer Crawford states: "I have long maintained that interactivity is the essence of the gaming experience, and that the quality of the interaction determines the quality of the game" (2003a: 84). A more interactive game isn't necessarily the one with the flashier graphics, but the game that responds the most to the player. What matters is that the player can affect the outcome. Crawford proposes a workload versus payoff model for determining the effectiveness of a game's interactivity, which is very similar to the concept of challenge and skill alignment required to determine a state of psychological "flow." The gamer does not wish to become aware of the interface as she plays, as this would break immersion: "For many video game designers, it is important to ensure that there is no explicit detachment and distance from the contents of the game" (Newman 2004: 17–18). Interactivity in gaming is designed to ensure immersion and challenge. Immersive theatre can also be designed to allow for this kind of engaged experience.

The difference between a game and simply *play* is that while a game has a way to win or to lose, play has no winning beyond what a player may understand the term to mean. Open-ended or "sandbox" games do not have explicit ways to win but gamers may aim for certain goals they set for themselves. The relationship between a player and the rule(s) of play are themselves a site for interactivity, or player-led modification or manipulation:

once the rules [of a game] have been deduced and overcome, videogames may lose their appeal and new challenges may be sought, either through (purchasing) new games or the imposition of new ludus rules. [...] Deducing, collating, and working within or around a game's rulesets represents a large part of the pleasure of videogame play and further highlights the active, participatory role of the player. (Newman 2004: 21–22)

This game-within-a-game mode of interactivity—interacting *with* the rules themselves—could also occur in immersive theatre, particularly in shows that give no explicit instruction to audience members beyond the vague assurance that "tonight, your bearing shapes your fate" (the audio introduction to *The Drowned Man*). Repeat attendees in particular may set themselves additional challenges, games or goals: applying their own ludus rules on top of, as well as, or even overwriting, the production's implicit suggested modes of engagement. A sister activity to deliberately creating additional ludus rules is accidentally breaking the implicit existing rules—and breaking this boundary may not necessarily break immersion. Alston (2016) describes how the "mistakes" of an errant immersive spectator, accidentally wandering far from a piece of work's prescribed or preferred course, paradoxically emphasises the centrality of the audience member's role in creating immersive aesthetics.

It follows that interactivity has several forms, only some of which might be anticipated by the game/theatre designer; a participant might interact in ways which have not been designed for. Murray argues that "*Agency and immersion are mutually reinforcing.* When we engage with an immersive world and it responds to us as we expect it to, revealing deeper levels of content, greater detail in its coverage, we become more deeply immersed" (2012: 102; original emphasis). Murray calls this the "active creation of belief." Agency occurs when an interactor-player engages with an imaginary world and experiences a reciprocal response. For Crawford, reciprocity is also key to interactivity, fundamentally "A cyclic process in which two active agents alternately (and metaphorically) listen, think, and speak" (2003a: 76). By these definitions of interactivity, much immersive theatre may seem not very interactive at all.

The difference between games and puzzles provides a further distinction that is useful for considering interactivity and immersion in theatre. Puzzles are self-contained: they may enrich the feeling that play is occurring in a vast world; or stall or disrupt gameplay and add little to the overall experience, becoming redundant and defunct once completed.

Interactivity differentiates a game from a static puzzle. A player is able to control, or at least play a part in, a game's events. This kind of "active" interactivity is seen to allow for immersive experience by being linked to feelings of control and agency, a sensation of skill matching challenge. The assumption that there is an automatic correlation between interactivity and agency is under question in gaming studies—such assumptions should also be queried in regard to claims made by immersive or interactive theatre regarding audience agency or empowerment. Newman argues that discussing how interactive games are overlooks an even more fundamental point:

> Videogames are highly complex, segmented arrangements of elements. Some of these elements may be seen to be highly "interactive," requiring considerable player participation and responding to player action, while others… appear to demand little or no direct player input or control, nor do they respond to attempts to exert influence. Yet, this is not to say that the player is not actively interrogating the material, exploring it for clues to aid forthcoming play or reading a presented narrative in order to make sense of part events or those yet to come. (2004: 27)

The player's movement between various levels or types of participation—going between passive watching and active strategising, for example—creates a rewarding video game experience: a movement into, and out of, and into again, various levels of engagement with a game. Interactivity requires a response from the gamer, and their input is necessary for the game to continue, progress, be completed; but this, in itself, does not guarantee immersion. This is a useful framing of interactivity that runs parallel with the definition of immersive experience as a temporary, fleeting, intense, necessarily temporary phenomenon that exists as a series of graded states, not as a felt/not-felt binary. The movement between levels of interactivity—in a Punchdrunk show, for example, this could be a movement between passive watching, emotional engagement with a piece of dance, active searching through rooms, getting lost, following someone—is what creates an immersive experience, not the sensation of interacting (or not) in itself.

The idea that an audience member moves between different modes of interactivity resolves an apparent contradiction in the relationship between interactivity and immersive experience. Interactivity is not required to be consistent. In fact, moving between modes of interactivity might be more effective in allowing for immersive experience than suggesting an audience member/game player be fully in control of their own experience throughout. It may be helpful to draw a distinction between interactivity and activity. Writing from the perspective of interactive digital media design, Murray notes that interactivity is "a design term that is often used too loosely, and is sometimes confused with mere activity or potential actions" (2012: 426). If a game is defined by, or discussed primarily in terms of, the input and participation of the player, non-interactive cutscenes might be seen as problematic or annoying for a gamer, disrupting play. They are plain "activity," which they cannot influence and therefore cannot become immersed in. By this logic, the most frustrating moments of an immersive theatre production would be when an audience member comes upon performers dancing a scene and are required to give them space, as this stops them from moving freely around or actively engaging with individual performers or parts of the set. Watching the scene becomes an activity that they have little control over. But of course, watching a dance scene from close up can be deeply rewarding, engaging, impressive, emotional, real: so a simplistic interactivity/activity model cannot provide straight answers to the question of what kind of engagement will lead to a more affecting experience of immersion in the work. The quality and significance of the ways an audience member/player might engage with a piece of work are integral to the effect it has, rather than any one mode of interactivity (or activity) being automatically the most effective. Rather than being simply dismissed as interruptions, cutscenes might be considered alongside level breaks, save points or restarts as pauses that punctuate gaming and affect its tempo or the overall rhythm. They are all part of a game's structure, and these components combined with actual play make up the full experience of the game—not to mention their potential contributions to story, tone, atmosphere, worldbuilding. Movement between different modes of engagement, active exploring followed by a calmer minute of watching, makes for a richer experience than constant single level of activity or intensity. Just as video games are not all about interactivity, but contain movement between more and less interactive scenes, neither is immersive experience in theatre all about interactivity, but consists of movements across lowered barriers to immersion and into various (and varied) modes of engaging with performers or the performance space.

Salen and Zimmerman offer a four-mode taxonomy of interactivity:

Mode 1:   Cognitive interactivity; or interpretive participation
Mode 2:   Functional interactivity; or utilitarian participation
Mode 3:   Explicit interactivity; or participation with designed choices and procedures
Mode 4:   Beyond-the-object interactivity; cultural participation. (2004: 69)

This model incorporates the many definitions of interactivity that can be found across studies of both gaming and theatre rather than attempting to give a definitive, and therefore limiting, description of what interactivity can be. I have suggested already that Dixon's hierarchical continuum of interactivity (from navigation to collaboration) contains an implicit value judgement about the role of the user in regard to making meaning within the work. O'Grady points out that studies of interactivity in performance too often focus on the ways in which interactivity is possible, rather than on the "*quality* or *significance* of the interactions taking place" (146; original emphasis). The following chapters on interactivity use Salen and Zimmerman's system, drawing on its incorporation of "overlapping ways of understanding any moment of interactivity" (2004: 69) to consider quality and significance, not just interactivity *type*. Salen and Zimmerman point out that "*meaningful* play is tied not only to the concept of player action and system outcome, but also to a particular context in which the action occurs" (60; my emphasis). The four-mode system allows for imaginative/cognitive/sensory participation to be regarded as interactivity, as well as more explicit physical manifestations of interactivity (which all four of Dixon's modes resemble) and participation within a wider social context (as in the theatrical event).

IN(TERACTIVE) CONCLUSION

Interactivity—whatever is meant by it—does not, in itself, guarantee immersive experience. Certain modes or moments of interactivity may facilitate and/or allow for it more than others, being a way to lower barriers to immersive experience and draw an audience member into the work. Although interactive theatre and immersive theatre may be created to fulfil very different aims, interactivity is an aspect of immersive theatre, albeit it may take different forms and have different effects from show to show, and from person to person. Audience members might become imaginatively, functionally or explicitly engaged with a show—or some combination of the three—at any one time, whether imagining worlds and stories from clues planted in an empty room; walking around, opening doors and exploring the space; sharing a drink with a performer in a one-on-one; or idly wondering how, on a more practical level, the whole thing was put together. *Interactivity* can also describe wider cultural participation, and in this mode immersive experience is, or can become, a social experience.

The following two chapters explore case studies from Punchdrunk to explore the complex relationship(s) between interactivity and immersive experience in more detail. Chapter 3 looks at interactivity and immersion in *The Drowned Man*, considering how it was constituted and performed, and the effects various mode of interactivity may have had on immersion. Chapter 4 considers the fourth mode in the model—beyond-the-object interactivity or cultural participation—beginning with *Faust* and *The Masque of the Red Death* and then, via *Sleep No More*, returning to *The Drowned Man*. Chapter 4 therefore traces a trajectory of the company's history and development in the near-decade between the earlier shows and their most recent productions, and this change in the company's status further informs how immersive experience is claimed to occur within their work, and who claims it.

References

Alston, Adam. 2012. Funding, Product Placement and Drunkenness in Punchdrunk's *The Black Diamond*. *Studies in Theatre & Performance* 32 (2): 193–208.

Alston, Adam. 2016. Making Mistakes in Immersive Theatre: Spectatorship and Errant Immersion. *Journal of Contemporary Drama in English* 4 (1): 61–73.

Bartley, Sean. 2013. Punchdrunk: Performance, Permission, Paradox. Borrowers and Lenders, Athens: Oct 2013, Volume VII, Issue 2.

Bramer, M.A. 1983. *Computer Game-Playing: Theory and Practice*. Chichester: Ellen Horwood.

Broadhurst, Susan and Josephine Machon. (eds.) 2006. *Performance and Technology: Practices of Virtual Embodiment and Interactivity*. London: Palgrave Macmillan.

Broadhurst, Susan and Josephine Machon. (eds.) 2012. *Identity, Performance and Technology: Practices of Empowerment, Embodiment and Technicity*. London: Palgrave Macmillan.

Crawford, Chris. 2003a. *On Game Design*. Indianapolis: New Riders.

Crawford, Chris. 2003b. Interactive Storytelling. In *The Video Game Theory Reader*, ed. Mark J. P. Wolf and Bernard Perron, 259–273. New York: Routledge.

Dixon, Steve. 2007. *Digital Performance: A History of New Media in Theatre, Dance, Performance Art and Installation*. Cambridge: MIT Press.

Dovey, Jon, and Helen W. Kennedy. 2006. *Game Cultures: Computer Games as New Media*. Maidenhead: Open University Press.

Gardner, Lyn. 2007. The Masque of the Red Death Left Me Punchdrunk. *Guardian*, October 4.

Griffiths, Alison. 2008. *Shivers Down Your Spine: Cinema, Museums and the Immersive View*. New York: Columbia University Press.

Huizinga, Johan. 1950. *Homo Ludens: A Study of the Play Element in Culture*. Boston: Beacon Press.

Izzo, Gary. 1997. *The Art of Play: The New Genre of Interactive Theatre*. Portsmouth, NH: Heinemann.

Klich, Rosemary, and Edward Scheer. 2012. *Multimedia Performance*. London: Palgrave Macmillan.

Machon, Josephine. 2013. *Immersive Theatres: Intimacy and Immediacy in Contemporary Performance*. London: Palgrave Macmillan.

McGonigal, Jane. 2011. *Reality is Broken: Why Games Make Us Better and How They Can Change the World*. London: Vintage.

McKinney, Joslin, and Philip Butterworth. 2009. *The Cambridge Introduction to Scenography*. Cambridge: Cambridge University Press.

Montola, Markus, et al. 2009. *Pervasive Games: Theory and Design: Experiences on the Boundary Between Life and Play*. Burlington: Morgan Kaufmann.

Murray, Janet H. 2012. *Inventing the Medium: Principles of Interaction Design as a Cultural Practice*. Cambridge, MA: MIT Press.

Newman, James. 2004. *Videogames*. London: Routledge.

O'Grady, Alice (ed.). 2011. Interactivity. In *Performance Perspectives: A Critical Introduction*, ed. Jonathan Pitches and Sita Popat, 146–175. London: Palgrave Macmillan.

Packer, R., and K. Jordan (eds.). 2001. *Multimedia: From Wagner to Virtual Reality*. New York: W.W. Norton and Company.

Perron, Bernard. 2003. From Gamers to Players and Gameplayers: The Example of Interactive Movies. In *The Video Game Theory Reader*, ed. Mark J. P. Wolf and Bernard Perron, 237–258. New York: Routledge.

Pitches, Jonathan, and Sita Popat (eds.). 2011. *Performance Perspectives: A Critical Introduction*. London: Palgrave MacMillan.

Popat, Sita. 2006. *Invisible Connections: Dance, Choreography and Internet Communities*. London: Routledge.

Ridout, Nicholas. 2009. *Theatre & Ethics*. London: Palgrave Macmillan.

Rose, Frank. 2011. *The Art of Immersion: How the Digital Generation Is Remaking Hollywood, Madison Avenue and the Way We Tell Stories: Entertainment in a Connected World.* New York: W.W. Norton & Co.

Rose, Frank. 2012. How Punchdrunk Theatre Reels 'em in With Immersive Storytelling. Wired. Accessed 12 Mar 2012.

Salen, K., and E. Zimmerman. 2004. *Rules of Play: Game Design Fundamentals.* Cambridge, MA: MIT Press.

Schani, Hadassa. 2004. The Theatrical Event: From Coordination to Dynamic Interactivity. In *Theatrical Events: Borders, Dynamics, Frames*, ed. Vicky Ann Cremona, Peter Eversmann, Hans van Maanen, Willmar Sauter, and John Tulloch, 111–129. New York: Rodopi.

White, Gareth. 2013. *Audience Participation in Theatre: Aesthetics of the Invitation.* London: Palgrave Macmillan.

CHAPTER 3

Interactivity and Immersion in *The Drowned Man*

Taking a setting inspired by the gothic Hollywood of Nathanael West's novel *The Day of the Locust* (1939) and Buchner's *Woyzeck's* (1879) fragmented narrative of jealousy and military trauma as the grounds for its plot, *The Drowned Man* (31 London Street/Temple Studios: 2013–2014) took place across five floors of an old post office building in central London. It was Punchdrunk's largest show to date, in both scale and audience capacity, and it ran for a year after several extensions to the original run. Audience members were presented with a mask and invited to wander through a series of spaces that made up the fictional Temple Studios and the secret, hidden world(s) around it. This included film sets, private studio rooms, a costume department and a grand dressing room on the Hollywood side; and a real world side including a caravan park, town centre and doctor's surgery. More abstract spaces with eerie imagery also lent a sense of menace across the show: a witch's hut; scarecrows; a desert across the top floor, coated with sand. The story that looped through the show, which audiences were allowed to find, follow or explore at will, contained two main plots which roughly followed that of *Woyzeck*. Two Woyzeck equivalents (William and Wendy) journeyed through the space, experiencing the world of the film studio and its sinister underbelly, their actions coming together at the end in a finale of desperation, murder and dance.

This chapter applies the multivalent model outlined in the previous chapter to *The Drowned Man* to discuss interactivity and immersive experience within the walls of an immersive theatre production. It uses the first three modes in the four-mode model:

© The Author(s) 2017
R. Biggin, *Immersive Theatre and Audience Experience*,
DOI 10.1007/978-3-319-62039-8_3

Mode 1:   Cognitive interactivity; or interpretive participation
Mode 2:   Functional interactivity; or utilitarian participation
Mode 3:   Explicit interactivity; or participation with designed choices and procedures. (Salen and Zimmerman 2004: 69)

The next chapter will widen out to consider social contexts, interactivity beyond the theatrical encounter. This discussion is interested in interactivity and immersive experience in regard to audience agency, empowerment and freedom in the moment(s) of performance. Running through the chapter is a questioning of the assumption that interactivity in and of itself is centrally important to immersive theatre's effect(s). *The Drowned Man* was not interactive in an explicit sense, as the audience did not have power to change or control any of the action. This observation is not necessarily a criticism of immersive work; interplay between interactivity and passivity can be what gives immersive experience its power. *The Drowned Man* could be highly interactive in an imaginative and interpretive sense, and certainly required a high level of interactivity in a functional sense. What may be more interesting than defining how interactive a production is, is asking how the *idea* of interactivity is situated among larger claims for immersive theatre.

Cognitive Interactivity

> This is the psychological, emotional, and intellectual participation between a person and a system. Example: the complex imaginative interaction between a single player and a graphic adventure game. (Salen and Zimmerman 2004: 59)

How might cognitive interactivity, or imaginative participation, occur or manifest in *The Drowned Man*, and what relationship might it have with immersive experience? The creation of an individual narrative via an audience member's route through the show, or the process of piecing together separate fragmented rooms/scenes into a wider world or story: these are common grounds for discussion of *The Drowned Man* and other immersive productions that emphasise audience exploration across wide spaces and fragmented narratives (such as Machon 2013). Immersive experience in *The Drowned Man* was facilitated (in part) by this mode of interaction—in part, because emotional and intellectual engagement does not have a physical manifestation. In *The Drowned*

Man, imaginative engagement was necessarily linked with physically navigating the space. Worldbuilding, clue-solving, path-finding, room/object/performer-discovering and the general exploratory nature of navigation have the potential to facilitate imaginative engagement.

Imaginative engagement is linked to structure. Discovering a scene, an audience member might not necessarily know the character, their story so far, or—if the scene is *in media res*—even what is currently going on. The audience were introduced to the main players of Temple Studios at the beginning of the show by a performer in the lift: this introduction preceded entry to the show proper and gave a brief outline of the plot dynamics. The (deliberately) disorientating effects of the production mean it is still possible, or inevitable, to happen upon a scene not quite knowing where you are. The potential for imaginative engagement remains with anonymous characters. Knowing a little about them might be a key part of being able to follow one story, but cognitive interactivity can occur without this information. Reading a scene—for example, a medical examination in the Doctor's surgery that drew on the imagery of Leonardo Da Vinci's *Vitruvian Man*—as an abstract meditation on medicine and the human form is just as complex an act of interpretation as reading the scene as a key moment in William's life, if you have been following the character of William and understand that he has recently returned from war. Both these approaches to imaginative interaction require a level of engagement that suggests immersive experience. Barriers to immersion arise when one way of engaging with the show becomes coded as the "better" or "correct" way. Giving out a plot synopsis at the beginning, for example, as *The Drowned Man* did to the waiting queue to enter, suggests some knowledge of the plot is required to fully engage. The ability to interpret a scene, to imaginatively participate with it, could become blocked by the anxiety that there is a better way to engage with the scene, perhaps with the show as a whole, and that you did not know it.

This is an important aspect of the relationship between cognitive engagement, imaginative participation and immersive experience, and leads to the question of how immersion is described (or implied) in a show's own discourses. An emphasis on freedom in inviting an audience to go their own way exploring a show suggests that there is no wrong way to experience it. This suggestion may stand in contradiction if it is also implied that anything needs to be understood to enjoy the show fully: whether that is an outline of the plot and introduction to the main characters, or an understanding of implicit rules regarding audience behaviour within a theatrical form. Does a plot synopsis give audience members a path from which they are free to deviate, or does it suggest that if they cannot find these stories they have not experienced the show as fully as they might have? The former could lower barriers to immersive experience; the latter might raise them high. Imaginative immersion can also be broken by a more pragmatic sense of scope:

> It's difficult to give yourself over to theatre when your overriding emotion is anxiety. Anxiety that you're not seeing the crucial key that will unlock the piece; that you're looking too hard at something that means nothing; that you might have to get involved at any moment; or that you're missing out on something more exciting happening in another room. (Jones, "Is Theatre Becoming Too Immersive?," 2013: n.p.)

This is far from a revered gaze that results from admiration for an overwhelming spectacle. The difference may be down to whether an audience member feels they are supposed to follow or understand a certain aspect or whether being unable to see everything is understood to be key to a production's power. They may be told one thing but find the other is heavily implied.

Disorientation was a key motif of *The Drowned Man*, both in the stories and world of the characters and in the production's physical layout. Barrett has called *disorientation* part of any Punchdrunk experience: "If you're uncomfortable, then suddenly you're eager to receive" (in Hoggard 2013: n.p.). As discussed previously, barriers to immersion can be lowered but immersive experience cannot be guaranteed and it certainly cannot be forced. A sense of force will break immersion very quickly. The opening moment(s) of *The Drowned Man* provide a useful example for thinking through imaginative immersion and disorientation.

The show had a series of beginnings. Audience members were released from a lift onto one of the floors, bringing a randomised element to where, geographically, their experience began. Even before the lift however, the audience moved through a dark, narrow maze-like series of corridors to get to the first small space (gradually meeting several other masked spectators, who they will eventually get into the lift with). These moments were characterised by calm and quiet semi-darkness, before a voiceover introduction to the fictional world of the show. They offer a transition experience between the pragmatics of the ticket queue, cloakroom and so on, and the exploration of the show proper. The introductory voiceover, by a character within the fictional world (Mr. Stanford), introduces the film studio (Temple Studios) and the conceit that their latest picture (also called "The Drowned Man") is about to finish filming. The lift then opens, and audience members are given a more personal introduction by the character operating it before being spat out at various floors to (finally) "begin" their exploration of *The Drowned Man*.

These varied beginnings contained deliberately disorientating elements while providing a layout of the rules of engagement designed to make the experience less disorientating. In the lift audience members were given an in-character assessment of the main players at Temple Studios and advised that it is better to split up: an introduction to the logistics of the show as well as an introduction to the power dynamics of its fictional world. The opening voiceover introduced the tone of that world (along with the possibility of an unreliable narrator) alongside aesthetic and atmospheric introductions in the sinister music and dim lighting. *The Drowned Man* had multiple beginnings, which contained invitations to explore, imagine and interpret the show while also advising on how engaging with the show smoothly might best be achieved.

Through these graded starts, *The Drowned Man* enabled imaginative interactivity. The task of interpretation and exploration were immediately set up and allowed for by a mixture of deliberate disorientation and carefully mediated instruction. These invitations for imaginative engagement (cognitive interactivity) can be seen as lowering barriers to immersion, by gradually taking audience members away from the real world in which they put the masks on and bringing them into (the world of) Temple Studios. It is possible that barriers to immersion are set up here, however. When the rules of engagement are strict, anxiety over the consequences of breaking them or witnessing others breaking them (whether accidentally or deliberately) can lead to imaginative engagement being broken.

Key to this book's conceptualisation of immersive experience is its existence as a series of graded states, not a felt/not-felt binary. The gradual building up of information about the production/world/characters while wandering through *The Drowned Man* might facilitate a slow entry into an environment that invites immersive experience: exploring the different atmospheres from room to room, space to space; following characters, or making the decision to wander at random instead, can lead to a sense of immersion in the production. There are many examples of this kind of interpretive participation within *The Drowned Man*: piecing together characters' stories to get some sense of a whole; following an individual character and focusing on their journey instead; exploring rooms; reading letters; watching duets or group performances; scenes of dance, scenes of dialogue; piecing together the relationship between the two worlds of the show, inside the Studio and outside; following all the references to horses in the decor; or all the references to black magic; or following themes—fame, unhappiness, jealousy. Any and all these means of navigating the show might lead to immersive experience and losing track of time, an effect of total immersion in the activity (Brown and Cairns 2004). An audience member has some degree of freedom over how closely they pay attention, and what they pay attention to. They might focus on the structure of the show as a whole, following actors to get a sense of the logistics; or vary between exploring in this way and focusing on a greatly detailed part of the set design. Or the invitation to engage in all this varying exploration, while appearing open-ended, might create a feeling of frustration in being overwhelmed or lost.

Referring to *The Masque of the Red Death*, Barrett stated the production "failed" if an audience member was to "suddenly remember they're in London in 2007" at any point (in Gardner 2007: n.p.). Later, *The Drowned Man* had a similar aim: "We're trying to build a parallel universe. [...] For a few hours inside the walls, you forget that it's London 2013 and slip into this other place" (Barrett in Hoggard 2013: n.p.). These goals demonstrate a desire for intense engagement—total immersion at all times—with the fictional world of the show: total cognitive interactivity, total interpretive participation. This understanding of immersion could be nuanced by incorporating the concept of Real World Disassociation or RWD (Jennett et al. 2008), a state in which engaged players/spectators can choose to pay attention only to very relevant distractions. Remembering that you are in London in 2007 or 2013, and then throwing that thought away again to get back to the Masque or the Studio, might demonstrate a more thorough experience of immersion than if this thought never occurs.

Having discussed the importance of disorientation, and how it may create a receptive state of mind for cognitive interpretation and allow for (lower the barriers to) immersive experience, it is worth considering briefly the seemingly contradictory the idea of an audience member knowing the layout or design of the show and to an extent knowing what to expect. Beyond reaching this point by exploring the show or even attending it multiple times, this perspective was allowed for within *The Drowned Man* itself. The Drafting Studio, a space on the basement floor which only Premium ticket holders could access, contained a diagram outlining where the characters were at any time, their looped actions spelled out across a grid. The character who runs this room shows an audience member where they are in the timeline, advises them to go and see what she has just told them will happen next. Such a diagram enabled rehearsals for the show; incorporating it into the performance added something of the mastermind element—beyond the fictional world of Temple Studios which had the sinister studio manager Mr. Stanford as its mastermind, but as a production more generally with an author known as "Punchdrunk" in the role. The diagram lent a sense of inevitability to the action, and the sense of being partial to secret knowledge may make for a compelling immersive experience in the space, watching a scene having been told it was going to happen, perhaps alongside other audience members who did not receive the tip-off. Of course, discovering the workings in this way makes explicit the audience member's lack of agency to change or alter the course of the action. If interactivity is more rewarding when it is collaborative, the relationship between this kind of experience and immersion in the world might appear mutually exclusive—a detailed diagram of the production somewhat going against the exploratory nature of imaginative participation in a fictional world. Perhaps the tip-off itself becomes the collaborative element: interactivity between authorial mastermind and (lucky) (Premium) ticket holder.

Functional Interactivity

> Included here: functional, structural interactions with the material components of the system (whether real or virtual). For example, that graphic adventure you played: how was the interface? How "sticky" were the buttons? What was the response time? How legible was the text on your high resolution monitor? All of these elements are part of the total experience of interaction. (Salen and Zimmerman 2004: 59)

In any theatrical event, and especially work that takes on immersive/pervasive/interactive labels, utilitarian participation is a formative part of the experience. This mode of interactivity is concerned not with the imaginative but with the real. Physical barriers to immersion fall under this category and many are straightforwardly real-world: could you see over everyone else? Was the mask comfortable? Were you able to navigate that space with the odd floor without tripping? This mode of interactivity is concerned with what must happen *before* any suspension of disbelief, plunging into a new world or going off to explore can occur. It asks what a spectator must grow accustomed to before any imaginative work can take place—how they navigate and negotiate the physical, structural or logistical rules of the performance. Questions of accessibility are also raised by considering interactivity in this mode. Much immersive theatre relies heavily on audience members having the physical means to move themselves through the building or negotiate multiple sets of stairs, and depends upon their feel comfortable (or the right kind of uncomfortable) in darker, closer, more intimidating spaces. For audience members who cannot achieve these goals, utilitarian participation offers a perspective for why immersive experience becomes impossible—barriers are raised beyond hope of passing in the very form of the production.

What might the relationship be between interactivity and immersive experience in *The Drowned Man*, in reference to utilitarian participation?

Barriers to immersion play a large part in this mode. The means of participation in the show were primarily logistical. They are also about preparation: the queue; the cloakroom; any physical discomforts or boring necessities surrounding the initial activity of *getting to the space* also come under this category. As discussed previously, *The Drowned Man* had a series of beginnings that aimed to lower the barriers to immersion caused by this initial business, steadily moving the audience from the real world to its fictional one. Premium ticket holders had a separate entry and cloakroom, making entry a little easier (awareness of this tiered system might make Standard ticket holders more aware of their own entry system). And the in-character introductions were means of lowering barriers to immersion regarding physical navigation as well as laying out the fictional story.

Punchdrunk's decision to mask spectators has been discussed as providing a liberating anonymity (White 2005). More problematically it has been called an aid to voyeurism, a portable fourth wall separating spectators from the show in an alienating fashion: "By issuing masks to spectators, the company introduces, as it understands, a fourth wall stand-in" (Gordon 2013: n.p.). In terms of functional interactivity a potential problem is physical discomfort, which makes it difficult to forget the mask and be able to become engaged in the space beyond it. Punchdrunk have been continually refining the style of mask they use, and *The Drowned Man*'s carnivalesque mask came away from the face over the mouth (although it remained non-compatible with glasses). Masking audience members has become a known Punchdrunk convention, and they are given out along with the rules: do not remove it during the performance; don't speak to performers; tell the black-masked ushers if you have any problems. This means of introducing one of the most important physical ways audience members navigated the show could become, potentially, an intimidating list of Dos and Don'ts which act as barriers to immersion. The way the masks are introduced—and whether they are seen as an everyday convention or an exciting artistic decision, a chore to be dealt with or an exciting idea that adds to the fun; or some combination of these; or no big deal either way—will affect how "well" they work at a purely utilitarian level.

Rules of engagement—whether stated or implied—are key to experiencing immersive productions. Utilitarian participation is concerned not only with the physical and functional—such as discomfort with the mask—but also with emotional or psychological well-being: becoming anxious that you are missing something more exciting elsewhere; or that you have got the wrong kind of lost; wanting to go back to a certain room and being unable to find it. A key problem for a show on the scale of *The Drowned Man* is ensuring audience members can still feel the excitement of intimacy and secrecy in a much bigger space. *The Drowned Man* dealt with the size of the building by creating smaller spaces within it: a large sandy desert-like landscape and a town centre existed alongside many much smaller rooms, mazes and spaces. The effect(s) of disorientation might also allow size to become more of an elastic concept that does not directly affect the experience of moving through individual rooms and settings.

At a utilitarian level of participation, other audience members may also provide barriers to immersion. This was particularly the case for *The Drowned Man* as it invited both those well accustomed to the rules of play (long-term immersive theatregoers and/or fans of the company), and people experiencing a Punchdrunk show for the first time. Observations of certain audience behaviours can also suggest there are more rules to experiencing the show than might first appear. Susannah Clapp commented on the changing nature of a Punchdrunk audience in *The Drowned Man* (the first sentence placing this changing audience in the context of work with an increasing sense of "re-tread"):

> This is billed as Punchdrunk's biggest show, but the expansion is of square feet rather than imagination. [...] Now aficionados poke eagerly into a place, suss out whether there is any action and move on. They run. They follow the action in packs. They elbow. Maddeningly, some hold hands. They know how to winkle out a narrative. There is less baffled loitering and fruitful lingering. That is something of a loss. (2013: n.p.)

There are no explicit rules against any of these behaviours, but they are perceived as inconsiderate, towards both the performers and the rest of the spectators. Frustration over this kind of behaviour reveals a series of implicit assumptions about ideal audience behaviour. In addition, black-masked ushers move audience members away from sites of imminent dance sequences or instruct them not to talk; as well as implicit assumptions of how best to watch, there are explicit rules that enforce considerate spectatorship. The notion that you might find a performer and follow them becomes a kind of unwritten rule for the way a spectator "should" experience *The Drowned Man*, rather than being merely one way to experience the show, a choice no better or worse than others. Follow a character and see the most action: and by doing so, get the most out of the production. The result is large groups of white-masked audience members following performers around, making it seem impossible to stumble upon a private moment or accidentally find yourself the sole spectator of a scene, or (on a more functional level) to have a good view of the character you are following. This behaviour prioritises finding performers over wandering through the space in your own time, as well as prioritising performers over set and design. The "rule" that audiences are split up into individuals was not always followed in *The Drowned Man*: couples clung together; groups hung on to each other; people talked, sent tweets and texts. On the surface it might seem as if this behaviour can only detract from any chance of immersion, as well as bothering others and detracting from theirs. But remaining with friends should not be dismissed outright as "not doing it properly." I have seen an audience member's friends laugh with her for screaming; I have seen people wave to a couple taking a few minutes' rest on a swing seat, who waved back. These moments were not really occurring in the fictional world of Temple Studios, and might be technically against certain implied rules of engagement; but they were valid and meaningful exchanges of human connection. Immersive experience is constantly (re)negotiated in the moment by audience members, at times with each other.

Finally, the decompression or interval space provides a break in regard to functional, utilitarian interactivity and immersive experience. In the bar, masks can be removed, talking and socialising is allowed, and drinks are available. This release from the quiet intensity of the rest of the show might allow for both states to be experienced more fully.

Explicit Interactivity

This is "interaction" in the obvious sense of the word: overt participation like clicking the non-linear links of a hyper-text novel, following the rules of a board game, rearranging the clothing on a set of paper dolls, using the joystick to manoeuvre Ms. Pac-Man. Included here: choices, random events, dynamic simulations, and other procedures programmed into the interactive experience. (Salen and Zimmerman 2004: 59–60)

This kind of interactivity takes a physical manifestation. It is the mode of interactivity where the participant's contribution and effect is the most obvious. Most work—theatrical or otherwise—that calls itself *interactive* will use this mode: a player/participant is given something specific to *do*. Imaginative immersion can be engaged without physically doing anything (and it can occur from a proscenium arch seat or in front of a computer screen: it is not inherent to any one art form). Navigating the space of immersive performance is also a valid mode of interactivity, although it does not guarantee explicit interactivity. As immersive experience exists as a series of graded states, this utilitarian/practical form of participation is required before explicit interactivity can occur: for example, a participant needs to be comfortable in the mask (or at least willing to wear it) before they are allowed to enter the space. Moving through a production could also be included in the explicit mode of interactivity, as it entails making decisions about navigation, or which character or detail of the set to spend time with—engagements with the show that are affected by individual choices. However, at times what resembles explicit interactivity may only *appear* to be related to choice or freedom, particularly in relation to one-on-one scenes.

The relationship between explicit interactivity and immersive experience in *The Drowned Man* appears straightforward: the invitation to go where you wish and to pay attention to whoever or whatever you wish— to imaginatively engage with the show and its characters—are means of empowering audiences to make choices about how they engage with the production. They are designed to create a sense of freedom, to allow for excitement and exploration. One-on-ones occur when coincidence of position and timing result in an audience member being taken into a smaller space with a performer to experience a short scene alone. The intensity of these scenes is highly conducive to facilitating immersive experience, although perhaps not to audience agency. These scenes are pre-scripted, and although there may be space for an audience member to respond their input does not determine the outcome and the performer remains in control at all times. These moments can feel intimate and secretive, which may be made explicit by the performer locking the door once they have taken their chosen spectator inside. Just as mental "flow" is created when the challenge of an activity is equal to its perceived achievability, a hierarchy of experience to reward becomes clear: an audience member who accepts the invitation to wander will have the more fulfilling immersive experience, and may even "win" a one-one-one. This relationship between interactivity and immersion is a commonly suggested one: Punchdrunk's company description (on the *Sleep No More* site, Punchdrunk.org among other places) of making "theatre in which roaming audiences experience epic storytelling inside unique sensory theatrical worlds" suggests that physical signifiers of interactivity (roaming, sensory stimulus) are an integral part of the experience. Explicit interactivity results in an active, rather than a passive, spectator: so the logic goes.

Although interactivity may appear to be linked to immersive experience, many immersive productions are not particularly "interactive" at all, at least not in the sense defined by this mode. They may include explicit participation in a navigational sense, but audience members are not invited to influence, change or complete anything. *The Drowned Man* was highly interactive in the sense of imaginative engagement and interpretation, and it required co-operation with the practical rules of play. But in the sense of explicit interactivity, the show did not provide as much freedom as might be assumed from statements about liberated, automatically active audiences in "productions where the audience is physically present, so that they are driven by a base, gut feeling and making instinctive decisions. That sort of show leaves a far larger imprint on you than just watching something" (Barrett in Kelly 2015). The goal here is not to debunk assumptions about empowerment as an end in itself: rather I am interested in questioning whether, in terms of immersive experience, it actually *matters* how interactive *The Drowned Man* and other immersive productions are.

Apart from one-on-one scenes, explicit interactivity occurs when an audience member shares a moment of eye contact with a performer; when they rifle through a drawer full of letters; when they decide to go through this door rather than that one. Interactivity with designed choices and procedures, in *The Drowned Man*, refers to the wider layout of the space and the looping structure of the choreographed scenes. This layout is not influenced by an audience member's choice, although they have a certain amount of agency over where they go within that layout. Neither can a spectator inform any of the action: in a literal sense, the scenes would continue just the same if they were not there. The procedures of being an audience member in *The Drowned Man* are the routine activities: don the mask, explore, interact—with the space, possibly with a performer—and allow your imagination to engage with the world that is being presented. Routine is not intended to imply tedium in this context, but to suggest that these are the base level rules of engagement with the production.

A question might be whether making these decisions about where to go, and so on, is what allows for immersive experience. As already suggested, experiencing anxiety about somehow making the wrong choice raises barriers to immersion and may break it. Emphasis on going along an individual path and choosing what to look at is intended to be a liberating freedom rather than a constricting one—but choice paralysis could be a barrier to immersion. Wishing you were somewhere else—sensing there is something exciting going on that you are missing out on—are not sensations that are conductive to immersive experience. They are instead a powerful reminder of the limitations on your current circumstances, the opposite of losing yourself in a task. The layout and structure of an immersive production with looping scenes provides an audience member with a wide range of potential choices and procedures—but this type of interactivity in itself cannot guarantee immersive experience. Honour Bayes' reading of *The Drowned Man* perceived a gap between the level of interactivity promised and the level received, an unsatisfying experience cancelling out the potential for an immersive one:

> *The Drowned Man* is strangely unsatisfying and for me this is because of what I perceive as an increasing shift of focus within Punchdrunk's work from creating human connections to building movie set worlds … my sense throughout was of that the type of voyeurism being encouraged was disempowering rather than thrilling … a little contact would do so much to enable the actual thing live up to the heart-racing promise of this production's electric trailer. (Bayes 2013: n.p.)

A key aspect of this mode is the player/participant faces *designed* choices and procedures. To making *The Drowned Man* Punchdrunk created an environment and choreographed a series of stories within it. The structure of the building implied a series of choices available regarding where an audience member might go. Framing this sense in the main body of the show—of freedom to create your own experience or build your own narrative—was a strong sense of authorial control at either end. As well as the show's carefully crafted beginning(s) the entire audience was brought together for the finale. The opening and closing scenes did not require explicit interactivity on the audience's part: they could not alter what happened in these scenes, barring making the choice to crash the stage. But these scenes allowed for the longer, more exploratory part of the show to be bracketed by a strong sense of the production (or, through it, Punchdrunk) taking charge of the event and of how the audience will experience that event. The final scene was the opposite of the graded beginnings at the start of the show, and brought events to a climax in terms of performers (all together for the first time, as indeed are the audience members), the stories (the Woyzeck characters—William and Wendy, if you know their names—finally facing each other), spectacle (the sheer size of the space and energy of the choreography) and sound. The final dance sequence had clearly been designed with maximum audience experience in mind, and just as in any theatrical spectacle it allowed for immersion (leading to a revered gaze) in its size, energy and scope: immersive experience does not have to occur in a tiny, dark, intimate space with room only for two. Many group dances in *The Drowned Man* (a line dance; an after-party) were scenes of virtuoso movement and dramatic spectacle. Finale scenes like this may get their power from the implication that they are the "reward" for experiencing the rest of the production. Scenes like this require the audience to stand back and watch, much like the passive spectators immersive theatre is often claimed to work against.

Barriers to immersion, in the context of interactivity, occur when a participant experiences trouble, discomfort or dissatisfaction. Somewhat paradoxically, although physical manifestations of interactivity must be engaged with and overcome in order to be immersed, immersive experience is defined by being in-the-moment in a psychological or emotional sense, in effect its result is forgetting the physical conditions around you. Utilitarian participation needs to be mastered and then forgotten about to enable imaginative or explicit participation. One-on-ones in *The*

Drowned Man were not guaranteed by merely attending the show: the result of being in the right place at the right time, they could be seen as the reward for being a dedicated enough explorer, for lucky timing, or for visibly wearing a Premium ticket holder's ID card (or a combination of the above). If they are seen as a reward, not achieving one is inevitably coded as failure, breaking immersion in the moment or making for an unsatisfying experience as a whole. (For further issues concerning Punchdrunk one-on-one performance, and particularly ethics, see Gordon 2013 on intimacy and voyeurism; Silvestre 2012 on responsibility and care; Alston 2012 on consumer consumption.) Immersion might also be broken by a lack of empathy: engaging with the story of a character can keep a spectator immersed, just as it can in a naturalistic production in a proscenium arch. The broken-up scene structure means such an emphasis on story may not necessarily be how the show is best experienced. Reviewers have recognised that attempting to experience immersive productions this way is a set-up for disappointment; or they did exactly this, and were disappointed. Compare Clapp (2007): "If you doggedly try to map Poe's narratives onto Punchdrunk's scenes you will have a frustrating evening" with Billington (2010): "Then you go in search of the nine scenes to which Webster's story has been reduced in Ian Burton's libretto." Caring about characters should not be dismissed as unnecessary to immersive theatre. Being affected by the emotional power of a scene or performance might constitute strong immersive experience in a spectator: the challenge might be reaching the point where this can be the case. An episodic structure or the nature of audience behaviour might work against this kind of engagement becoming viable. The movement and behaviour of an audience can never be fully predicted (Eglinton 2010; Machon 2013) and the process of creation, devising and rehearsal, with modifications and changes to reflect, incorporate or respond to audience behaviour(s) throughout the run of a production represent a continual attempt to keep barriers to immersion as lowered as possible.

The Drowned Man invited and facilitated a great amount of interactivity in imaginative and utilitarian modes. In the explicit mode, the show could be considered not particularly interactive. Its audience could choose where to go but they could not affect the action, and were not presented with the illusion of affecting the action. They were ghosts drifting through Temple Studios, watching its characters re-enact looping scenes of action and dance. Salen and Zimmerman's phrase "*designed* choices" is useful here to understand what is meant by freedom in this context, and its apparent links to empowerment or agency. *The Drowned Man* presented carefully designed choices or options to its audience in terms of its physical structure and looping scenes; its audience to some extent could choose what to do within the time allowed, but there were many rules of engagement to be followed—some clearly stated, some implied. Rooms were occasionally locked, some hidden. And whatever freedom there might have been during the majority of the performance, the opening scenes and the finale bracketed that sense of choice with strong authorial control. A cynical reading of immersive theatre might suggest that by not being fully interactive in an explicit sense risks creating the passive audience members that the work claims to dismantle; rewarding after all those who submit the most to its rules. But immersive experience can exist in that movement between passive and active engagement: between freedom and following rules; making choices within given pre-designed constraints. When considering immersion and interactivity within the walls of an immersive theatre production, what matters is less how interactive a production actually *is* at any given moment, and more the question of how it manipulates various modes of interactivity to allow for the experience(s) of its audience.

These three modes—imaginative participation, functional participation and explicit interactivity with designed choices—are useful to consider as separate aspects of interactivity that function simultaneously within an immersive production. Separating them allows for a more detailed consideration of what an audience member is immersed *in* at any given moment, and what the affects are: that is, does being able to walk through a space create a type of interactivity that allows for immersive experience, and if not, what is the relationship between physical and mental/imaginative exploration? Rather than celebrating a direct correlation between interactivity and agency, varying degrees of engagement aid the graded states of immersive experience. Moving in the course of one production between following a performer, reading a letter on a dressing table and taking in a large dance scene could result in a more powerful immersive experience by virtue of its gradual changes in tone and form. Alternatively, a spectator might be at their most active (cognitively, imaginatively) while passively watching a dance scene than when they aimlessly wander through rooms in no particular order, wondering whether they are missing something better. Immersive experience might occur best when there is interplay between a feeling of free choice and designed control, surrendering to a structure that is already in place.

REFERENCES

Alston, Adam. 2012. Funding, Product Placement and Drunkenness in Punchdrunk's *The Black Diamond*. Studies in Theatre & Performance 32 (2): 193–208.
Bayes, Honour. 2013. Why Punchdrunk's Latest Left Me Cold. *The Stage*, July 24.
Billington, Michael. 2010. The Duchess of Malfi. *Guardian*, July 14. http://www.guardian.co.uk/stage/2010/jul/14/duchess-of-malfi-review. Accessed Jan 2013.
Brown, Emily, and Paul Cairns. 2004. A Grounded Investigation of Game Immersion. CHI 2004 Extended Abstracts on Human Factors in Computing Systems, 1279–1300.
Clapp, Susannah. 2007. Into the Velvet Darkness Punchdrunk's *Masque of the Red Death* Turns the BAC into a Carnival of Sumptuous Horrors. *Guardian*, Sunday October 7.
Clapp, Susannah. 2013. The Drowned Man: A Hollywood Fable; The Machine; The Masque of Anarchy—Review. *Guardian*, Sunday July 21.
Eglinton, Andrew. 2010. Reflections on a Decade of Punchdrunk Theatre. *TheatreForum*, Issue 37, pp 46–56.
Gardner, Lyn (2007). The Masque of the Red Death left me Punchdrunk. Guardian, 4 October.
Gordon, Colette. 2013. Touching the Spectator: Intimacy, Immersion and the Theater of the Velvet Rope. Borrowers and Le`nders. Accessed Nov 2013.
Hoggard, Liz. 2013. Felix Barrett: The Visionary Who Reinvented Theatre. *Guardian*, July 14. Accessed July 2014.
Jennett, Charlene, Anna L. Cox, Paul Cairns, Samira Dhoparee, Andrew Epps, Tim Tijs, and Alison Walton. 2008. Measuring and Defining the Experience of Immersion in Games. *International Journal of Human Computer Studies* 66 (9) (September 2008): 641–661. Accessed Nov 2010.
Jones, Alice. 2013. Is Theatre Becoming Too Immersive? *Independent*, Wednesday March 6. Accessed Apr 2014.
Kelly, Guy. 2015. Punchdrunk Visionary Felix Barrett: If Audiences Get Used to the Rules, Change Them. *Telegraph*, June 19.
Machon, Josephine. 2013. *Immersive Theatres: Intimacy and Immediacy in Contemporary Performance*. London: Palgrave Macmillan.
Salen, K., and E. Zimmerman. 2004. *Rules of Play: Game Design Fundamentals*. Cambridge, MA: MIT Press.
Silvestre, Agnes. 2012. Punchdrunk and the Politics of Spectatorship. *Culturebot*. Accessed July 2013.
White, Gareth. 2005. Odd, Anonymised Needs: Punchdrunk's Masked Spectator. In *Modes of Spectating*, ed. Oddey and White, 219–229.

CHAPTER 4

Fan Interactivity: Communicating Immersive Experience

I am in dark, twisted love with your theatre group.

The previous chapters have considered interactivity as it may occur during an immersive theatre production. In this final discussion I widen the lens to incorporate the production as a whole, and the notion of interacting *with* it as well as within its walls. My discussion draws on a qualitative analysis of a very specific kind of discourse to consider how the live performance event might be valued and communicated beyond the moment of encounter. Fan communication with Punchdrunk via their website during the runs of *Faust* (21 Wapping Lane, 2006–2007) and *The Masque of the Red Death* (Battersea Arts Centre, 2007–2008) reveal how audience members describe immersive experience. Themes across the comments can be used to build a vocabulary of what is valued in immersive experience, with consequences for theorising the value and effects of immersive theatre. There are practical ramifications to studying these kinds of discourses, but paying attention to fan response can contribute greatly towards a further understanding of how immersive experience is both created in the moment of theatrical encounter and discussed and shared afterwards.

Comments submitted to punchdrunk.org.uk during *Faust* (2006–2007) and *The Masque of the Red Death* (2007–2008) are valuable documents for considering relationships between audience and production, framing immersive experience as something to be communicated outside of the performance space. Their language and the subject matter reveal, or

© The Author(s) 2017
R. Biggin, *Immersive Theatre and Audience Experience*,
DOI 10.1007/978-3-319-62039-8_4

make manifest, a relationship to the shows, individual performers within them, and Punchdrunk as a company. Trends across this discourse, such as descriptions of overwhelming sensory excitement or childlike fascination, reflect the ways immersive theatre as a whole is often described, understood and talked about within fan discourse. And outside of it: marketing rhetoric around immersive theatre frequently draw upon similar themes of individuality, excitement and exploration. Further trends in subject matter across the comments include cryptic references to one-on-one encounters, the joy of discovery and accounts of the social resonances of visiting a show with a group. Fan discourse of this kind is more than an honorary curtain call or giving of thanks. It functions as a means of claiming ownership over immersive experience and a means of effectively beginning a dialogue or conversation—initiating interactivity—with a production, theatre company or other members of the fan community. My discussion is only an initial exploration of fan studies in the context of immersive theatre, and this is an area of enquiry which would greatly repay further study.

There is considerable theoretical basis for the study of fan interactivity. Jenkins notes that fans "become active participants in the construction and circulation of textual meanings" (1992: 24). Fans often have a highly sophisticated critical gaze towards the work they love—rather than the passive non-critical adoration of the fan stereotype. Hills (2003) and Duffett (2013) consider the state of fan research and culture, and Barker and Mathijs (2007) propose methodological approaches to long-term research into fan response. Lewis (2002) emphasises active, reciprocal relationships between fans and the producers of the original work. Abercrombie and Longhurst provide a continuum of audiences that outlines a movement towards active production as consumers become fans. "Consumers" rise through enthusiasts, cultists and fans, with "petty producer" at the far end of the spectrum, engaged in actively producing additional texts (1998: 141). Studies of theatre fandom are rarer, and Freshwater argues for paying more attention to theatregoers: "audiences are beginning to be trusted by practitioners and by industry. But it seems that theatre scholars have yet to develop this trust" (2009: 74). Discussions of immersive theatre and Punchdrunk have been considered from the perspective of anonymity (White 2009) and intimacy (Gordon 2013), and it is possible to chart changes in audience behaviour as the company's work becomes more popular (Silvestre 2012; Jakob-Hoff 2014).

Abercrombie and Longhurst consider fans and enthusiasts "a form of skilled audience" (1998: 121). Clapp comments on the changing nature of a Punchdrunk audience in her review of *The Drowned Man*:

"aficionados poke eagerly into a place, suss out whether there is any action and move on […] There is less baffled loitering and fruitful lingering." She concludes that this development is "something of a loss" (2013: n.p.). Her comments suggest something intrinsic to the *experience* of immersive theatre is lost when its audience is increasingly aware of certain rules of engagement. In turn, this implies an understanding of what those rules of engagement are perceived to be. Clapp prioritises slow exploration over excited and deliberate searching, but why not try to search, find, discover as much as you can? I do not suggest there is an intrinsically "right" or "better" way to engage with immersive theatre: however, audience members who feel they have had a *successful* Punchdrunk encounter often draw on implicit assumptions about what the rules of engagement are—and feel that in doing so they have gained an understanding of what "the best experience" actually *is*. The fan mail texts discussed in this chapter reveal the ways audience members place value on performance experience, and how they communicate this value. What constitutes immersive experience is implied in how they describe it. Fan (inter)activity is in ongoing creative dialogue with immersive experience.

The Drowned Man's opening voiceover advises the audience on navigating the show: "I urge each of you to steer your own course. Tonight, your bearing shapes your fate". In separating spectators into individuals, Punchdrunk attempt to make literal the theatrical truism that every spectator has their own unique experience. Crucially, this is accompanied by an awareness of others having their own similar-but-inevitably-different individual experience. *The Drowned Man*'s voiceover is given to a group, and other masked audience members are seen during a journey through the show. *The Masque of the Red Death* and *Faust*, considered in this chapter, as well as *The Drowned Man*, have built into their very form this awareness of multiple similar-but-different individual experiences. It is an awareness that demand to be talked about afterwards, compared and contrasted. Immersive experience in these productions has a life beyond the show, not just in memories but through discussion. Experiences are created in the moment and projected beyond. In addition to conversation and comparison, the construction of communal realities occurs in the creation of art and fiction inspired by the shows and shared between fans, and in the co-creation of comprehensive diagrams, plot outlines or synopses of the action.

The social element of fan engagement is worth considering, in spite of a common emphasis on the singular audience member on an individual journey:

even if you're holding hands with your loved one when you arrive we'll make an effort to try and separate you because you'll have a better time when you're fighting for yourself and you're selfish for once. (Barrett: at "Experience Economy" Remix Summit, 2014)

Jenkins provides a reminder of the importance of fan communities' social qualities: "For most fans, meaning-production is not a solitary and private process but rather a social and public one" (1992: 75). Popat's discussion of online dance communities proposes interactivity as a means of experiencing rewarding social engagement, as well as an opportunity for developing creative practice: "in a situation where the group members perceive themselves to be connected in some way, a single individual interacting on behalf of the group can lead to a strong sense of participation being felt by others within that group" (2006: 32–33). Individual experiences within the moment of the live encounter have social values as well as private ones. Much of the fan mail discussed later in the chapter refer to friendship, family, work or school groups, and the richness of the experience for being simultaneously separate and shared.

Punchdrunk only kept a minority of the vast number of comments they received, and so the audience response data had already been curated into a smaller selection prior to my own research. My discussion is drawn from an archive of little over a hundred. These often contain highly personal recollections of an audience member's experience, and frequently use the language of shared relationships, particularly when discussing one-on-one scenes. This is especially relevant in relation to a theatrical form that invites the creation of relationships. A website form allows communication in an instant: a relationship between audience member and company, established in the performative moment, is made manifest as soon as the comment is sent. Many responses emphasise this proximity to the moment of encounter: "I've just got back..." or "Last night..." They are also mostly very short—rarely more than a few lines. Together they build up an impressionist description of audience members' best experiences of *Faust* and *The Masque of the Red Death*. Through this interaction audience members share individual experiences of theatrical immersion, the act of communicating revealing the values placed on this experience.

Drawing on the discourse of fan mail has some practical ramifications. Most obviously they were written for Punchdrunk, and not intended to be read by an outside party. As part of the Punchdrunk Archives they are extremely useful for thinking about how audience members communicate immersive experience, and Punchdrunk has given permission for them to be disseminated for this purpose. They were already anonymous, and I have changed any names or personal details.

Secondly, they may imply a certain bias: positivity shines out from them all. Negative experiences would be unlikely to be communicated or archived. Voluntarily contact after the event generally indicates a positive experience, a particular eagerness to respond to Punchdrunk's invitation for multisensory exploration and to lose themselves in the work. However, fans and enthusiasts is only one type of attendee within a larger audience. Not everyone will respond positively. Nield (2008) and Freshwater (2009) discuss potential negative effects of too much physical freedom, leaving audience members alienated, unsure, certainly not immersed. While acknowledging that positive responses are not the only sort possible, or that they are in any way definitive, and recognising the potentially limiting specificity of the fan demographic, it is still useful to build the vocabulary that enthusiastic audience members use to place value on immersive experience. As members of a "skilled audience" (cf. Abercrombie and Longhurst), fans experience work they love with a detailed and critical eye.

The most common purpose of these comments was to provide simple feedback of short, intense praise.

> I have just been to the Masque of the Red Death this weekend and was completely blown away by the production! An absolute inspiration!

> The Masque was the best thing I'd been to in years.

> I enjoyed "The Masque of the Red Death" more than immensely.

> Astonishing. Please do something else soon.

> I was at The Masque of the Red Death last night and it was quite simply the most amazing show I've ever seen in my entire life.

> I have just had the most brilliant night out I have had in a long time.

What these share is an evaluation of the *overall* experience. More is revealed through longer comments that reference the specific elements people loved. Particularly mentioned are the relationships audience members felt they formed with single performers. Most often this occurred in one-on-one experiences. These moments are often remembered as a formative element of the theatrical experience: something the audience member particularly wants to tell Punchdrunk about, and for which they want to thank them and/or the performer:

> I finally managed to see The Masque of the Red Death. Amazing. I wish I could go back and dance with Tom Lawrence again! Thank you.

> That Red Masque show was great. The man (actor!) who locked me in a closet with himself (scared the living daylights out of me for 30 secs) must shake his hand! Or buy him an absinthe—top show cheers PJB MUST BRING MY PALS TO SEE YOUR NEXT PROD!!

In recollection the spectator separates the fictional character from the charisma of the performer, which has implications for how immersive experience manifests in the moment. Although frequently positioned as an overwhelming experience that leaves little room for additional thought, immersive experience does not exist as a binary with critical distance. These audience members have a sense of the artifice of the production, as well as sharing the memory of a particularly intense moment of performativity. Reason (2010) identifies a similar process when he who dismantles the theoretical binary between critical distance and immersion in his discussion of dual perception in young audiences.

There is also a sense of shared knowledge when one-on-one encounters are mentioned: the performer and/or the anonymous mastermind Punchdrunk are expected to know exactly what is being referred to. Rather than sharing details explicitly, these comments hint at a secret that only the intended recipient would be able to understand.

> LOVED the show, especially your attic vault and the bedrooms and the tall blonde young guy who gave me a very seductive experience in the boudoir room!

> A quick note to say congratulations on the production! I attended last night at the BAC and came away feeling that I had experienced something very special. A particular mention of thanks to the actors behind "Madeleline" and "the Nurse" characters whose interaction with me on a 1:1 basis left me thoroughly moved by the intensity and immersive nature of their performance. From the man in the red sweater and stripy scarf!

These are comments that create interaction, not merely share description. They have the tone of the in-joke, the cryptic reference or secret code, in accord with the atmosphere of secrecy and discovery that characterises the invitation offered by the work. Some comments place the author in a temporal relationship with the production, giving the specific date they saw it: perhaps revealing an assumption that a certain interaction or moment occurred only once across many performances. It is assumed that the performer will remember exactly the interaction and audience member that is being talked about. This is particularly relevant in relation to a theatrical form that so emphasises the importance of emotional, visceral reactions that are positioned as unique experiences.

Making these observations is not to diminish audience members' experiences. Rather, the intention is to reveal the extent to which immersion might depend on a sensation of true uniqueness in the interactivity—whether or not this was actually the case in terms of exactly how the scene was created, rehearsed and performed. "A one-on-one, for me, is the purest form of Punchdrunk; it's distilled Punchdrunk" (Barrett in Machon 2013: 162). It may not matter if the experience created is truly bespoke: what is at stake is that is *felt* to be personal.

One-on-one scenes represent interaction at its most explicit in terms of the attention paid to the audience member, and the sense that it makes a difference that they are there. In the fan mail texts, however, immersive experience is not only expressed in terms of relationships to performers. Another trend among the comments—and one that complicates the notion of immersive experience as a private sensation—is that many are very social, placing the author within a wider group. While expressing joy in their individual experience, they situate themselves in relation to a wider community:

> I came to see Masque last night and would just like to say congratulations on what was, for myself and the friends I went with, quite simply the most amazing night out we've had in years. Part dream part film set, in our wildest dreams we could not have come up with anything remotely as fantastic. Can we come back, please?

As well as sharing memories of *The Masque of the Red Death* with Punchdrunk, these comments gesture towards memories that exist between the audience members, or thank Punchdrunk for providing an amazing individual experience that is a joy to share with others:

> I'd love NOTHING more than to go back there, but part of me feeling like that's cheating. Greedy even. Like going back in time and meddling with events, not to your advantage nor disadvantage, but just because you can. If I think about it rationally, I'm MORE than satisfied with my memories of that one night. As well as the stories of S—'s, S—'s and L—'s (My companions TO, but not AT, the Masque) experiences of the Masque, which I'm sure we will talk about for years to come. Only trouble is, it's hard to be rational about something as breathtakingly indulgent as this! This was so close to my heart it's uncanny! Thanks, LOADS!

The importance placed on individual experience, with each audience member actively encouraged to make their own journey through the show, informs how the production will be talked about and remembered afterwards. Arriving in a group, and then either splitting up or not, affects how the show is experienced. It is the difference between, as the previous comment puts it, companions *to* and companions *at* the Masque. Choosing to separate is a decision. It may be aided by suggestion in the form of ushers, voiceovers, reviews and word of mouth; but it is, still, a decision that consciously has to be made by participants. Audience members can always determine to stick together if they want, and many do. The decision therefore reveals ideas about "correct" rules of engagement with the work. Comments that inform Punchdrunk of this perhaps also express the spectator's sense that they have understood what the correct rules of engagement are, and followed the suggested route to the best possible experience. The author thanks Punchdrunk for providing an event that leads to group reminiscing, storytelling, comparison and reflection: the individual experience in itself becomes the basis for further social interaction.

> My partner and I attended last week—we decided to split up immediately and each go on our own journey throughout the production—which was a great idea—on the way home we were abuzz with how different the experience had been for each of us—some rooms having not been visited by one—and a discovery being made by the other—we had had the most incredible and unrivalled theatrical experience [...]
>
> I went to see Masque of the Red Death on Saturday. To say I found it completely bizarre is to undervalue the different approach to theatre. I have to say thank you as I went as one of a group of five and we all had different experiences and saw something different to the point we could have gone to five different events. The finale, big band and dj were

fantastic and worth going for those performances in their own right. My only regret is that we were too late in the season to see it once more to attempt to see other rooms I didn't find at my first attendance.

The very existence of these comments suggests that sharing memories with Punchdrunk can be just as much a part of the pleasure as sharing with friends after the show. The sense of discovery as one travels through the production might indeed be heightened if a spectator explores as a lone wolf: but by splitting up, a spectator can learn about not only their own experience but that of their companions. The above authors might call upon other audience members to fill them in on the "other rooms [they] didn't find" and immersive theatrical experience extends beyond the confines of in-the-moment, and beyond the individual.

The comments function as honorary curtain calls when a scene or moment of interaction leaves a spectator unable to thank the performer via conventional applause. Describing particular moments, or the production overall, in terms of a sense of sensory/emotional overload suggests that, for some, immersive experiences are a state of intense engagement. Describing this experience either with friends or through writing to Punchdrunk afterwards functions as a means of claiming ownership of one's own immersive experience: a means of stating, and underlining, that such an experience took place.

As well as friendship or family groups several comments refer to school outings, either from a student or the group leader. In either case, they often refer to having gathered inspiration for their own projects. Thanks are given not just for the show itself, but for the resonances that continue afterwards. The following examples reflect a desire to continue engaging with immersive experience from the perspective of creation and design, and are characterised by a sense of shared, communal discovery:

> I took my group of A level students to see your production last night. We came away inspired, moved and very excited, thank you. Feelings like that are not evoked very often from a piece of theatre. It was a triumph.

> Hi—I just wanted to say myself and my whole drama class came to see The Masque of the Red Death, and we all thought it fantastic, we've never ever seen anything like it before. You've really opened our eyes to what theatre can do, and really inspired us as we're starting our A-level devised coursework projects at the moment! Thank you, and good luck with all your shows and future projects!

Another frequent trait within descriptions of immersive experience is an emphasis on a state of *childlikeness*. A further relationship might be created, or made manifest, here: the relationship between the author and their previous experiences of theatre and performance.

> Saw the performance last night and was blown away. It's good to know that at 43 years of age I can still be surprised and challenged. Thanks!

Comments that refer to friendship or school groups are the few contexts where the age of the author is directly implied or stated. But a childlike openness and willingness to explore are often seen as ideal, with many comments referring to the spectator being in this state. Experience, and age itself by virtue of the childlike metaphor, become unhelpful baggage: pre-formed ideas of what theatre ought to look like. Only letting go of these preconceptions enables a full commitment to getting the most out of the show, in order to return to the "childlike excitement and anticipation of exploring the unknown and experience a real sense of adventure" that is promised on Punchdrunk's website (2014). These comments reveal how immersive experience manifests outside the spatial and temporal boundaries of the performance space. The following comments all refer to something resembling an immersive theatre hangover after engaging thoroughly with a show. Whether the metaphor is parallel universe or dream, the experience has left them physically changed:

> Last night was a dream sequence I am unable to leave behind. All day today has been like the dream and the reality is me still in those corridors looking for another room watching from behind my mask the life and death struggle of the actors. Truly brilliant theatre as it hits hard into the sub-conscience and stays there. Please put me in as a friend of Punchdrunk.

> Thank you very much for "The Masque of the Red Death". I went to see it three weeks ago, and I still feel as if I'm waking up from a dream. You have given flesh to all my darkest gothic fantasies! I'm coming back to "Masque" in March, and bringing lots of friends. Can't wait to see it again, and I'm really looking forward to your next projects.

> My wife and I are still reeling from our experience at the Masque of the Red Death last night. It was simply sublime, and we're pleased to be attending it again in April for our anniversary.

> Thank you for one of the most amazing experiences at Masque of the Red
> Death; I'm still feeling withdrawal symptoms. I've never known theatre to
> be so addictive!

> I attended the 29th December performance and was wondering if you
> could divulge the recipe for the perfumer's atomizer cologne. I think it's
> lavender and rose, but I'd love to replicate it for personal use. Thank you
> and can't wait to attend your next production.

> I've just had the privilege of performing with some musicians at your late
> night Masque soiree at the BAC. We also saw the whole show and I just
> wanted to say it was the most amazing thing I have ever attended and I
> loved it! Atmosphere detail and the whole psychology of the interactivity—
> just jawdroppingly brilliant. Head's still buzzing about it now! I actually
> feel I left the country… Big thank you to the inspired creators and per-
> formers and just, well all involved!

Some spectators, of course, do attend multiple times, rather than simply wishing they could or remaining for various reasons reluctantly satisfied with their limited time. These audience members will have a different frame of knowledge to build on each time they experience the show, and different expectations that affect how they engage with the work. Further study of immersive experience of repeat visitors will be an interesting area to explore further.

A comment that begins by placing the author in a group (of students) introduces a final trend. Punchdrunk are placed in a relationship to a broader theatrical tradition:

> Dear Punchdrunk, I went with my school's A-level drama students to see
> your and BAC's production of The Masque of the Red Death and quite
> simply since than my eyes and soul have been opened to what theatre and
> performances should really be like: emotional, inspirational and immensely
> powerful. Thank you Punchdrunk!

"What theatre and performance should really be like" refers to the emotions stirred and the visceral reaction experienced, rather than what actions specifically happened in the show: the compliment is built on atmosphere and emotional impact. It is the same decision, and has the same effect, as choosing to write *a very seductive experience* instead of describing what constituted it. The emphasis is on how the performance felt rather than what it specifically included. Immersion is an experience rather than a specific series of actions.

The following comments situate their praise of *The Masque of the Red Death* in relationship to wider ideas of what theatre could or should be, finding that its very form opens up different *uses* for theatre. These respondents inform us that they had the "best" experience possible. The production revolutionised what theatre can be capable of, or confirmed an earlier idea of what makes good theatre:

> Hello, I was recently abroad based in London this fall and was fortunate enough to see my first performance of Punchdrunk. I would just like to thank you for an amazing, unforgettable experience that has challenged my definition of live theatre. Thank you so much.

> Hello, I came to see Masque of the Red Death on Friday and thought it was a theatrical revolution! I absolutely loved it, and it has filled me with inspiration.

> Everyone involved. This was by far the most extraordinary night I have ever spent in the theatre. Your production gave me the same joy that I had when I was 5 years old and decided I wanted to work in the theatre. What you have created here should be at the core of ALL we do in the theatre. Thank you for making it so clear what we should all be aiming for. I look forward with great anticipation to your next work. With the utmost respect and admiration.

> I was completely blown away by The Masque of the Red Death, it has changed my perception of theatre forever. Thank you and well done to those involved for all the hard, brilliant work you do.

These comments do not mention specific events, instead describing the overall sensation of experiencing the production. Immersive experience is communicated in visceral, emotional, psychological terms, and it is something of a paradox for makers of immersive theatre that this experience, although facilitated by a production's form—and even defined by it—is not necessarily the automatic result of logistical, atmospheric or structural signifiers. Being able to physically travel through rooms, interact with performers and so on are not enough in themselves to create and maintain immersive experience, although *immersive* tends to be applied to productions that include these things. These techniques allow for immersive experience but do not guarantee it. The previously mentioned comments adhere to the "correct" rules of engagement with immersive theatre by conflating form, content, and effect.

A final comment is worth quoting in its entirety. It discusses the material conditions of viewing; hints at the experience within a production; suggests cognitive and sensory immersion, and willingness to navigate both; initiates a relationship between participant, production, and company:

> Last night I attended the Masque of the Red Death. It was my first venture to a Punchdrunk performance, and I was lucky enough to attend only because my friend had won tickets via the Goldbug website. I just wanted to thank you for creating such an awe-inspiring production. For three hours, I was totally absorbed in the performance, and rendered completely oblivious to the world outside the show. As a child, I had a magical imagination—I spent hours roaming the countryside with my siblings, creating alternative worlds that only we inhabited, but as I've grown, my ability to disassociate myself from the wider world has diminished. For the first time in decades, I was a child again. I know this sounds rather trite, but it's the best way I can describe the effect your performance had on me. I was terrified, excited and confused; totally lost in a world that I could never have conceived of myself. Today, I am back in the real world, gazing onto the urban jungle of London from my apartment and mourning my return to the present. Thank you for opening a window into the past.

Of interest here is *how* the experience has lingered; not just that it *has*. The comment uses the language of dreams, and "mourning" is particularly striking. It communicates a sense of loss, but through (recognition of) that loss, a sense that something else has been gained. Choices of words and imagery reveal how immersive experience lingers afterwards, and this in turn reveals what function the immersive experience might be playing for them and what values are being places on it.

> Saw Faust last night: alone. Best Valentine's Day I've ever had.

> My friend was right—Faust is better than sex.

Even when measuring immersive experience against *other kinds* of relationship, the latter comes out wanting.

Conclusion: "Thank You Punchdrunk!"

Faust and *The Masque of the Red Death* were popular shows that led to a rise in Punchdrunk's prestige and visibility, and established several theatrical, atmospheric and logistical trademarks that have persisted through their work. While not a definitive list, the traits and themes described previously demonstrate how spectators communicated immersive experience within, and to, these shows. Of course, the comments in this chapter may have been made by one-off visitors to the site who may not self-identify as fans. But today, the Punchdrunk fan community is much larger and more prominent, and would allow for comprehensive study. Writing on the politics of spectatorship in immersive theatre, Silvestre (2012) describes the activities of *Sleep No More* "superfans":

> Since the show opened in New York [in 2011], it has acquired a cult following of "superfans" who attend the show repeatedly and extend the experience online. One superfan, a woman in her fifties, travels in from out of town to see all the weekend shows—up to 12 h of SNM in two days. Another superfan I spoke with has attended the show 37 times and counting, and runs a blog called *They Have Scorched the Snake … but not killed it, bitches!*, where fans share their experiences of the show, confess crushes on performers, and post fan-art and fan-fiction. On other blogs such as *The Bloody Business*, the participants engage in role-play, take on personae such as "Thane of Glamis" or "Cawdor," and joke about 12-step programs to quit the *SNM* habit. (2012: n.p.)

Since this list was written some can say they have seen *Sleep No More* over a hundred times. Further research on immersive theatre fandom would build an understanding of how these particularly invested audience members value and communicate experiences of immersion, and what leads to such high levels of investment.

Fan interactivity with immersive theatre and with Punchdrunk reaches other fields. Jakob-Hoff cites a computer game designer who has been "directly influenced by *Sleep No More*" (2014), and Erin Morgenstern's fantasy novel *The Night Circus* (2011) cites a debt to the company in its closing acknowledgements. Morgenstern credits Punchdrunk productions with her desire to (re)create her own: "special recognition" is due, she says, to "the immersive experience of Punchdrunk, which I was lucky enough to fall into thanks to the American Repertory Theatre of Cambridge, Massachusetts" (295–296). Visitors to the novel's *Cirque des Rêves* experience physical immersion in the world of a magical, nocturnal circus. Once inside, characters experience visceral sensations that sound very much like the immersion described in Punchdrunk's fan mail; those who love the circus the most join the Dreamers, who follow the circus around the world to visit as often as they can. The novel is a piece of Punchdrunk fan fiction. The mysterious circus is not based on a specific show but its atmosphere, organisation, sudden appearance and strange beauty is the invention of an artist enamoured with the company's work. Morgenstern's novel allowed readers to become immersed in a fictional immersive experience. Fan response to Punchdrunk is developing in terms of the number and dedication of long-term fans and the making of work influenced by the company, in theatre and other media: Punchdrunk fans are producing professional work as well as personal responses, active producers of texts.

Considering the specific type of discourses made manifest in fan mail texts also serves to complexify some of the claims made on behalf of immersive theatre. Immersive theatre often emphasises the benefits of individual, multisensory experiences: the unique personal journey. Stubbornly choosing to stay in a group, for example, is therefore coded as leading to a disrupted, blocked or otherwise lesser, fundamentally worse experience. While Punchdrunk enthusiasts often do seem to have internalised this expected mode of viewing, individual journeys are often synthesised as part of a communal experience. The relationship between immersive experience and emotional distance comes further into question, with many respondents describing their experiences with a critical detail that suggests a dual perception between, for example, actor and character. This implies a conception of immersive experience often missing from wider discourse: one where immersion and distance do not work as a binary, but instead have a reciprocal relationship, informing each other in the moment.

Assumptions about the relationship between participatory performance and audience empowerment are under investigation elsewhere (Nield 2008; Freshwater 2009; White 2013; Alston 2016). Examining direct communication from enthusiasts of Punchdrunk to the company opens up an avenue for further exploration into these claims, with the texts in this chapter providing a comparative measure of a successful experience: one where the immersive experience lingers as the memory of a dream, or the hangover from an overwhelming state of emotional engagement, now left behind.

References

Abercrombie, Nicholas, and Brian Longhurst. 1998. *Audiences: A Sociological Theory of Performance and Imagination*. London: Sage.

Alston, Adam. 2016. *Beyond Immersive Theatre: Aesthetics, Politics and Productive Participation*. London: Palgrave Macmillan.

Barrett, Felix. (2014). Felix Barrett, Artistic Director, Punchdrunk. Speaking at Remix Summit: *Experience Economy: Creating Extraordinary Moments and Stories that Get People Talking*. https://www.youtube.com/watch?v=xCRcuHiDEYs. Accessed Mar 2014.

Barker, Martin, and Ernest Mathijis. 2007. *Watching the Lord of the Rings: Tolkien's World Audiences*. New York: Peter Lang.

Clapp, Susannah. 2013. The Drowned Man: A Hollywood Fable; The Machine; The Masque of Anarchy—Review. Guardian, Sunday 21 July.

Duffett, Mark. 2013. *Understanding Fandom: An Introduction to the Study of Media Fan Cultures*. New York: Bloomsbury.

Freshwater, Helen. 2009. *Theatre & Audience*. Basingstoke: Palgrave Macmillan.

Gordon, Colette. 2013. Touching the Spectator: Intimacy, Immersion and the Theater of the Velvet Rope 2013. Accessed November: Borrowers and Lenders.

Hills, Matthew. 2003. *Fan Cultures*. London: Routledge.

Jakob-Hoff, Tristan. 2014. At the gates of Temple Studios: Where Gaming and Theatre Collide. Eurogamer, 2 May 2014 235. Accessed May 2014.

Jenkins, Henry. 1992/2012. *Textual Poachers: Television Fans and Participatory Culture*. London: Routledge.

Lewis, Lisa A. (ed.). 2002. *The Adoring Audience: Fan Culture and Popular Media*. London: Routledge.

Machon, Josephine. 2013. *Immersive Theatres: Intimacy and Immediacy in Contemporary Performance*. London: Palgrave Macmillan.

Morgenstern, Erin. 2011. *The Night Circus*. London: Vintage.

Nield, Sophie. 2008. The Rise of the Character Named Spectator. *Contemporary Theatre Review* 18 (4): 531–544.

Popat, Sita. 2006. *Invisible Connections: Dance, Choreography and Internet Communities*. London: Routledge.

Punchdrunk. 2014. *About*. https://www.punchdrunk.org.uk/about/. Accessed July 2014.

Reason, Matthew. 2010. *The Young Audience: Exploring and Enhancing Children's Experiences of Theatre*. Stoke on Trent: Trentham Books.

Silvestre, Agnes. 2012. Punchdrunk and the Politics of Spectatorship. Culturebot. Accessed July 2013.

White, Gareth. 2009. Odd, Anonymised Needs: Punchdrunk's Masked Spectator. In *Modes of Spectating*, ed. Oddey and White, 219–229. Bristol: Intellect Books.

White, Gareth. 2013. *Audience Participation in Theatre: Aesthetics of the Invitation*. London: Palgrave Macmillan.

CHAPTER 5

Follow the Story: Narrative and Immersion

The role of "story" in immersive theatre is one of continual interest. How does story work in this form of theatre; is it important anyway; what does *story*, in this context, even mean? What concept of *story* is being grappled with during a state of immersive experience—or must story be forgotten about in the moment to let the experience happen? Is emotional engagement intended to come from caring about a character's fate, solving a mystery or some other narrative "hook"—or does emotional immersion arise from something else? And what are the underlying politics of all these options?

The following three chapters lay out some suggestions for theorising immersion and narrative. This chapter introduces key concepts from narrative theory and past and current models of the relationship between discourse and plot, story, character and causality. Drawing on Cobley (2001), Abbott (2002, 2011) and Herman (2009), and the methodology of the "fuzzy-set" definition offered by Ryan (2011), the chapter lays some theoretical ground for considering immersive experience and narrative. My main discussion is interested in how immersive experience might occur in the interplay between the physical immersion of an audience member in the performance space, her movement through the atmospheric/logistical score of the production, and the crafting of story events with this audience member in mind from the perspective of makers. Overall I argue that form and story structure have a reciprocal relationship in facilitating immersive experience. (Chapter 6 considers the common immersive theatre trait of presenting story events out

© The Author(s) 2017
R. Biggin, *Immersive Theatre and Audience Experience*,
DOI 10.1007/978-3-319-62039-8_5

of chronological order; Chap. 7 applies a gaming model to the "role of story" question.)

This chapter considers narrative and immersive experience using Punchdrunk's *The Crash of the Elysium* (Salford Quays 2011) as a case study. The show had a fundamentally linear structure: the audience were led throughout by guides and followed a single path. This form makes the show a useful model for considering the relationship between an audience's journey through an immersive space and the structure of story events within that space. In *The Crash of the Elysium*, these were experienced simultaneously: in both story and spatial terms, Punchdrunk were incharge of the plot and the path through which that plot was revealed, explicitly leading the audience on the course through it. The sense of a clear trajectory from A to B, the concept of narrative as "a sequence which starts and moves inexorably to its end" (Cobley 2001: 9), is made literal in *The Crash of the Elysium*, physically embodied by audience members and performers.

One additional aspect of *The Crash of the Elysium* was vital to immersion in its story. The production was set in a well-known pre-existing fictional universe: and a very contemporary one, with a recognisable brand and extremely active and engaged fan base (as opposed to the pre-existing classic textual worlds of Shakespeare and Poe—although those canons have their superfans too, of course). The relationship between *Punchdrunk* and *Doctor Who* is a further site for investigation of the interplay between physically immersive worlds, a constructed discourse within and through that world (the plot of *Elysium* and how it was encountered by its audience) and the wider pre-established fictional universe(s) in which the story was set: a universe with recognisable aesthetics, in-world rules and dynamics, well-known characters and iconic sound effects.

An Introduction to Narrative Theory(s)

Defining Narrative

For a history of recent developments in narrative theory, and particularly the influence of Genette, see Fludernik (2008); for an overview of historical perspectives and current approaches, see Herman (2009: 23–36). Abbott (2002) provides a useful definition: "narrative is *the representation of an event or a series of events*" (12; original emphasis). This definition opens up two areas for immersive experience to take place: in the event or series of events (the structure and order of scenes) themselves, and in the effectiveness of their theatrical representation.

Herman (2009) develops a definition that contextualises immersive experience and narrative: narrative is "a mode of representation that is situated in [...] a specific discourse context or occasion for telling." The representation "focuses on a structured time-course of particularized events": these events introduce disruption into a storyworld, and the representation (narrative) "conveys what it is like to live through this storyworld-in-flux" (189). Further to the notion of narrative as a mode of representation, Herman's definition introduced the concepts of a "storyworld" which then becomes a "storyworld-in-flux," a model that emphasises the importance of causality and disruption (which could also be called *conflict*) into the making of a narrative and reader/audience experience of that narrative. Also key to Herman's definition is the exploration of, and representation of, "what it's like" (xvi) to experience the disruption of a storyworld. This experiential aspect of narrative forefronts reader/audience engagement, highly relevant to immersive experience in story.

The term *storyworld* is useful when considering immersive experience and narrative in theatrical performance. The term refers to "the world evoked implicitly as well as explicitly by a narrative," but it might also refer to a pre-existing storyworld drawn on in the creation of a specific text (Herman 2009: 106). *The Crash of the Elysium* had its own internally coherent storyworld that was created, maintained and developed by the interplay between performers, text and design. But it also evoked, and worked within the perimeters of, the wider pre-existing and well-established *Doctor Who* storyworld. It did this implicitly by incorporating a science-fictional aesthetic into its design; but primarily the *Doctor Who* storyworld was explicitly evoked. The connection was of course central to the commercial positioning of *Elysium*, and the production included televised scenes with actors and sets from the show and incorporated well-known tropes and imagery into its design, musical score and text: "To the Tardis!" The opportunity to step into a beloved world and actively experience these famous aspects was an integral part of the show's appeal. Immersive experience and narrative in the context of *The Crash of the Elysium* was facilitated by interplay between previously known elements and tropes which were there to be recognised, and unknown elements and story events which were there to be discovered. The familiarity came from *Doctor Who*; the mystery was Punchdrunk's.

Cobley (2001) emphasises the role of representation in narrative, and the way narrative functions in three dimensions: "narrative is a particular form of representation… it is necessarily bound up with sequence, space and time" (3). The concept of *sequence* is important: the organisation of events and the way those events are encountered affect how a narrative affects a reader. The notion of *sequence* becomes embodied in immersive theatre, as the audience member is invited to move through space to physically encounter story events: indeed, they must move in order to experience these events. A narrative is a representational form which presents a sequence of events (Abbott and Cobley). Sequence, space and time are necessarily bound up with the form of immersive theatre: the question then becomes one of how sequence, space and time affect immersive experience.

From Herman, the concept of *storyworld* can be added to this definition: a narrative draws on a wider storyworld to create a discourse and/or evoke a fictional storyworld as part of that discourse, representing events that occur in that storyworld in response to disruption or conflict. Cobley adds the notion of the *ending* event as a specific type of narrative event. Narrative form depends on, and adjusts in response to, its technological context (the media used to tell the story):

> [Narrative] *re*-presents time, space and sequence; it facilitates the remembrance and exploration of identity; it imbues its representations with causality; it envisages an end; and it does all of these according to the specificities of the technologies in which it is embedded. (2001: 228; original emphasis)

A final model will complete the definition of narrative used throughout the following discussion. Marie-Laure Ryan's (2011) methodology for approaching narrative resembles a model of immersive experience as a series of graded states. Ryan argues for a "fuzzy-set definition" of narrative, proposing a series of categories and questions that go towards considering how much of a narrative any given text is, and what kind of a narrative it is: the key question should not be merely whether any given text is a narrative or not. Such a prescriptive approach is not particularly fruitful, or ultimately useful. Instead, Ryan proposes that *narrative* is a more flexible category: "Because judgments of fictionality affect what the reader will or will not believe, they are much more important than judgments of narrativity" (2011: 32). Similarly, Abbott argues it is restrictive to require narratives to contain more than one event or to suggest causality between events in order to qualify as narratives (2002: 12), suggesting instead a wider scope to allow for a greater range of texts. A definition of narrative drawn from these models must incorporate this flexibility. Narrative is a representation of a sequence of events; narrative occurs within and creates a storyworld; it exists in space and time; it is bound up with sequence and causality: and it changes its form depending on its context. My approach is (to use Ryan's phrasing) "fuzzy-set": less concerned with whether an immersive theatre production contain narratives per se, and more with how ideas of narrative are useful for considering immersive experience within it. *Plot*, *story* and *discourse* are useful concepts for considering what kind of invitation an immersive production offers its audiences. The various narratives of a show—whether defined as the story-as-told (performed, enacted), story-as-experienced (what "story" an audience member builds for herself), the structure of story events and how an audience member engages with this framework (the physical journey through the space) or some combination of all of these—might all be considered in relation to immersive experience, which is part of "what the reader will or will not believe."

Ryan identifies three ways a spectator/reader might become involved with narrative: "spatial immersion, the response to setting; temporal immersion, the response to plot; and emotional immersion, the response to character" (2001: 121). *Immersion* can describe both a physical and a mental state, so it is helpful to consider immersion in narrative using these separate categories. The first concept seems particularly apt: while prose fiction and a computer game do not physically surround a reader, immersive theatre and virtual reality are able to create a space that is immediately and literally present and all-encompassing. However, for immersive experience as a *mental* state to occur within that space, merely being in the room is not enough: the audience member's response to their environment determines whether the space facilitates immersive experience, and the level of such experience that might be reached.

A final narrative concept, highly relevant to much of Punchdrunk's immersive theatre, and therefore worth adding to any working model of narrative that will be used to consider their work, is *suspense*. Ryan's discussion of pace and suspense makes clear the relationship between narrative immersion and a varying of intensity:

> This experience of being transported onto the narrative scene is so intense and demanding on the imagination that it cannot be sustained for a very long time; an important aspect of narrative art consists, therefore, of varying the distance, just as a sophisticated movie will vary the focal length of the camera lens. (2001: 139)

Immersive experience as a highly intense, temporary and fleeting state, that must necessarily be temporary, becomes relevant here. This definition also recognises the importance of the writer's craft in creating narrative suspense by manipulating form and structure. Immersive experience requires varying pace and intensity in order that the experience not become overwhelming (or sublime; or "revered"). Immersive experience exists as a series of graded states—of which either the author/creator or the spectator/reader (in a theorisation of the active, empowered audience member) is in control.

Ryan distinguishes four types of suspense: *what* suspense (what will happen next?); *how* suspense (how did it come to be like this? /how did this happen? the reader desires to learn what prehistory results in the present moment); *who* suspense (commonly found in the whodunnit: there is no sadness in the murder, merely interest in the puzzle); and *metasuspense*, "critical involvement with the story as verbal artefact"—such as wondering how the author is going to finish the story, what will become of all the plot threads (2001: 143–145). It is possible to feel multiple types of suspense simultaneously: to wonder what will happen as, for example, you follow a character through a door ("what suspense"), in what state your character's emotional journey might end up ("how suspense"), for the Punchdrunk fan to wonder how on earth they will top their show of the previous year ("metasuspense").

Story, Plot, Discourse

An ever-present complexity in narrative studies is the relationship between *plot, discourse, narration* and *story*. Some narratologists use terms taken from Russian Formalism, such as *fabula* and *sjuzhet* meaning story and plot, respectively (Barry 2002: 223). Abbott shows the importance of making the distinctions at all:

> The distinction between plot and story, like that between narration and story, is an implicit presumption that a story is separate from its rendering.

Just as a story can be narrated in different ways, so it can be plotted in different ways. This analytically powerful distinction between story and its representation is, arguably, the founding insight of the field of narratology. (2011: 40)

This is further complicated by the fact that the discourse (the wider story) only makes itself known in the telling, as it is only through the story (reading/encountering story events) that a reader is able to deduce the discourse. The concepts can be separated, but are interrelated.

Abbott suggests a distinction between story and discourse: "The difference between events and their representation is the difference between story (the event or sequence of events) and narrative discourse (how the story is conveyed)" (13). A writer often invents the story that is going to be narrated, fictional actions gradually revealed via the organisation of the discourse. Narrative discourse—the representation of events, how the story is told—is closer to what the reader actually experiences. It is through narrative discourse that a reader comes to experience a story, and it is narrative discourse that a writer or artist is able to consciously manipulate and organise; narrative discourse is "infinitely malleable" (Abbott 2011: 15). A key approach of narratology is therefore distinguishing the difference between the story itself, and the story-as-discourse (Abbott 2011; Genette 1980; Chatman 1978). There is a difference between the story events themselves and the story-as-told. The story events have to happen chronologically, but the story-as-told might present them to its reader in any order. The way an author, artist or theatre company manipulate and design story events affects the reader or audience member's experience of, and relationship to, the discourse.

To consider this in the context of immersive theatre is to physically embody the distinction between story and story-as-told (or story-as-encountered). Immersive productions might separate story from discourse, by creating and ordering events and inviting audience members to build their own discourse or plot. In the structural/logistical form most common Punchdrunk—large-scale, exploratory spaces with action scattered through it—the *story* is what is happening across the building, and as an audience member wanders through the space, they build their own *plot*. There is construction and craft in how these story events have been made, designed and ordered, but less a sense of deliberate design in the path an audience member takes: indeed, they are invited to "steer [their] own course" as *The Drowned Man* had it.

The wider storyworld is the building of the production and is certainly a storyworld-in-flux, with enacted conflict, emotion and drama coursing throughout it. In this theorisation, then, an audience member is in control of her own experience of the wider discourse: she is free to become her own narrator. The wider storyworld has already been made, of course: the audience member has as much control over characters' actions as she would while watching a well-made play in a proscenium arch, or reading a murder mystery paperback. But the invitation is to freely navigate—to freely *plot*—an individual journey through this presented world. The offer is to build an individual discourse.

Framing an audience member as the narrator of events within an immersive storyworld-in-flux helps explain a problematic way these story events might be navigated: one that can result in frustration or disorientation and ultimately raise of barriers to immersion. Rather than enjoying the sense of freedom to create their own plot and see whatever scenes they come across, a desire to understand the wider storyworld places the story and the plot (the events of the show and the audience member's own narrative discourse as built by their individual journey) in conflict with each other. This will adversely affect immersive experience as it raises barriers to immersion that interrupt any sense of psychological "flow." *Flow* occurs when there is a sense of matching challenge and skill in an activity: it may not be explicitly coded as a game or challenge, but the sensation of being "unable" to do something is a key barrier to immersion at the level of accessibility and in this context, a conflicting relationship between *story* and *plot* means a large immersive theatre production presents an impossible task to its audience members, demonstrating the existence of a storyworld full of events it is impossible to successfully navigate. Unable to see everything, blocked from building up an understanding of the "whole story" via the path of an individual discourse: when the sense of a wider story and an audience member's sense of her own plot come into conflict the result is a sense of missing or unclear narrative—anxiety over doing it wrong or being in the wrong place—a botched immersive experience. This problem is a greater risk when, for all the invitations to exploratory freedom in the marketing of a production, and however explicitly phrased in an opening voiceover, there *does* seem to be a proper way to do it.

Cobley's explanation of the relationship between *story, plot* and *narrative* allows for all three terms to be taken into account, and applied more precisely to immersive experience:

"story" consists of all the events which are to be depicted. "Plot" is the chain of causation which dictates that these events are somehow linked and that they are therefore to be depicted in relation to each other. "Narrative" is the showing or the telling of these events and the mode selected for that to take place. (2001: 5–6)

In this model, both *plot* and *story* are concerned with what the original storyworld is and what the original events are—*narrative* is how the story and the plot are (simultaneously) conveyed to a reader. This organisational aspect is key to considering narrative and immersion: a writer (or a director, or a theatre company) has invented, crafted and ordered events which the reader/audience member encounters. The sequential element is important, as is the extent of a sense of causality between events. This model might explain why story, plot and narrative can work together in theatre to facilitate immersive experience rather than block it, as an original selection and organisation of events is experienced by an audience member as they move through the space. It becomes possible to distinguish between the creation of a wider storyworld (*story*), the design of several story events that are enacted across the space and/or embedded in its mise-en-scene (*plot*), and the audience member's own experience of these events, some of which they see and some of which they miss (*narrative*).

In *The Crash of the Elysium*, *story*, *plot* and *narrative* did function together and were experienced simultaneously: a physically linear show, the audience experienced the story events in the order Punchdrunk determined they would, led throughout by actor-guides who, in the fiction of the show, were exploring this strange world at the same time as their charges. Narrative and immersive experience were closely intertwined in this production, which was built with the purpose of avoiding any chance of lost, aimless wandering, working to minimise any conflict between the events of the story and the physical events provided by moving through the space.

The Importance of Causality

If a *story* is, fundamentally, a series of events (as suggested in Abbott's deliberately wide and all inclusive definition), then in a *plot*, one event naturally leads to another. The distinction is demonstrated neatly by Forster:

"The king died and then the queen died" is a story. "The king died, and then the queen died of grief" is a plot. The time sequence is preserved, but the sense of causality overshadows it. [...] Consider the death of the queen. If it is in a story we say: "And then?" If it is in a plot we ask: "Why?" (1963: 87).

One of the most cited works on the study of narrative, Barthes' "Introduction to the Structural Analysis of Narratives" (1966), also considers causality a key component to how humans engage with narrative. Indeed, for Barthes a "confusion of consecution and consequence, what comes *after* being read in narrative as what is *caused by*" (94; original emphasis), is central to narrative. Other studies of narrative suggest the importance of causality to meaning-making. To Brooks, plotting (defined as the act of shaping or crafting a narrative) is how a story is given meaning: "Plot as I conceive it is the design and intention of narrative, what shapes a story and gives it a certain direction or intent of meaning" (1984: xi). Narrative is structured into plot: the reader encounters plot and follows it, creating meaning and interpretation as they go. Brooks describes plotting as "that which makes a plot 'move forward', and makes us read forward, seeking in the unfolding of the narrative a line of intention and a portent of design that hold the promise of progress toward meaning" (xiii). Ricoeur also suggests meaning and causality are connected: he defines following a story as "understanding the successive actions, thoughts, and feelings in question insofar as they present a certain directedness. [...] There is no story if our attention is not moved along by a thousand contingencies" ([1970] 2000: 259).

Causality allows an audience member to become immersed in a linear narrative. As demonstrated in Forster's "Why?", wanting to know the reason for one event following another is a strong reason for continuing a story to the end: it can even persuade a reluctant reader to finish a story they are otherwise, for whatever reason, not enjoying. If events can be experienced in any order, a certain sense of causality might be lost: or if events, embodied by a performer's actions, are known to be on repeating loop, a sense of causality in the story they are enacting might become questionable. An internally coherent fictional world lowers barriers to (psychological, cognitive) immersion and a well-plotted story that allows the reader to deduce the fictional world as they explore. The plot need not be linear (see Pinter's *Betrayal* or Churchill's *Top Girls* to name two obvious examples of non-chronological scene structuring), but the story told by the plot, the story that is *revealed* as the plot goes along, will be. Causality in the context of immersive theatre can provide a means for immersive experience (as one discovery or encounter leads seamlessly to another) or raise barriers to immersion (as a frustrating attempt at interactivity leaves an audience member wondering why something happened, or did not happen, to them). The difference between a production's storyworld and an audience member's journey through the space can become as a site of problems in terms of interpretation, of frustration or of anxiety over understanding. Narrative comes from, and is the result of, the desire to find sense and meaning:

> our narrative perception stands ready to be activated in order to give us a frame or context for even the most static and uneventful scenes. And without understanding the narrative, we often feel we don't understand what we see. (Abbott 2002: 11)

Conflict between the wider story/structure of an immersive production and an audience member's journey through the space will adversely affect immersive experience; story and plot become separated to the detriment of the overall experience.

However, this separation might also lead to a different conclusion. The non-linearity of story events, and the relationship between the story events and an audience member's experience of these events (some found, some stumbled upon, some followed for a while) might be precisely what *is* immersive, rather than being what interrupts or frustrates immersive experience. The sensation of searching and finding and engaging with the story as part of the formulation of an audience member's own narrative discourse becomes a similar task to solving a puzzle or playing a game. The question then might be which lens a piece of work is inviting its audience to look through: a story formed of causality, or a game made of mystery-solving. Either can be immersive; two approaches in conflict may not be.

Character and Plot

Aristotle's *Poetics* prioritises plot over character: "plot is the course and (as it were) the soul of tragedy; character is second" (trans. 1996: 12). Characters are agents that function to further the plot:

there could not be a tragedy without action, but there could be one without character. [...] the most important devices by which tragedy sways emotion are parts of the plot, i.e. reversals and recognitions. (12)

Later discussions trouble this binary: screen- and play-writing guides often emphasise that "plot is character in action" (McKee 1999; Fountain 2007); character not only creates the plot but *is* the plot, bring about story events by choices and actions.

In explicitly interactive theatre (with a presentation of choices that lead to varying outcomes) audience members resemble these Aristotelian agents. They function to further the plot and/or initiate the events of the performance. In immersive theatre, however, audience members more closely resemble the second model: by wandering freely and choosing to explore they bring about their own experience, curating their own series of events as they discover them. As discussed previously, immersive theatre and particularly the work of Punchdrunk tends not to include explicit interactivity, and could be considered not interactive at all, however much it may create a sensation of genuine interactivity. Immersive theatre productions do allow for a great amount of imaginative participation, and Punchdrunk shows facilitate participation in the wider culture of the production. In terms of performers' characters and the wider plot, many of Punchdrunk's larger productions tend to follow an Aristotelian model; a performer's movements are pre-set and structured across the space of the building, and their adherence to following this prescribed course brings about the performance events. An audience member may experience a show this way too, sensing various performers' movements in terms of a wider pattern. But in the moment of performance, the fictional story of an individual character may resemble the second model as well, as they are seen to experience emotions, make choices, perform actions and experience consequences. An audience member following an individual actor closely may experience the show's story primarily in this mode.

A Linear Case Study of Narrative and Immersion: *The Crash of the Elysium*

The Crash of the Elysium was part of 2011 Manchester International Festival at Salford Quays, transferring to Ipswich for the 2012 Cultural Olympiad. Primarily a children's show (although "family" and adult-only performances did occur, the latter by popular demand) the show was an adventure set in *Doctor Who* universe; a collaboration between Punchdrunk and the BBC, executive producer Stephen Moffat and series screenwriter Tom MacRae. Starting off as a (deliberately rather boring) lecture about a missing Victorian steamship which is quickly interrupted, the audience are informed that they are urgently needed for a special mission: and as a team they explore the wrecked *Elysium* ship, encounter footage by Matt Smith's Doctor, find the Tardis and defeat the Weeping Angels. For the purposes of considering narrative and immersion in *The Crash of the Elysium*, it is helpful to consider *story*, *plot* and *narrative* separately, even if they are experienced simultaneously in the moment of theatrical encounter. The puzzle-solving approach to piecing together information can also be enjoyed in linear storytelling, especially if the content involves solving a mystery (What happened to the *Elysium*?) or searching for a lost object (Where is the Tardis?). Just like immersive experience itself, immersion in storyworld and immersion in the structural mechanics of how one might "play" within a production are not a binary choice; rather, interplay between them facilitates immersive experience. *The Crash of the Elysium* allowed for immersion in terms of both content and form, storyworld and discourse.

Although from the beginning there was speculation about the fear factor (the Manchester International Festival website waning that: "Like any *Doctor Who* episode, children will find this event both scary and exciting"), care was taken of the audience throughout. Lyn Gardner noted that "performers have been chosen for their child friendliness, and … parents are being advised on how to prepare their children" (2011: n.p.). The audience were led by in-character guides who spoke and engaged with them throughout, and in the fictional story of the show the audience find themselves crucial agents in restoring balance to the storyworld-in-flux. These conventions broke with the usual Punchdrunk formulation of audience members as wandering ghosts, allowing for more active engagement. The show's form did not allow the free wandering that might characterises a sense of audience choice.

Throughout the show the audience were instructed to line up, take instructions, stay together, be careful and for everybody to signal *ok* before the group moved on. These gestures and signals were effective safety precautions built into the show's performance vocabulary to continue immersion in the fictional world. The guides never left the audience completely on their own, and a medic (a real-life first aider, who is also explained to be a medic within the fictional world of the story) travels with the group. Immersive experience and narrative worked together to ensure audience well-being, fictionalised as dynamic mission-solving teamwork. Even though there were some instances of time-travel—the audience escape the Weeping Angels by jumping to a Victorian fairground, and then appear to leap forward into a far-future spaceship before returning, as the performance ends, to the present—the show was fundamentally linear through the story it tells, and was physically linear throughout in terms of how the audience plotted their way through that story. Causality was maintained throughout the narrative discourse.

The concepts of barriers to immersion and the model of immersive experience as various levels of intensity and engagement lead to the challenge, for makers, of lowering these barriers in order to facilitate immersion in their audiences. Structure and craft are required in the composition and rehearsal of scenes and performances, with the aim of bringing about immersion in narrative as the audience follow a *plot* and experience a *story* that takes place in a wider *storyworld*. *The Crash of the Elysium* provides a useful approach to this challenge of form and story. The relationship between story of the show and the *plot* through that story by actors and audience, due to the show's linear structure, meant performance events could also function as narrative events. They worked together to facilitate immersive experience and lower barriers to immersion. The audience travelled through a series of atmospheric spaces and experienced different kinds of interactivity (television screens; in-character guides asking their advice; crawling, running, lining up in the space) which can allow for immersive experience in terms of exploration, discovery and excitement. (Or, should it go wrong, a breaking of immersion due to fear or confusion.) These events were also narrative events that allowed for immersion in a world and a sense of "what it's like" to experience the storyworld-in-flux (cf. Herman 2009), building to a climax of spectacle, music and narrative/character, the final scene functioning as both a performance event and a narrative ending that brought the experience of the show as well as its story and plot to a close.

A rough story outline is also an audience movement outline. The deliberately boring prologue—a professor's lecture on the history of the crashed *Elysium*—presented a world that was ready to be broken, making the call to adventure even more exciting (and even necessary): in a strong inciting incident the guides enter the lecture space, recruit the group and the real adventure begins. The narrative event was made physical in the speedy journey out of the white-walled classroom and through the wreckage of a derelict ship. The first video communication from the Doctor set up the world ahead and hinted at its dangers ("*don't* blink") and in asking the audience for help finding the Tardis, the relationship between them and the guides is firmly established: the audience's active engagement is required and they are important for restoring the fictional order. The protagonists are established (the audience, their guides), as is the conflict between the secondary characters (the Doctor, River Song) and the antagonist presence (the Weeping Angels—alien monsters that take the form of stone statues, moving at the speed of a blink). An attack by the Weeping Angels results in a trip to the Victorian age: a second act climax in which everyone is thrown off the path, and seem to be the furthest yet from their goal. This predicament within the narrative was again made physical and literal in the shape of the show: by running away from the Weeping Angels, the audience seem to go off their planned path. When the Tardis returns them to a far-future spaceship (the production's final performance space, apart from one corridor back into the real world), everyone puts their hands on a tree to join their powers together and bring the plot to a final climax, music and lights lending to the tension and gravitas of the moment. The actor-guides and the interventions from screens add plot exposition and intensify the conflicts and what is at stake for the *Doctor Who* characters. Balance restored, the audience make a final dash through a corridor of trapped statues—making literal the successful change they members have achieved in the storyworld. The end of the story is also the end of the audience's plot, and this is made very clear both in content and form as the guides salute and say goodbye.

Immersive experience can, of course, occur in a linear plot: in *The Crash of the Elysium*, the linear plot enabled intense engagement through a clear sense of causality, as well as making the audience appear to be the agents of change in the storyworld-in-flux. Punchdrunk manufactured the overall movement score and progression of the show and little was left to chance, just as in a linear playtext, with some deliberate spaces for improvised conversation and discussion with the guides. Audience members were free to create their own sense of change and effect upon the immediate experience of the show in the moment of performance—the show facilitated, for its young participants, high levels of imaginative participation, of cognitive interactivity.

One example illustrates a moment where narrative and immersive experience were incorporated into the rehearsal process. After the first filmed section from the Doctor, early in the show, the guides inform the audience that their mission is to find the Tardis. The guides ask if anyone can provide information about this unknown object: "we don't know what it is; we don't know what it looks like," encouraging them to respond to this prompt. In a rehearsal of this scene, this line was improvised to include "we don't know what colour it is." Although someone outside the storyworld of the production is likely to know the Tardis is blue, within the world it was too specific a question—if you don't know what something is, do you think to wonder what colour it is? The line was eventually rejected as overly leading: it was a line belonging to the real-life production, not to the fictional world. This decision represents a movement between levels of interactivity (a child might be more able or willing to give a definite answer to the closed question of "what colour is it") and narrative coherence.

Elysium: An Internally Coherent Immersive World

An immersive space is physically internally coherent, existing within strongly defined spatial and temporal boundaries. Immersive experience is also a temporary sensation, all the more intense and powerful for its being finite or (in the case of peak experience or flow) fleeting. Add to that the provocation that an internally coherent world is a requirement for effectively immersive fiction. In terms of storyworld, the rules of *The Crash of the Elysium* also had to feel complete and make sense: the show needed a story the audience could follow, not just in terms of their physical route, in order to become successfully immersed in the storyworld and experience the storyworld-in-flux.

The world of *The Crash of the Elysium* had a further imperative to aim for internal coherence by way of its taking place in the well-known, pre-established universe of long-running children's television programme *Doctor Who*. This is a universe with known characters and relationships, dynamics, boundaries and rules. The Tardis and the Weeping Angels are recognisable figures with known skills and abilities; the audience would be likely to have seen them functioning as plot elements in the television show, and now they find themselves incorporated into a plot in which these characters also feature. The show's aesthetic elements are also recognisable, not just its characters but its sets and its soundtrack.

Within this known and recognisable universe the story of the *Crash of the Elysium* sits—its challenge was to not shift or alter the universe of the show, but to fit within it. The collaboration between Punchdrunk and *Doctor Who* was of course a foundational aspect of the show and the cornerstone of its marketing. The world of the story had to fit within this universe, and allow its audience to function as important agents whilst not upsetting the dynamics of the wider *Doctor Who* universe. For an audience member, the excitement of being involved in an adventure might go hand in hand with being aware of anything that is wrong, inaccurate or disrespectful. Drawing on a recognisable brand can be both a bonus and a challenge in terms of keeping everyone happy.

In rehearsal, the deliberately created space for off-script improvised dialogue and answers to questions were subject to scrutiny. Inconsistencies in the script were discussed at length and the rules of *The Crash of the Elysium*'s universe worked out in order that any tricky questions could be answered. Whether or not these questions came up during performances, the anxiety to get this element right demonstrates the importance of story-based internal coherence and the potential dangers of a script with internal inconsistencies on an audience who might well be likely to spot them and point them out. The relationship between the actor-guides and audience relied on the exchange of information, exposition and occasionally the deliberate suggestion of ignorance or powerlessness which could only be solved by one of the audience members. The manipulation of story events and plot elements went towards creating a narrative that, in terms of content and internal dynamics, made recognisable sense, functioning logically within the *Doctor Who* universe. This was as important in the show's making as the process of creating physical immersion, tension and atmosphere. The wider cultural narrative of the television programme and its history was incorporated into how the show was structured, rehearsed and performed.

Elysium: Structural and Soundtrack Linearity

The creation of the show also involved working towards narrative linearity in terms of crafting the audience's physical journey.

The rhythm of the show was created by its soundtrack. Every beat of the audience's journey along their route was accounted for, and rehearsed to be maintained. The audience were moving along a predetermined path led by the actor-guides, but the scenes themselves were cued by musical/sound-effect scores and lighting, which were cued (in secret) by the actors. The soundtrack functioned as a score throughout the audience's journey, adding pace and tone to the structure of the scenes. Music and sound are capable of creating highly immersive effects (Di Benedetto 2010; Radbourne et al. 2014): lowering barriers to immersion; creating an internally coherent world (drawing on the soundtrack of the television show—recognition becoming an added stimulus); creating mood and atmosphere. The soundtrack functioned as a structural aid within the scenes themselves as well as across the show as a whole. This allowed for immersion in the storyworld through which the audience were led by the actor-guides, learning the story (the Doctor's relationship to the *Elysium*, the alarming news about escaped Weeping Angels, etc.) through their own plotted course through the performance. The rhythm of the score was matched to the timing of the actors, significant story events occurring to create moments of excitement (immersive experience in the space), participation (immersive experience in the performance) and adrenaline (story experience—what will happen next?).

This was a well-known and easily recognisable soundtrack: music from the show and famous SFX functioned as performative intertextual references that situated the production within the universe/wider storyworld of the television show. This affected the production's internal narrative consistency, but there is also an interesting relationship to be distinguished between immersion in a fictional narrative and a fictional world, and a real-world event. Immersive experience can manifest as temporarily forgetting about outside world. As demonstrated, the production was crafted and rehearsed to ensure the audience remained in the world of *The Crash of the Elysium* throughout. However, the intertextual references drawn on in performing and attending the show came from real-world experience of fictive world exposure: the generic and aesthetic elements of *Doctor Who* narratives influenced immersive experience in the production. The real world cannot be entirely forgotten about—disassociated from—during *The Crash of the Elysium*, since it is a fictional world *from* the real world that is the setting for its story, a very famous fictional world that is referenced and drawn on all the way through. Immersive experience when watching television might appear to be more passive than experiencing a *Doctor Who* adventure in the real world, and physically it is less immediately active (even when going to hide behind the sofa); but engagement with the story elements, aesthetic and soundtrack while watching the television show might also make for a powerful immersive experience in *narrative*, and in the enjoyment of spending time with recognisable characters in a well-known wider storyworld. The relationship between narrative and immersion in *The Crash of the Elysium* was supported by the structure of the show, internally coherent performances and rules of the storyworld-in-flux, and the relationship between the performers and the audience members—which emphasised the vital importance of the presence of the latter.

Conclusion: Narrative and Immersion, Form and Story

Machon's description of *The Crash of the Elysium* hints at an interpretation of the relationship between narrative and form:

> an immersive event that exploits the action-led, mystery-solving narratives of Doctor Who via the Punchdrunk process to encourage high-paced interactivity. The format borrows from Punchdrunk's recent explorations in pervasive game-playing […] Rather than via Punchdrunk's trademark complex layering in form and content, audience-participants are engaged by the dynamic clue-solving participation, involving interaction with the Doctor via a series of video messages, and sensory stimulation. (2013: 3–4)

Machon suggests the show emphasised—and facilitated—interactivity in both content and form. The mode of an audience member's engagement with narrative was certainly more active and communal than the solitary, slow-paced exploration of Punchdrunk's larger shows made of "complex layering." The content and form of *Elysium* did suggest interactivity: in narrative terms, the actor-guides clearly communicated to the audience that their role in the story was important; in form terms, some moments of interactivity went beyond imaginative engagement and required real physical input. However, the production's content was tightly controlled throughout, and this interplay between narrative score and physical show structure led to the facilitation of immersive experience.

Immersive experience came about at the moment where spontaneous reaction in audience members met the carefully rehearsed and well-crafted environment which had been specifically designed to bring about such a spontaneous response. This phenomenon lowered the barriers to immersion. The barriers were physical (to be able and willing to move through the space following the actors) and atmospheric/narrative-based (to be engaged in the story and interested in the wider storyworlds of

Elysium show and *Doctor Who* universe). The audience's journey was structured in terms of the story they were experiencing. The story and the show were one and the same, proceeding at the same time, at the same rate and through the same space. The relationship with the actors was also direct, due to the intended audience for the work. The relationship between rehearsed movements and space for interaction and dialogue between audience and actors was factored into the show, and the relationship between narrative and immersion needed to be navigated throughout the rehearsal process. The audience were invited to change the world of the story and influence the outcome of its events, while also being technically and structurally cared for; working through a pre-rehearsed and pre-cued set of events, effects and encounters.

Not all Punchdrunk shows are this linear in form, or focus so much explicit attention on their audience. The next chapter will investigate what happens to story, plot and audience experience when the form of an immersive production is quite different.

References

Abbott, H. Porter. 2002. *The Cambridge Introduction to Narrative*. Cambridge: Cambridge University Press.

Abbott, H. Porter. 2011. Plot, Story and Narration. In *The Cambridge Companion to Narrative*, ed. David Herman, 39–51. Cambridge: Cambridge University Press.

Aristotle. [330BC?] 1996. *Poetics*, trans. Malcolm Heath. London: Penguin.

Barry, Peter. 2002. *Beginning Theory: An Introduction to Literary and Cultural Theory*. Manchester: Manchester University Press.

Barthes, Roland. [1966] 1988. Introduction to the Structural Analysis of Narratives, trans. Stephen Heath. In *Image Music Text*, 79–124. New York: Noonday Press.

Brooks, Peter. [1984] 1992. *Reading for the Plot: Design and Intention in Narrative*. Cambridge, Mass: Harvard University Press.

Chatman, Seymour. 1978. *Story and Discourse: Narrative Structure in Fiction and Film*. Ithaca: Cornell University Press.

Cobley, Paul. 2001. *Narrative*. London: Routledge.

Di Benedetto, Stephen. 2010. *The Provocation of the Senses in Contemporary Theatre*. London: Routledge.

Fludernik, Monika. [2005] 2008. Histories of Narrative Theory (II): From Structuralism to the Present. In *A Companion to Narrative Theory*, ed. James Phelan and Peter J. Rabinowitz, 36–59. London: Blackwell.

Forster, E.M. 1963. *Aspects of the Novel.* London: Penguin.
Fountain, Tim. 2007. *So You Want to be a Playwright?* London: Nick Hern Books.
Gardner, Lyn. 2011. The Crash of the Elysium: Punchdrunk Children Only. *Guardian*, June 8, 2011.
Genette, Gérard. [1972] 1980. *Narrative Discourse,* trans. J.E. Lewin. London: Basil Blackwell.
Herman, David. 2009. *Basic Elements of Narrative.* London: Wiley-Blackwell.
Machon, Josephine. 2013. *Immersive Theatres: Intimacy and Immediacy in Contemporary Performance.* London: Palgrave Macmillan.
McKee, Robert. 1999. *Story: Substance, Structure, Style, and the Principles of Screenwriting.* London: Methuen.
Radbourne, Jennifer, Katya Johanson, and Hilary Glow. 2014. The Value of Being There: How the Live Experience Measures Quality for the Audience. In *Coughing and Clapping: Investigating Audience Experience,* ed. Karen Burland and Stephanie Pitts, 55–68. Surrey: Ashgate.
Ricoeur, Paul. [1970] 2000. Narrative Time. In *The Narrative Reader,* ed. Marin McQuillan, 255–261. New York: Routledge.
Ryan, Marie-Laure. 2001. *Narrative as Virtual Reality: Immersion and Interactivity in Literature and Electronic Media.* Baltimore: John Hopkins University Press.
Ryan, Marie-Laure. 2011. Toward a Definition of Narrative. In *The Cambridge Companion to Narrative,* ed. David Herman, 22–35. Cambridge: Cambridge University Press.

CHAPTER 6

Exploring Multistories: Narrative, Immersion and Chronology

Describing the suitability of Büchner's *Woyzeck* as a Punchdrunk source text (for 2013's *The Drowned Man*), Felix Barrett draws on the play's fragmented structure and chronological ambiguities:

> Büchner died before he finished it and just left a series of scenes with no order. And it doesn't really matter which order you digest them in—still the conclusion is inevitable and it's always the same. That is the Punchdrunk way. (in Hemming 2013: n.p.)

This chapter is interested in immersive experience, narrative and time, and in particular what happens to them in the context of a structural trademark of many Punchdrunk shows. Most of their large-scale productions have taken a similar form: in *The Drowned Man* (2013–2014), *Sleep No More* (2011–), *The Duchess of Malfi* (2010), *The Masque of the Red Death* (2008) and *Faust* (2005), performers enacted scenes on repeating loops throughout a large building, travelling in predetermined paths from one event to the next, with audience members invited to wander through the space at will, finding moments of performance whenever and wherever they managed to do so (and missing them, of course, if they didn't). No two audience members (unless doggedly sticking together) therefore encounter the same events in the same order or at the same time, making each visit to the show unique in a literal sense. Finally the whole audience is brought together for a grand finale, having each seen, to an extent, a different show until that point.

© The Author(s) 2017
R. Biggin, *Immersive Theatre and Audience Experience*,
DOI 10.1007/978-3-319-62039-8_6

Rancière proposes that "an emancipated community is a community of narrators and translators" (2009: 22). Bartley uses the term "narrator-visitor" for members of a Punchdrunk audience (2013), a term that reflects the emphasis placed on the opening invitation, issued to an audience member along with their mask, to go forth and create their own sense of story. What happens to immersive experience when the events of that story are encountered out of their original order—or if there is no sense of an "original order" at all? This chapter considers the negotiation between apparent interactivity, the slippery notion of audience empowerment and the phenomenon of being "immersed" in story or acting as the emancipated narrator of your own story within a wider theatrical environment. This is a negotiation that becomes particularly interesting if, after all that, it remains "the Punchdrunk way" that "the conclusion is inevitable and it's always the same."

My discussion draws on concepts proposed by Genette and Riceour on the relationship between narrative and time to discuss moments of performance in Punchdrunk's *It Felt Like A Kiss* (2009) and *The Duchess of Malfi* (2010). *The Duchess of Malfi* was in the structural tradition described previously, with looping scores of action from performers (the usual actors and dancers, plus opera singers and musicians: the show was a collaboration between Punchdrunk and English National Opera) which audience members were invited to explore freely. *It Felt Like A Kiss*, however, is not listed in the above roll call of Punchdrunk shows with looping performer tracks. It was a linear show in terms of structure, and it featured (barring a few surprises) no actors. The audience were invited to explore the path in their own time in the tradition of Punchdrunk's typical "narrator-visitors," but there was only one path to follow (with a few subtle emergency doors for anyone requiring an early exit). The audience's relationship with the physical space was therefore key to how they were invited to engage with the production. In both shows audience members wandered through a building and "discovered" scenes—but only in *The Duchess of Malfi* could this be said to truly resemble discovery in the sense Punchdrunk usually mean it, as in *It Felt Like A Kiss* the path through the production was more controlled.

There is also, when considering immersion and idea of story, a question of prior knowledge of the text Punchdrunk are adapting. Both these two productions drew on stories with which an audience member might be expected to be at least partially acquainted; a Jacobean tragedy in the case of *The Duchess of Malfi*, and American post-war history in *It*

Felt Like A Kiss. The level of familiarity with the source text may affect a spectator becoming immersed in the show on its own terms, or delighting in the way Punchdrunk are ringing the changes on something she knows well.

I conclude my discussion on immersive experience and time by considering the idea of the ending. Comparing the finale of both shows (one successful, one unsuccessful) demonstrates two approaches to manipulating the relationship between immersive experience and an audience member's sense of chronology. At the end of *It Felt Like A Kiss* audience members left the building individually, having been deliberately split into individuals in the final sequence. *The Duchess of Malfi* did the opposite, ending in a more typical finale mode with everyone brought together for the first time, ushered into a large (previously inaccessible) space. In considering the way these productions ended, I argue that immersive experience is profoundly affected by the relationship between the physical structure of the show (the logistics of navigating it), and the narrative events enacted by performers or embedded within the mise-en-scene of the space. When chronology is disrupted, structural and logistical elements of the show *become* the narrative events. The manipulation of structure and time is a key way theatremakers might engage audiences.

A Short Introduction to Narrative and Time

The relationship between narrative and time is fundamental to narratology: "*narrative is the principle way in which our species organizes its understanding of time*" (Abbott 2002: 3; original emphasis). For Brooks, the relationship between narrative, plot and time reveals a central exploration of the human condition: "It is my simple conviction [...] that narrative has something to do with time-boundedness, and that plot is the internal logic of the discourse of mortality." Plot is "the product of our refusal to allow temporality to be meaningless" (1984: 23, 323).

Aristotle's *Poetics* emphasise the importance of *completeness* in plots: "a whole is that which has a beginning, a middle and an end" (1996: 13), but this does not mean the *telling* of a story has to conform to the same structure. Heath notes that "Aristotle is often quoted as if he had said that a play has a beginning, a middle and an end. This is wrong. It is the plot, the underlying sequence of actions, that has that structure" (trans. 1996: xxiii–xxiv). A playwright, novelist or theatre company decide which events of a story to show, and in what order, to best create their preferred dramatic effect: a creative act of meaning-making involving *how* a story is told, as much as the story itself. Punchdrunk's non-chronological productions do contain characters who enact scenes that can be classified as beginnings, middles and ends. The difference is an audience member might not encounter them in that order, or might only encounter some of them. They instead encounter events that are the beginning, middle and end *to them*, building their own story through the production. The *Poetics* also discusses unity of time and action in performance: "the structure of the various sections of the events must be such that the transposition or removal of any one section dislocates and changes the whole" (trans. 1996: 13). *The Crash of the Elysium*, for example, was a linear show in terms of structure: unified in time and action as it began and concluded in the space of a single journey, the adventure occurring, for audience members, in real time. But common to Punchdrunk's work are productions that break this rule in the way they invite engagement with scenes, the "transposition or removal of any one section" built into their structure.

The previous chapter outlined some concepts from narrative theory that are useful for thinking about immersive experience and story. To think about immersive experience, story and time, more tools are needed. Literary theorist Gérard Genette's structuralist analysis of narrative (his focus is prose fiction) gives several "problems" of narratology, including time:

> the problems of narrative discourse can be classified under three main headings: the categories of time (temporal relationships between the narrative [story] and the "actual" events that are being told [history]); of mode (relationships determined by the distance and perspective of the narrative with respect to the history); and of voice (relationships between the narrative and the narrating agency itself: narrative situation, level of narration, status of the narrator and of the recipient, etc.). (1970: 93–94)

From Genette's *Narrative Discourse* (1980) come the concepts of types of narrator (homodiegetic and heterodiegetic); evocations that disrupt the chronology of a story's telling (analeptic and proleptic); frame and embedded narratives; and the difference between mimetic and diegetic narrative modes. These concepts expand the vocabulary available for considering narrative and chronology in immersive theatre.

A homodiegetic narrator is present as a character in the story. A heterodiegetic narrator is an outsider (243–245). An omniscient narrator is by definition heterodiegetic. As they create their own plot as they move through the space, the audience member in immersive theatre in essence functions as the narrator of their own experience: the question then becomes one of type. Especially in the immersive form considered in this chapter, masked and anonymous audience members, Punchdrunk's "narrator-visitors," are heterodiegetic—experiencing the world of the show from outside. When a character makes eye contact and/or initiates a one-on-one scene, a spectator temporarily becomes homodiegetic: the movement between these two modes might go towards drawing an audience member into immersive experience. Finally, above and beyond the audience members and performers in a Punchdrunk show, a vast and semi-anonymous character called "Punchdrunk" functions as omniscient heterodiegetic narrator.

Genette recognises a difference between the time of the story (the narrative) and the time of the telling of the story (the plot). Stories often begin *in media res*—halfway through the action, the joy for the reader/spectator partly in the catching up—and the telling of a story may include *analeptic* scenes, evoking events that went chronologically earlier in the larger narrative, and *proleptic* scenes which evoke events or action yet to come (40). Punchdrunk's larger shows certainly (seem to) begin *in media res*: both literally in that the productions often stagger the times of entry, and in sensation, in that scenes will often be encountered halfway through due to the logistical structure of the show.

In his discussion of narrative levels (228–231), Genette distinguishes between primary narrative and secondary narrative, also known as frame narrative and embedded narrative (this distinction is further clarified in Barry 2002: 235–237). The frame narrative is the wider setting or interpretive framework, or (cf. Herman 2009) the storyworld. The secondary or embedded narrative is the plot—the story that is actually being told, actually being experienced, the sequence of events drawn from this wider storyworld. A character's looping scenes in *Sleep No More* and *The Drowned Man* is an embedded narrative within the larger frame narrative of the McKittrick Hotel and Temple Studios respectively; an audience member searching through drawers and reading letters will encounter hints at further narratives embedded in these larger framing storyworlds. These smaller instances of story could also be considered "a narrative within a narrative" or a meta-narrative (Genette 1980: 228n), and it is possible for frame and embedded narratives to interplay. A frame narrative is intrusive when it interrupts a secondary or embedded narrative. An intrusive frame narrative might occur when solo exploration is interrupted, or an audience member suddenly comes upon a scene in the midst of the action. This movement between the frame narrative and various embedded narratives can either lower or raise barriers to immersive experience depending on whether they are a welcome or refreshing addition or surprise, or a rhythm-breaking interruption. Key here is whether the audience member (feels she) has control over the movement between these narrative modes.

Finally, Genette distinguishes between mimetic and diegetic narratives, or "showing vs telling" (162–170). In prose fiction the difference between mimetic and diegetic narration manifests in, for example, direct speech "vs" reported speech. Mimetic and diegetic are useful terms as they lack the implicit value judgement of "showing vs telling" (see numerous creative writing guides advising that "showing" is the better method). In an immersive production the detailed (small, filmic) performances of the actors and much of the set design (adhering to what Punchdrunk's website calls "cinematic" realism in its levels of detail) functions in mimetic mode; and the more surreal or abstract sets, or scenes of contemporary dance, are a diegetic demonstration of story events, emotions and themes. Barry suggests mimesis and diegesis "need each other, and often work together so that the join between them can be difficult to discern" (2002: 232). If the actors in a Punchdrunk production are engaged in mimetic performance and the dancers are concerned with diegetic performance, while the two modes also coexist across the design, the sensation of movement between them create a richness of experience rather than one "mode" being inherently more immersive.

For the philosopher Paul Ricoeur, narrative and temporality have an important relationship:

> the art of storytelling places the narrative "in" time. The art of storytelling is not so much a way of reflecting on time as a way of taking it for granted. ([1970] 2000: 259–260)

Ricoeur defines plot as "the intelligible whole that governs a succession of events in any story"; a plot "places us at the crossing point of temporality and narrativity" (259). Manipulating the relationship between narrative time, event chronology and the structure of scenes is a means of creating immersive experience across an entire production, as well as for more intense moments of immersion during events and scenes within it. Key to immersive experience is its temporary nature, as fleetingness and intensity dovetail. The distinction between story-time and event-time is explicit when scenes may be experienced in different orders by different audience members. Events that are significant in terms of the story's narrative may not impact an individual spectator's own plotted course. If they do find a scene of high narrative importance, they may not necessarily know (or care) what it means.

Immersive Experience, Structure and the Question of Chronological Order

Immersive experience is a fleeting state of engagement which can assume different forms and various levels of intensity. Immersive experience, narrative and time have a reciprocal relationship characterised by oscillation between differing states. Frances Babbage describes the relationship between show structure and narrative events in Punchdrunk's *The Masque of the Red Death*:

> in place of controlled narrative composition, the company substitute event composition—and for that event to be possible, narrative "wholeness" was sacrificed, perhaps gleefully abandoned. (2009: 17)

An abandonment of narrative coherence does not mean an abandonment of any coherence; Babbage notes that *Masque's* organisation was "highly sophisticated" (17). The elaborateness of the production, its scope or level of detail, affected how an audience member might engage with the scenes or events rather than any emotional attachment to the individual story of the characters or the wider storyworld of Poe. Evocations that disrupt the chronology of a story's telling (Genette's analeptic and proleptic) may not be scenes that are deliberately intended to reflect events that have happened or are yet to come, but are a side effect of this form of event composition. Productions like *The Masque of the Red Death* or *The Duchess of Malfi* evoke a sensation of an overarching narrative architecture and an overall finite timeframe. Musical cues and repeated images may occur throughout the space, but whether scenes are analeptic or proleptic in an audience member's own journey depends on when and where they happen to encounter them during the performance.

An audience member moves between types of narrator, during one-on-ones or other small interactions becoming a homodiegetic participant who a performer temporarily treats as belonging to the story and the storyworld. After this, a return to spend time as a heterodiegetic spectator who watches from inside the world of the production physically but not belonging to it in the same way as the characters. These graded states of relationship within and to the production and its storyworld and characters facilitate immersion by offering different levels of intensity. Movement between these types of narrator may be a barrier to immersive experience if it occurs in a way that jars or is otherwise unwelcome. The sensation of being moved between states in a way that produces discomfort or disorientation, being forcefully moved by an usher for example, affects the overarching narrative discourse by disrupting the immediate moment-by-moment navigation of the space. The difference between mimetic and diegetic narrative modes of discourse has the potential to affect immersive experience, and the relationship between immersive experience and story—and the act of movement between these states might facilitate immersive experience more than either can achieve individually.

Causality is what separates a story from a mere series of events. An effect of encountering story events out of order (or rather, in the case of well-known texts such as Poe's short stories, presented in a new order) is that a sense of causality is lost. The extent of the sense of this may depend on a performer's interpretation of their character's action loop. Some performances will create a sense of flow across a character arc, while some move between scenes in a more episodic manner, performing one and then the next with little performative cohesion. Both approaches are valid and both may occur in the same production. It becomes a question of aim, and neither approach is guaranteed to lead to immersive experience in spectators. One action appearing to naturally lead to another becomes problematic if there is also a strong sense of a tightly organised performance score from which performers (and audience members) are unable to deviate. There is still be a sense of causality, but in the context of the real-world production—drawing attention to the overall structure of events, scenes, characters and design, the crafting of the overall score—and away from the fictional *storyworld* that is being depicted. This could be theorised as movement between the embedded narrative and the frame narrative.

Plot (as defined by Ricoeur as the structure and organisation of story events) places a reader at a crossing point of temporality and narrativity.

Physically moving through a space contributes to an immersive sense of chronology because we are always aware, not just of character arcs or the time spent in a single room or wandering through a certain space, but of the overall theatrical arc of the show. It will not last forever, and an audience member gets to explore only within a finite time frame. The theatrical event has an end-stopped chronology even as the actions within it occur on a loop and go through repetitions—the event is also likely to have a climactic ending which the performances are working towards. Just as immersive experience is not a felt/not-felt binary, the sensation of moving between specific (finite) encounters and being aware of the wider (finite) theatrical arc of the show has the potential to produce a richness of experience—moving between these states of awareness characterising immersive experience in the temporality of the production. Referring to Riceour's model of time a psychological formation, Erikson suggests:

> to refer to theatre as a "time-based art" seems a misnomer, simply because it is not the case that performance is somehow based on or grounded "in" time: rather performance actually produces time (or, if you will, a sense of time—but what's the difference?) for the audience through the principle of tension and release. [...] if what Ricoeur says is true, then one can ask if producing an experience of time for the spectator and producing time for the spectator aren't in fact the same thing. (2012: 89)

Watching performance that appears to be occurring in a separate time (the fictional time and setting of the storyworld) to the spectator's own time (the real-world time of the performance) is a potential site of negotiation between immersion in the production and in narrative.

Cognitive science may provide further tools for considering theatrical structure and time. The relationship between immersive experience and chronology can be explained as a cognitive process. Hogan differentiates story and discourse in a way consistent with other discussions of narrative: "A central distinction in narratology is that between story and discourse, what happens and the presentation of what happens" (2003: 115). The reader of a text is "presented with an array of materials—partial, fragmentary, disordered, perhaps contradictory, untrustworthy, or irrelevant. From this, it is up to us to figure out 'what happened'" (116). Hogan describes this process of making sense of narrative as resulting from "procedural schemas," "cognitive structures of action [... that] allow us to construct the story from the discourse" (117). An important cognitive task as a reader or viewer of a text is "assigning *significant* temporal relations" to a series of events (122; original emphasis). The temporality of story events is therefore important to how a reader interprets a text at a cognitive level. A problem with considering immersive experience and chronology this way is it risks an essentialist interpretation of cognitive behaviour as by its logic, any event that requires a certain amount of cognitive behaviour is immersive and such reasoning makes it difficult to distinguish different kinds of engagement with the structure or chronology of a theatrical production. It also collapses art and life into one: for example, Hogan notes the cognitive work required to distinguish discourse and story is the same that occurs in a court jury sorting through evidence (deciding what is relevant, putting together "what happened" from scattered fragments, etc.) (115–116). It is difficult to consider procedural schemas in the context of theatrical performance as the cognitive behaviour is essentially the same.

As the brain sorts discourse from story and creates meaningful temporal relationships between events, nonlinearity in theatrical form can be theorised as an aid to immersive experience. But nonlinearity can also be theorised as presenting a tantalising puzzle to be explored further or solved. Moving the model from story to game, a deliberate lack of linearity becomes an integral part of the enjoyment, not a frustration or a block. In the context of gaming, the concepts of narrative immersion and sensory immersion are highly relevant to the question of what a participant is actually immersed *in*. Real World Disassociation (RWD) is a useful concept for considering temporarily and the relationship between a source text's storyworld, the presented and performed story and storyworld in an immersive theatre production, and an audience member's plot through and across these.

RWD is a phenomenon that occurs at high levels of immersion (Cairns et al. 2006; Jennett et al. 2008). Characterised by an extreme engagement or sensation of psychological "flow," reminders of the real world, which would normally be expected to jolt someone straight out of an immersive experience—such as becoming aware of an usher, or obtrusive behaviour of fellow audience members—might not necessarily adversely affect experience. Bartley suggests "[t]he most pervasive form of limitation imposed on narrator-visitors in *Sleep No More* is the presence of Stewards" (2013: n.p.), and these limitations seemingly imposed upon the production from above by Punchdrunk come into conflict with an audience member's own journey towards immersive experience: "the narrator-visitor cannot escape the influence of Punchdrunk's restraints" (2013: n.p.). RWD can explain a process where distractions and difficulties might be spotted and then ignored: that is, deemed insignificant to the audience member's plot through the production's storyworld and therefore rejected or let go in order for immersion to continue *in spite* of an awareness of these limitations or restraints. In the context of immersive performance and narrative, RWD explains how an audience member might retain awareness of real-world events and continue to experience a sense of immersion in a fictional landscape, atmosphere or story. An audience member may negotiate with their immediate surroundings to retain engagement in the storyworld (narrative immersion) and the atmosphere (sensory immersion), or move between both. Finally, it is worth repeating that RWD is theorised as only occurring when a high level of immersion has already been achieved: so a production may need to work towards this first, before trusting that an audience member's state of wonder will automatically rule out any distractions.

An example action that illustrates the relationship between narrative immersion and sensory immersion could be drawn from any of the Punchdrunk productions listed at the beginning of this chapter: an audience member opening and going through a door. Opening a door and entering a new space is an action that marks a liminal transition moment in an audience member's narrative discourse or plot through the show. The action is of course a literal one that is required to further the successful navigation of the physical layout of the space. But it also acts as a metaphor for a scene change, or a time change: it is a new event in an audience member's narrative discourse. Immersive experience itself is liable to change or develop as you open a door and walk through: if this new room/space is as yet unknown, (or if it is significantly different, such as having performers in it for the first time), the moment demonstrates a development in the audience member's own narrative. From what they find, they will deduce a story or explore a wider storyworld that performers enact in the space or that designers have embedded into the mise-en-scene, or both. Opening a door is an example of content and form simultaneously facilitating immersive experience, operating as both an architectural/design event and a story event.

The concepts outlined so far are useful for considering time, structure and organisation in a production that invites exploration through its physical structure and featuring a story broken up by unusual or unexpected chronology. However, this chapter began with Punchdrunk's artistic director stating that, however the rest of the show is experienced, the ending is "always the same." Therefore it seems appropriate to turn focus to a discussion of endings, with a view to examining how they might enable or inhibit immersive experience by the way they treat the relationship between story and structure.

Two Immersive Endings

It Felt Like A Kiss (2009) and *The Duchess of Malfi* (2010) had endings that demonstrate different relationships between immersive experience and the way an audience encountered the story events. The former created a synthesis of story, plot and narrative that resulted in an effective relationship between time and immersive experience; the latter suffered from conflict between an audience member's physical journey-score through the production, the company's design of the immersive space and the structure of story events.

An ending defined as the final event, chronologically, that occurs in a *story*; it can also be the final event, not necessarily chronologically, that is told in a *plot* or narrative discourse. The two are often experienced simultaneously, the telling of a story ending with the final event of that story. However, distinguishing the difference allows for narrative discourses that play with chronology, like the Punchdrunk structure considered in this chapter does. The ending of a story will be the last chronological event that occurs in the wider storyworld; the ending of a plot is the last event that a reader/audience member actually experiences.

The ending is the most important event in a narrative discourse. It will be the last impression a reader or spectator receives of the work. It is also important in terms of story events: the ending happens at the end of the story, but more importantly, the ending *can only* happen at the end of the story. The final event changes the world of the story irreversibly. At the moment of its happening, the ending must seem surprising. The audience should not have been able to predict it with detailed accuracy ahead of time. But neither should it be inappropriate: once the final event has been revealed, it must become clear that the whole of the previous story event have been leading up to it, and in retrospect it is clear that the story could not have ended in any other way (these rules from McKee 1999: 309). And as Ricoeur states, "rather than being predictable, a conclusion has to be acceptable. Looking back from the conclusion to the episodes leading up to it, we have to be able to say that this ending required these sorts of events and this chain of actions" (1970 in McQuillan 2000: 259). From narrative theory to contemporary screenwriting gurus (McKee and others), these are the elements that not only make for a good ending, but make for an ending at all.

I want to conclude my discussion of immersive experience, narrative and time by considering the final events or scenes of two productions. The first occurred in a show with a linear path where the audience were not led by any performers. Indeed, the show featured few performers at all, with the exception of some actors in an ushering role (putting audience members into groups ready for the ending) and a single surprise performer during the final event. *It Felt Like A Kiss* had an ending that, like Riceour's description of a conclusion, was not predictable—but acceptable, in retrospect, in the context of the narrative discourse that had gone before it. It maintained an internally coherent world. *The Duchess of Malfi* had an ending that followed the (by then typical for Punchdrunk) finale convention, which combined spectacle with narrative. This ending was not as successful in creating immersive experience because physical plot and narrative plot were at odds with each other.

First—a linear immersive narrative ending. *It Felt Like A Kiss*, Punchdrunk's collaboration with the film-maker Adam Curtis for the 2009 Manchester International Festival, had a section that illustrates the description of an ending, above: an event that changed both the story and storyworld that had gone before. Images and sets echoed and repeated across the time and space of the production, and the ending used these to create a synthesis between narrative discourse and the audience's plot through the building.

The show begins with a lift-ride to the top of the building. The first rooms the audience wander through are the rooms they will encounter again later, at the ending. They depict an American household in the 1950s: bedroom, lounge, dining room. Beyond the dining room and through the front door, the audience find themselves outside this dream house, even down to the picnic on the green lawn. These spaces are without people, although a mannequin watches the television screen in the lounge. A laudanum bottle, the abandoned state of the picnic, and the sinister all-pervading soundscape makes this moment in the show highly atmospheric, but not actively frightening.

Fast forward to the "interval" space, decorated like a high-school hall with paper streamers and a mirrorball, done up and ready for prom. This was where the Adam Curtis film (also called *It Felt Like A Kiss*) played on a continuous loop. Footage from this film occurs on television screens throughout the show, and the show in turn echoes the film in many of its spaces, settings and soundtrack. One such example: the film shows Doris Day opening a door, with the same number as the door that led the audience into that first bedroom and then living room of the house.

Fast-forward again to an event in the second half of the show. A group of nine audience members have been put together and sent through a human-sized rat maze, the climactic event of which is a high-speed high-panic chase that felt straight out of the horror-schlock B movie. At the sound of a chainsaw, the group starts to run. They run out of the maze and find themselves travelling through a series of rooms: some of these rooms look exactly like rooms that were encountered earlier, although with some distinct changes. There is more rat's maze to be navigated before the show ends properly and the audience members sprint out into daylight: but this moment of running through familiar-and-yet-unfamiliar rooms illustrates the point I wish to make about narrative endings, physical endings and immersive experience.

During the first half of the show audience members were invited to explore the show at their own pace and in their own numbers. Now a group has been formed that has been through the first rat's maze, running from the sound of a chainsaw. They run out of the maze and seem to run into rooms they have been in already, with the same dimensions and overall layout as the American household they travelled through at the top of the show. They are at this moment in the living room. The living room is different; it is messy, the furniture has been overturned. They have a moment to pause and breathe and perhaps assume that the chase is all over when the television screen suggests that they run, and the chainsaw revs again. The group sprint out of the living room and into the dining room, through it without stopping, and out of the house. Instead of a front lawn with a picnic they are now in a moonlit forest. Running through this takes the group into the second rat's maze area. As I stated previously there is a while to go yet, and not least more maze to get through: but these moments signal that a finale is approaching via the combination of repetition and change. This repetition at this stage of *It Felt Like A Kiss* created immersion in narrative by signalling a same-but-different story event that implied a relationship to time.

An ending occurs at the end because it changes the world of the story irreversibly. This stage of *It Felt Like A Kiss* was not the ending in the strict temporal sense (that was the final maze section), but its events signified an ending by combining repetition and change. When the audience first wandered through these rooms as a 1950s dream house, the show was only just starting. When they travelled through them about two hours later, things had changed. They had "been through" a lot; many different rooms, corridors, spaces, experiences; they had experienced much of *It Felt Like A Kiss*, including Curtis's film.

Circumstances had changed. They were not with the same people they had come in with. (For the finale, we were sorted into groups of nine.) They were in a heightened state of fear of agitation, running, perhaps screaming. The rooms had an identical layout, but were different in their decoration: the furniture was entirely gone from the dining room, leaving only the layout of the space to make it familiar. The tiny children's bedroom had been trashed; empty squares replaced the pictures on the walls. The space was "the same," in the sense that the audience were running through the identically built rooms. But the audience "saw" it differently. The rooms looked different, but this was only partly because they were physically altered (messy, empty); the rooms were also different because the way the audience were looking it had changed, because of everything that had gone before and their new (more panicky) circumstances. This repetition with differences enabled the audience to see things differently, and not only because there were different things to see. The irreversible change to the story's world (defined earlier as what makes for a satisfying ending) was both physically and emotionally apparent. The design, structure and narrative of the show (both the storyworld and the audience's own plot through that world) synthesised together to facilitate a highly intense immersive experience. (In terms of technicalities, this effect was of course created by re-building the same top-floor sets on the ground floor. Add disorientation to things the audience went through.)

It Felt Like A Kiss created a satisfying ending that achieved the same function (irreversibility, ringing the changes) in terms of both story and plot. Punchdrunk's next show *The Duchess of Malfi* (2010) is an interesting example of multiple narratives existing at cross-purposes within the same show and acting to raise barriers to immersive experience rather than to lower them. A narrative discourse of my own illustrates how the immersive plot and the narrative plot functioned without a satisfying synthesis.

The instructions at the beginning of this show were a mixture of invitational (go where you wish) and didactic (do not talk or remove your mask; do not touch the performers). They did not suggest a specific quest—such as finding and learning what happens to the Duchess of Malfi. From the opening invitation, it was promised that there was no right or correct way to navigate the space and no right or correct way to navigate the show. (Beyond the rules not to actively sabotaging the shoe by blocking the performers, talking, etc.) If it is possible to, for example, never see the Duchess, it becomes a barrier to immersion for an audience member to sense that finding the Duchess is going to be the way to get the "full" or "best" experience of the show.

Michael Billington's review of *The Duchess of Malfi* described the process of immersive spectatorship as if it had begun with a sequence of clear instructions that had been deliberately snared by the theatremakers: "then you go in search of the nine scenes to which Webster's story has been reduced" (2010). The show did of course share the title with Webster's play and in doing so invited an engagement with its story, but audience members were never told explicitly "to go in search of the nine scenes," or even that there were nine scenes: and a quest this specific will lead to disappointment when it inevitably remains uncompleted. It is much easier to see all of the scenes of a story when they are played in front of you one by one in the order the playwright put them. Naturally therefore, Billington found Punchdrunk's version wanting: for him the show was "a fragmented, fitful experience that lacks the emotional intensity of a linear work of art" (2010).

The assumption of a quest to find all the scenes reveals preconceptions about the work, and the way the work needed to be approached to get the best experience from it. Billington's approach to the show meant that, in narrative terms, Punchdrunk were doomed to lose from the start. I would argue that the way the production treated Webster's playtext did lead to an unfulfilling narrative experience, but not quite in the way Billington suggests.

As previously discussed, an ending event happens at the end of a story and irreversibly changes all that has gone before. A description of the show and an illustration from my personal plotting through the events of this production illustrates how immersion and narrative (both in terms of the show's storyworld and my journey through it) were at odds.

A confession: until the finale of *The Duchess of Malfi*, I didn't see the Duchess at all. I believe this happened through no fault of my own. I simply never found myself in the same room as the performer playing that role. We both moved through the performance space and our paths never crossed. If at the beginning of the show I was told my quest was to find her, I might consider not finding her a failing: if an usher had advised that it might be fruitful to find and then pursue the Duchess' own narrative journey (plotting my own course the best I could to make her plot and mine the same), I might look back on my encounterless experience with the conclusion that it was my fault and that I might have done better. I hadn't searched hard enough, or figured out how to go to the right place; I hadn't done the right thing to have the most satisfying experience. I might wish the show had provided more help, but I had at least known what I needed to do. But I received no such instructions, and wandered around encountering other characters instead. Before the show's finale I did not feel my lack of meeting the Duchess was adversely affecting my experience of the show.

The climax of Punchdrunk's *The Duchess of Malfi* was a narrative ending as well as a finale of spectacle. It was also a finale of audience, as this moment was the first time the whole (very large) group occupied the same space. For an audience member unfamiliar with Webster's play (or one who had not seen the actress playing the Duchess at all that evening), watching this scene without an awareness of the play's story—of what was at stake for these characters—would be (and was) something of an unsatisfying experience. In the narrative of the show's spectacle, and design/musical score, it was certainly a grand finale and a satisfying one. The audience were together for the first time; the orchestra was fully assembled; in a true final reveal of spectacle, with a huge musical flourish the curtain was pulled on a warehouse-sized space full of hanging cadavers. In this sense, it was easy to know what was happening—the spectacular finale. But in a narrative sense there could easily be less immediate understanding: what had just happened between those characters? (Who are they? Am I *supposed* to know?) If I had encountered the Duchess before and perhaps learned something about her character, this finale might have meant more to me. It occurred to me then that I might have done the show "wrong." There didn't seem to be much I could do about it at this stage. The instructions at the beginning of the show had been deliberately open and vague, implying that whatever I found would be right *for me*; but the finale suggested that certain knowledge *was* required, and I was left with the distinct sensation that I hadn't done my homework properly.

A further way in which this ending lacked internal narrative coherence was in regard to the way the format of the show had been constructed and arranged before the finale took place. Looping individual characters' journeys during the show suggested, to me, that time itself in this world was fractured and cyclical, that the production was forefronting the idea of there being a deep and important relationship between the present and the past, between "now" and "history"—not just the characters' presents and their own pasts, but the contemporary audience looking back into their cruel world. (This was also suggested by elements of the design, which included modern computer wires curling up into a Jacobean forest.) Whether or not this potential reading of the production was a conscious part of the process of making it on Punchdrunk's side, the idea of cyclical, ever-repeating time was negated by an ending event explicitly showing the death of a main character. As mentioned earlier, a satisfactory narrative ending is one that changes the storyworld. But the story's own chronology (towards a tragic ending) and the show's emphasis on repeating ghosts of history made the emotional purpose of the finale less clear.

The production being an adaptation of a pre-existing text also affects the relationship between narrative and immersive experience. In *A Theory of Adaptation*, Linda Hutcheon proposes that "multiple versions of a story in fact exist laterally, not vertically: adaptations are derived from, ripped off from, but are not derivative or second-rate" (2006: 169). Even without imposing a value judgement on the texts, an audience member's understanding of the source text will affect how they engage with Punchdrunk's own interpretation of the source text, and their composition and structure of its scenes and events. Aebischer and Prince discuss Punchdrunk's *The Duchess of Malfi* in the context of contemporary adaptations of Jacobean drama and suggest the production was in line with popular responses to, and readings of, Webster's play:

> The co-production of *The Duchess of Malfi* by the ENO and Punchdrunk was representative of a larger trend, since it emphasised the non-normative sexuality of the lycanthropic Ferdinand. [...] Here was a production that not only enshrined, but that was contingent on, an understanding of The Duchess of Malfi as a canonical text exploring alternative, "queer" identities and sexualities. (2012: 2)

Writing about *The Masque of the Red Death*, which had a similar structural layout and logistical composition of looping scenes, and was also an adaptation of pre-existing text(s), Babbage notes that there were "narratives in play here that derive neither from host nor ghost, but are brought by the spectators themselves" (2009: 16). An audience member's sense of themselves as a heterodiegetic narrator of their own plot within Punchdrunk's production will be affected by their relationship to the wider existing storyworld(s) of Webster or Poe. Babbage writes that Punchdrunk's "fragile, hazy impressions of Poe's tales [...] left space for my own (pre)-readings" (18). *The Duchess of Malfi*, in contrast, demonstrated a clear interpretation of the themes and characters in Webster's play for Aebischer and Prince.

Optimum experience or "flow" in the context of psychological peak experience occurs when problems can be easily overcome with a feeling of challenge meeting achievement. Mental immersion is facilitated by clear, knowable goals and a sense of skills that reach them. Assumptions of the "goal" of an immersive production will influence how people approach the shows and navigate the space once inside. Narrative techniques can be used to draw on a larger storyworld (in this case, an existing Jacobean text) to create a story that an audience member navigates (taking in the design, moving through the layout of scenes, experiencing performances by singers, dancers and musicians), building their own plot or narrative discourse as they go. The story events of the production and an audience member's engagement with that production have a reciprocal relationship that, when they work together, may result in a highly engaging experience. When they are perceived to be at odds the result may be frustration or disorientation, or a sense of anxiety over doing the right thing, jolting a spectator out of any kind of immersion. For Ricoeur, narratives that evoke a sensation of experiencing "now" suggest a Heideggerian notion of making-present: he suggests that "These narratives [...] represent a person acting, who orients him-or herself in circumstances he or she has not created, and who produces consequences he or she has not intended. This is indeed the time of the 'now that...', wherein a person is both abandoned and responsible at the same time" ([1970] 2000: 261). A sense of choice and/or the freedom to wander has a relationship with the inevitability of how a story is designed and directed to be enacted in the space. This relationship—described as fundamental to "the Punchdrunk way" in the quotation at the beginning of this chapter—destabilises linearity and causality. An audience member who finds narrative, chronology and immersion to be at odds might feel something resembling Ricoeur's combination of abandonment and (unclear) responsibility.

References

Abbott, H.Porter. 2002. *The Cambridge Introduction to Narrative*. Cambridge: Cambridge University Press.

Aebischer, Pascale, and Kathryn Prince. 2012. Introduction. In *Performing Early Modern Drama Today*, ed. Pascale Aebischer, and Kathryn Prince, 1–16. Cambridge: Cambridge University Press.

Aristotle. [330BC?] 1996. *Poetics*, trans. Malcolm Heath. London: Penguin.

Babbage, Frances. 2009. Heavy Bodies, Fragile Texts: Stage Adaptation and the Problem of Presence. In *Adaptation and Contemporary Culture: Textual Infidelities*, ed. Rachel Carroll, 11–22. London: Continuum.

Barry, Peter. 2002. *Beginning Theory: An Introduction to Literary and Cultural Theory*. Manchester: Manchester University Press.

Bartley, Sean. 2013. Punchdrunk: Performance, Permission, Paradox. Borrowers and Lenders, Athens: Oct 2013, Volume VII, Issue 2.

Billington, Michael. 2009. It Felt Like A Kiss. Guardian, July 3 2009. Accessed June 2013.

Billington, Michael. 2010. The Duchess of Malfi. Guardian, July 14 2010. http://www.guardian.co.uk/stage/2010/jul/14/duchess-of-malfi-review. Accessed Jan 2013.

Brooks, Peter. [1984] 1992. *Reading for the Plot: Design and Intention in Narrative*. Cambridge, Mass: Harvard University Press.

Cairns, P., A. Cox, N. Berthouze, S. Dhoparee, and C. Jennett. 2006. Quantifying the Experience of Immersion in Games. Cognitive Science of Games and Gameplay Workshop at Cognitive Science 2006. Vancouver, Canada, July 26–29.

Erikson, Jon. 2012. Tension/Release and the Production of Time in Performance. In *Archaeologies of Presence: Art, Performance and the Persistence of Being*, ed. Gabriella Giannachi, Nick Kaye, and Michael Shanks, 82–99. London: Routledge.

Genette, Gérard. [1972] 1980. *Narrative Discourse*, trans. J.E. Lewin. London: Basil Blackwell.

Genette, Gérard. 1970. Time and Narrative in A la Recherche du temps perdu, trans. Paul de Man. In *Aspects of Narrative*, ed. J. Hillis Miller, 93–118. New York: Columbia University Press.

Hemming, Sarah. 2013. It's All About Presence: Punchdrunk Theatre Company's Felix Barrett Talks About Keeping Immersive Theatre Fresh and Why he wants to lose his Audience. *Financial Times*, 7 June 2013.

Herman, David. 2009. *Basic Elements of Narrative*. London: Wiley-Blackwell.

Hogan, Patrick Colm. 2003. *Cognitive Science, Literature, and the Arts: A Guide for Humanists*. London: Routledge.

Hutcheon, Linda. 2006. *A Theory of Adaptation*. London: Routledge.

Jennett, Charlene, Anna L. Cox, Paul Cairns, Samira Dhoparee, Andrew Epps, Tim Tijs, and Alison Walton. 2008. Measuring and Defining the Experience of Immersion in Games. *International Journal of Human Computer Studies*, 66 (9 September): 641–661, Accessed Nov 2010.
McKee, Robert. 1999. *Story: Substance, Structure, Style, and the Principles of Screenwriting*. London: Methuen.
Rancière, Jacques. 2009. *The Emancipated Spectator*. London: Verso.
Ricoeur, Paul. [1970] 2000. Narrative Time. In *The Narrative Reader*, ed. Marin McQuillan, 255–261. New York: Routledge.

CHAPTER 7

Play the Story: An Approach to Narrative in Immersive Theatre

Immersive productions can be read as games, and the overlap between the two forms has been noted elsewhere (Dickinson 2011; Gordon 2012; Green 2013; McMullan 2014; Klich in Frieze 2017). Immersive productions can even, with the addition of individual ludus rules, effectively be turned into games. A particularly clear example of the overlap is *The Golden Amulets of Agnes*, a fan-authored *Sleep No More* points system gamifying the theatrical experience by proposing rewards for certain achievements or encounters:

> *May I Have This Dance?* (20): Dance with any cast member.
>
> *Hail The New Thane* (20): Watch Duncan get murdered.
>
> *Love you /Hate you* (5): See any dance scene between characters that appears simultaneously amorous and violent.
>
> *Shut it!* (-20): Get caught speaking or with your mask off.
>
> *Out Of The Moment* (-5): Thinking about this point system during your stay.(Delirium Dog 2012: n.p.)

The "Out Of The Moment" anti-achievement humourously reminds any would-be players that the gaming frame is not, ultimately, the correct way to approach *Sleep No More*, however enjoyable it might be to consider in the abstract; a goal-driven ludic approach is understood to be at odds with what immersion in the production is actually supposed to resemble. The penalty for getting caught with a removed mask also implies that any additional approaches to *Sleep No More* must not occur at the cost of disruption to the production itself. A hierarchy of form is established, with the show's own rules of engagement placed firmly above any additional goals an individual might think about giving themselves.

This final chapter on immersion and narrative draws on game studies to explore one way of theorising immersive experience, theatrical form and the question of story. The (often troubled) relationship between narrative and ludology in computer games—respectively, the story told by a game and its mechanics of play—raises questions about what, in the heat of the moment, a player is actually immersed *in*: a story, or the *game* of finding/exploring/otherwise engaging with that story? A similar model can exist for immersive theatre, and raise similar questions. This chapter outlines the history of the "vs" relationship between story and gameplay before applying it to an analysis of immersive experience in *Sleep No More*, a production that made its relationship to gaming even more explicit than usual. Theories and methods from the field of game studies will continue to inform and influence makers of immersive theatre, and the narrative/ludology model provides a helpful means of approaching the consequences for audience immersion.

Introduction to the Narrative "vs" Ludology Debate

Early studies of computer games drew on pre-existing approaches and methods (mostly from literary studies and philosophy) in order to establish the field as a legitimate form of academic enquiry. Scholars explored parallels with other narrative forms, such as theatre (Laurel 1991) and literature (Murray 1997), to argue that games can be considered alongside these forms, and using concepts drawn from these sister fields. This approach was met with resistance from scholars who would later come to be considered ludologists (Aarseth 1997; Juul 2001; Frasca 2003a), who argued that games are worthy of study in and of themselves, rather than because of traits they happen to share with other pre-established forms. Computer games are not sub-films or not-quite-television and should not be read as such: they are a form capable of its own artistic and technical endeavours, requiring its own specialised vocabulary and expertise to study it appropriately. What makes games a medium—an art form—of their own, ludologists argued, is the existence of *gaming mechanics*:

puzzle, challenge, clear interactivity (of the explicit mode, with designed choices and procedures and quantifiable outcomes). Games' potential for immersion is concerned with cognitive/psychological immersion in the gaming mechanics and the present moment of play, not sensory immersion in detailed art design, or emotional engagement in the arrangement of narrative events. Ludology argues that games should be studied *as games*, not as a(nother) form of storytelling media. Those discussing parallels with (say) literature or theatre became "narratologists"—little more (from a ludologist perspective) than apologists for games, using narrative theory to provide a cloak of respectability and ultimately preventing the art form being considered on its own merits.

Jenkins has called the relationship between ludologists and narratologists a "blood feud" (2004: 118) and these arguments do imply a binary model to studying games, that any new researcher in the field must first pick a side. However, both approaches are attempts to answer the same question. As games are a form of media with the potential for immersion, what are players actually immersed *in*? Narratologists argue for games' abilities to tell stories and work with imagination and empathy, and that games deserve to be considered in this context (Murray 1997). Ludologists suggest the mechanics of gameplay are the most important aspect of studying games *as games*, and that this is the perspective that will best reward enquiry (Aarseth 1997; Juul 2001). Later, Frasca referred to "the non-existence of this ludological/narratological debate," and suggested that games scholars had never been hostile to the concept of studying games from a narratological perspective, in a paper called "Ludologists Love Stories, Too: Notes from a Debate That Never Took Place" (2003b: 3). However, Ryan suggests that, although the debate "may have been a one-sided affair, rather than a dialogue," it was never as neutral as Frasca retrospectively claims: "if these articles [by Frasca, Aareseth and Juul] don't take a stance against the idea of games telling stories, what will it take to start a polemic?" (2006: 296) she asks. Both Ryan and Jenkins situate themselves in a more neutral position, proposing that both perspectives provide useful tools for considering games. Ryan proposes a "functional ludo-narrativism" to allow both approaches to be included in reading and analysis: "By connecting the strategic dimension of gameplay to the imaginative experience of a fictional world, this approach should do justice to the dual nature of video games" (2006: 291). The field no longer requires newcomers to take sides in a blood feud, if it ever did, and is now open to nuanced perspectives on games, gameplay and narrative. The ludological/narratological debate, no longer at the forefront of study, continues to provide a useful model for approaching games: such as reading gaming mechanics as creators of implicit ideological narratives (Atkins 2003). The false binary has become a tool of nuance in itself.

Whatever the relationship between these two schools of thought for games scholars, the model of narratology/ludology as a binary or debate is useful for thinking about immersive experience in theatre. It provides an approach to considering how immersive experience is created, maintained and situated through a production. To illustrate, this chapter considers immersion in Punchdrunk's *Sleep No More* (McKittrick Hotel, New York: 2011–) in the context of this model. I discuss the production both in performance and in relation to an experiment in "remote and real world interconnected theatrical immersion" conducted between Punchdrunk and MIT Media Lab in 2012 (Higgin and Nightingale 2012). This experiment involved turning *Sleep No More* into a (primarily text-based) computer game that could be experienced at a distance from the show itself. I "played" the New York show from London. *Sleep No More* was adapted into a hybrid form of theatre and game: a process that required transferring the story, characters, aesthetic and tone (all subjects that would interest a narratologist) as well as the structural framework, logistics and practicalities of exploring the show (how you might "play" the show—the domain of ludology).

Narrative "vs" Ludology in *Sleep no More*

Punchdrunk first experimented with a virtual and real-world interconnected experience in 2008's *The Last Will*, the result of three months' research and development with Hide & Seek, HP Labs and Sleeper. "Players working in pairs of two [one physically present in the performance/game space, and one via computer interface] had to collaborate in real time, linked by sensors, comms & actuation technology, to unlock the secrets and escape the house" (Hide&Seek 2008: n.p.). The rooms had communicative "rules" that, once understood, enabled meaningful play; the exploration and discovery of this grammar in itself was a subject of play. In 2011 Punchdrunk experimented with real/online interconnected immersion in a project at Rose Bruford that riffed on the story of Bluebeard. And in 2012 the MIT Media Lab project created an experience that occurred between an online player and an in-show counterpart.

Sleep No More was experienced as a text-based computer game for virtual participants, and as an experience of the show for physically present audience members with added performative moments, props and interactivity via equipment incorporated into their mask.

The project's design and implementation involved considering telic and paratelic modes of play. Fernandez defines the difference:

> The telic mode tends to be more serious minded and focused on the future, while individuals in paratelic mode tend to be more playful, light hearted, orienting actions towards the present. (in Leino et al. 2008: 186)

Telic mode is when play consists of enjoying the movement towards a goal; paratelic is where satisfaction derives from play itself. Bartle's influential system divided players into four personality "types": killers, achievers, socialisers and explorers (1996). The approach to gameplay in the behaviour of each of these types grants them a different immersive experience in a game. Killers and achievers are telic; socializers and explorers are paratelic. The former are engaged in goals, know their targets and work towards them, and have specific reasons for engagement in the game; their immersion can be quite clearly linked to psychological "flow." The latter enjoy a lack of goals and pursue the activity or game for its own sake (or for its social aspects, or other outcomes that exist outside the reward remit of the game itself). The former play to win; the latter play to play. This model is useful not just for the idea of personality types and their respective approaches (Bartle's list was later expanded to eight, in reference to 3D and Virtual Reality gameplay [2003: 145]). The idea of an audience member's character and behaviour resulting in different ways of engaging with a piece of work enables us to see how immersive experience can come about in different ways, and also adds weight to the premise that immersive experience cannot be guaranteed by designers or makers and cannot be forced. It can only be allowed for, facilitated, made possible—and different "characters" or gamer/audience member "types" will respond differently to this very facilitation.

The *Sleep No More* project had three strands: an experiment to make a world as visual, ephemeral, as viscerally immersive, as the show in real life; heightening the *Sleep No More* experience in the physical world, with more interactions and extra narratives for participants; and finding a way to connect these first two goals. The project aimed to enable interaction between the two worlds and between the experiences of the two participants.

The live experience of *Sleep No More* involves multisensory stimulus, with a soundscape and set designs drawing heavily on light, atmosphere and scent. If sensory stimulation is a key aspect of facilitating immersion, then although it would be possible to film the production doing so would remove this important aspect of immersive experience. A film depicting a route through the show would resemble watching someone go through a ghost train with a night-vision camera: allowing an idea of "what happened" but losing any of the atmosphere or excitement of actually being there. A simple playback could not be expected to provide an immersive experience within a fictional or theatrical world. A project attempting to create a sense of immersion for a remote player would need to provide more than this. Higgin wrote in the *Guardian* that the project "wasn't about plonking a camera on a real-world participant and instructing them, drone-like, to move around the building. Instead, the challenge has been to recreate the infinite possibilities for journeys and experiences happening simultaneously across a Punchdrunk production" (2012: n.p.). The goal was for the online participants and the interconnected players to have individual experiences and form their own narrative(s), as well as experiencing some moments—and therefore to do some of their narrative-building—as a pair. The immersive experience being recreated, then, might be defined as this sense of making a singular, individual journey through a world: a setup that invites a participant to make choices about their movements and, through this, create an individual narrative.

The system was designed to be unnoticeable by other (non-playing) audience members and as unobtrusive as possible to those wearing them. The system had to work within the conventions of the production: namely, that audience members do not talk, and do wear masks. The result was a modified mask containing speakers, bone conductors and Bluetooth technology connecting the onsite audience member to Portal Objects in the production space and to the online participant. Portal Objects were items or props in the production that linked the in-show audience member to the remote participant and they included a typewriter, a mirror and Ouija board. The online participant was able to send messages to be typed up by the typewriter, appear ghostlike on the mirror or be spelled out on the Ouija board. *Operator* refers the controller of interactions between both participants.

The atmosphere of the physical setting was an important aspect of recreating *Sleep No More* virtually. This could have been attempted with a highly detailed, 3D-rendered exact copy of the rooms in the show—perhaps suffering the same limitations, described previously, as filming the show live. Instead, online participants experienced the atmosphere and setting more impressionistically. The decision to present the world of *Sleep No More* this way in virtual space helped to enable immersion more than a detailed 3D render would have. Such a more "realistic" aesthetic might have conveyed what the production looked like, representing the physical experience of wandering through its spaces. But the text-based system with its occasional imagery more accurately reflected the sensation of mystery and exploration that characterised immersive experience in the on-site production, and also the story that was created for the online participants of the project. The development from text to imagery also reflected the relationship created between the two linked players. The online player first experienced the show against a black background, with rooms and environments described with a few select details written in white across the screen. As the story progressed, the online player "looped" through several settings, returning to some spaces more than once. (Exploring and returning just as a real-life Punchdrunk participant might.) On the first loop the online player saw only black backgrounds and descriptive text, with no image content at all. From the second loop onwards some images gradually formed—these were the spaces where the online player's "real life" partner had visited. The online player's sensory perceptions could appear to have been provided or "granted" through the actions of their on-site partner.

As both the real-world and online experience of navigating the *Sleep No More* show featured elements of looping or scenes that were repeating-with-changes, it is useful to consider narrative/ludology in context of linearity and chronological order. One of the scriptwriters for the online experience describes the relationship between the online project's story and the practice of negotiating a story within the world of *Sleep No More*: "the experience for the online user seemed much more linear than a 'normal' SNM experience. [...] The story they uncover is nonlinear, but the story they create is more linear" (Punchdrunk 2012). Jenkins proposes a model of how gaming mechanics facilitate different sorts of narratives (again troubling the notion that narrative and ludology will always be in conflict). He notes "game designers have historically been more interested in issues of level design than of plot or character motivation": a game's setting or notional character dynamics may be evocative of a narrative situation but not engaged with directly in play, with the mechanics of gameplay being the most memorable for players (2007: 56). However, he adds that immersive gaming environments—virtual worlds a player can wander around in and interact with—do facilitate evoked, embedded or emergent narratives to emerge through gameplay, whether or not they were originally designed to do so. From this Jenkins suggests game designers ought to consider themselves "narrative architects" (60) who manipulate space and gaming mechanics in order to allow for engagement with story events.

Ludology/narrativity also describe how an audience member might approach "story" in environment and space. Jenkins offers a summary of how different types of storytelling are facilitated by immersive gaming environments:

> environmental storytelling creates the preconditions for an immersive narrative experience in up to four different ways: spatial stories can evoke pre-existing narrative associations; they can provide staging ground on which narrative events are enacted; they may embed narrative information within their mise-en-scene; or they provide resources for emergent narratives. (2007: 57)

These models are useful for considering immersive theatre as a form of "environmental storytelling." Productions can evoke existing texts, that is, narrative associations in the context of adaptation—*Sleep No More* draws most explicitly on Shakespeare and Hitchcock, but may also provide associations for an audience member with other Punchdrunk or immersive productions they have experienced; film noir; ghost trains; the staging history of *Macbeth*; and so on. Performers enact narrative events, within a space that has story events embedded within its mise-en-scene and overall design. An immersive production might also evoke narrative associations in a more general storytelling context, such as (as discussed in the previous chapter) opening a door functions as a narrative event in an audience member's individual discourse. At the same time, the structure of a production may provide gameplay/ludic elements. *Evoked* or *enacted* narratives reveal themselves as an audience member crosses the space: events in the plot become events in space, which they seek out, stumble upon or enact themselves. An *embedded* narrative implies a quest or goal that could lead to immersive gameplay experience in an audience member/player: an embedded narrative "doesn't require a branching story structure, but rather depends on scrambling the pieces of a linear story and allowing us to reconstruct the plot through our acts of detection, speculation, exploration and decryption" (Jenkins 2007: 59).

Although an audience member may read an immersive production as a game in these ways, the online participant in the *Sleep No More* project was provided with signifiers and tropes that explicitly suggested the form. This created potential for a problematic relationship between the gaming mechanics implied by the interface, and the story that had been written for the online participant to gradually uncover. The Portal Objects provided events of technical (ludic) achievement but were also intended to incorporate and express the rising momentum of the online participant's narrative discourse. Reading story elements or production events as part of a wider gameplay goal has the potential to break immersion with a sense of "failure" or being unsuccessful—it risks implying a much more binary model of whether a participant has a good or a bad experience, whether they have "done" the show correctly or not. Being explicit with gaming mechanics forefronts the quest nature of the experience (it may imply a deadline, a race, competition) rather than emphasising discovery, sharing or connection. In this way gaming mechanics may overpower any sense of narrative discourse, rather than allowing a participant to find narrative elements embedded within them or evoked by them.

Frasca (who was quoted at the beginning of this chapter arguing that there has never been a ludology/narrative debate) argues that "the biggest fallacy of 'interactive narrative' is that it pretends to give freedom to the player while maintaining narrative coherence" (2003a: 229). He proposes that traditional media (citing literature and drama as examples) are fundamentally representational, rather than simulational as a game might be. This means these forms cannot truly provide freedom for a player/reader, as the author/narrator decides in advance which events will occur and all that remains is for a reader to follow the author's storyline. Juul (2001) also prioritises ludology over the storytelling capability of games, suggesting that games cannot be considered a narrative form due to the relationship between storytelling, gameplay and time. Gaming happens in the present, even if a scene is nominally occurring as a flashback: and therefore gaming cannot achieve a sense of narration (and therefore cannot be analysed from the perspective of narratology), since it is impossible to narrate a story that has yet to reach its fulfilment:

[a] game constructs the story time as synchronous with narrative time and reading/viewing time: the story is now. Now, not just in the sense that the viewing witnesses the events now, but in the sense that the events are happening now, and that what comes next is not yet determined. (Juul 2001: n.p.)

These arguments presuppose an overly simplistic definition of the way drama and prose narratives tell stories, by assuming they deal with time and causality between events in a way that allows for no reader freedom. It is true that story events are crafted and organised in advance, but immersive experience in the moment is related to the interplay of a given event and an audience member/participant's reading of, and reaction to, that event. This is something that occurs very much in the "now," whenever the show was made or the story was written.

In the same way the sensation of immersive experience is always in the present, stories told about immersive experience—memories or retellings of immersive experience—evoke the present. Games do allow a player to influence outcomes, but only within boundaries defined and maintained by the mechanics. (How a player might beat a Super Mario level might be "not yet determined," as Juul states, but we know it won't be by buying a hotel on Park Lane.) Neither narrative nor ludology should be privileged for allowing total "freedom" in a reader/player: immersive experience is created in the moments of interplay between a reader and the text, and this can be facilitated by either approach or aspects of both. The *Sleep No More* project used the incorporation of gameplay aspects to create an experience that happened in the present. The project was designed to allow participants the sensation of uncovering events in a gaming context (Portal Objects as puzzles), a story context (Portal Objects as storyworld items) and to lower barriers to immersive experience in the sense of a fleeting, highly intense moment of engagement (interconnection and communication between the real-world and the remote participant).

Practical concerns are the first barriers to immersion in any form of media, making the use of hidden technology in the project potentially both a risk and a strength. Overly cumbersome, difficult, or faulty technology would keep both real-world and online participants away from being playing the game, never mind becoming immersed in it. It would also affect *Sleep No More*'s other audience members, not involved in the project, if the technology was too visible. The modified masks functioned as aids to gameplay and did not have any narrative importance in themselves—the speakers, bone conductors and so on were intended to deliver the sensation of experiencing story events. The online participant used a text interface to navigate spaces that paralleled the environments of the McKittrick Hotel in New York. The online participant would occasionally be informed that they had found an item or that they felt a chill in the air, and they would occasionally activate film footage from the show. These moments taken together aided in the gradual piecing together of a story, and the text-based adventure game imagery and tropes suggested solving this particular mystery was the quest or purpose of engaging in the project. The technology used in the project, then, was primarily not a narrative element but a ludic one—it had little to do with the story but was the means to allow participants to access it. For this reason it was important the technology be as fault-free as possible, ultimately becoming invisible behind the effects it delivered. Textual descriptions of space helped set the scene for the online participant; for the real-world participant, the Portal Object connections not only served to enhance ludic aspects of the game, but also served, as they were secreted within the real-world sets, to enhance the atmosphere and aesthetic of the physical show. The Portal Objects functioned as a means to enable the participants to connect with each other (a gameplay aspect) and to enhance the sensation of the storyworld they were both occupying (a narrative aspect). The design of spaces and general mise-en-scene, referential music and the atmosphere and colour palette in a show can all operate as elements of narrative. They create a wider storyworld and embed stories within them that an audience member can pick up as part of their own narrative discourse (should they wish to), just as description in prose fiction can enable narrative immersion by creating the sensation of a whole and internally coherent world. The technical details and equipment were intrinsic to manipulating barriers to immersion for the remote player and the real-life audience member, important for both story and game.

 The *Sleep No More* project created three types of audience member: online, on-site and on-site but unaware of the experiment. A model of engagement with immersive theatre involves movement between different modes of experiencing the work, as suggested by these types. A more "fluid" participant might choose to connect and disconnect to other participants at different times, or begin in one mode and move to the other: such behaviour suggests a physical embodiment of "ludo-narrativism" which allows both ludological and narratological aspects to facilitate immersive experience. Moments of explicit connection between the remote and the real-world participant (such as when the former sent messages for the latter to receive via typewriter) were concerned more with ludology than narrative, creating immersive experience in the gaming mechanics by suggesting a positive correlation between challenge and skill (and with the danger of breaking immersion if it did not work). However, should the technology be made subtle enough or the mechanics of engaging with technology be overcome, technology like Portal Objects can also facilitate narrative events.

An additional challenge for creating immersive experience in a form where narratology and ludology are both potential approaches is a theatrical question about representation, empathy and role play. Online participants in the *Sleep No More* project learned, or were informed as the story came together, that they had been playing the (important) role of Grace: a character who had been the subject of speculation and mystery until the reveal. The real-world participants were not given a fictional character in the same way, but continued to play themselves, as it were, exploring the world of the theatrical production. How these experiences could be interconnected, and allow both participants to experience immersion, becomes a question of narrative rather than gameplay, returning to the idea of empathy and suspense and requiring that *these* are the aspects that need to be manipulated to create audience engagement. In the *Sleep No More* project the online participant functioned (by the end) as a fictional character within the storyworld, while the on-site participants were free to engage with either the show or the more specific story about Grace they were building with their remote partner. This dynamic implies a desire that immersion in narrative is ultimately the most powerful or long-lasting effect of the project, story being forefronted rather than the ludological aspects of gameplay being the ends in itself. If gaming mechanics are intended facilitate engagement but are not the main purpose of the experience, the challenge for makers, then, might be in getting their participants to care.

GAMES AND STORIES: TWO KINDS OF TREASURE HUNT

Punchdrunk's *The Masque of the Red Death* incorporated the Gold-Bug treasure hunt, an overlapping that allowed for different readings across the space of Battersea Arts Centre (BAC). Reading the BAC as a treasure hunt site sits problematically with the slower, more exploration-oriented movement of those without specific goals in the space, making Gold-Bug chasers potentially detrimental to audience members not on the search. The two pieces—theatrical experience and treasure hunt—were at odds, reflected in contrasting behaviour between the spectators/participants operating on these different interpretive frameworks. Reading this problem from a narrative/ludology perspective, the majority of experiences of *The Masque of the Red Death* were narrative ones, characterised by the exploratory self-authored story and storyworld built up by a spectator's moving through the space. Although taking an audience member through rooms or story events in a non-chronological or fragmented order, the production is a linear narrative experience from an audience member's perspective (as discussed in Chap. 5). This approach comes into conflict with the ludology-framed challenge of playing a game, such as the Gold-Bug hunt, where the drive was to engage with the treasure hunt, moving through rooms quickly in search of clues. In a text where both interpretive frameworks are available, a production may choose to forefront one. In terms of technology design, the *Sleep No More* experiment aimed to reduce the possibility of audience members detracting from each other's experiences, manipulating elements within the production and its on-site and remote technology to allow neither narratology nor ludology to dominate at the expense of the other.

Although the MIT project resulted in a text-based computer game interface for its online participants, the project's goal was never to turn the show into a game but to somehow make an online/virtual/remote experience as exploratory and experiential as visiting the physical show, and it used computer gaming tropes to achieve this. A potentially frustrating outcome of reading a piece of immersive theatre as a game is the implied relationship to rules: a show that suggests there is no definite way, no correct method, to experience it, and yet *does* seem to reward certain actions with hidden rooms or one-on-one experiences, or simply in seeing more sights, might appear to be a game that *does* have rules that it is deliberately, and perhaps unfairly, hiding out of sight. The possibility of getting to, or reaching, a good experience or outcome contains within it the implication that it is also possible to fail to do this: winning only makes sense against losing. In an interview about *The Drowned Man*, Barrett and Doyle articulate a relationship between gaming and narrative in how the production might be experienced, emphasising audience choice:

"We've tried to invest in this idea from gaming that the further you unpeel the layers, the more secrets you'll discover," [Doyle] adds.

"The show goes vertically down as well as horizontally," says Barrett. "You can follow the story of our Woyzeck and it will be a great night out or you can go vertically down, lift away the topsoil and get to the other, hidden narrative underneath." (2013, n.p.)

This description shows the influence of gaming mechanics on how the show was put together and how audience members might be invited (or choose) to experience it. The non-linear structure and sheer size of large-scale immersive productions means it is impossible to see everything. Here it is suggested that there are different paths through *The Drowned Man*, literally of course in terms of which parts of the production to look at—but also metaphorically, and in terms of how far "vertically down" an audience member is able and/or willing to go. Coding these different layers of the production as narratives makes the relationship between ludology and narrativism a useful tool to approaching how immersive experience may function in the space. Not being able to see everything becomes an integral part of experiencing the show from a ludological perspective, as opposed to a problem that might arise by attempting to form a coherent narrative discourse that captures all of the production's wider story and storyworld. Paratelic gaming is *meaningful* play, play for its own sake rather than for the goal of winning, and *The Drowned Man* and *Sleep No More* can be read for their use of gaming mechanics without necessarily evoking competitive notions of right or wrong, win or lose. Deciding on, or making the assumption that there are, specific goals within a production will influence an audience member's experience; whether that goal is to find all the scenes, follow a specific character, wander aimlessly, wander with purpose, spend all the time in the bar or some combination of these: the experience will be(come) immersive if the show seems to reward the chosen means of engagement.

The disorientating effect of both content (scenes out of order, mystifying one-on-ones) and form (darkness, maze-like spaces, getting lost) might mean it is difficult to remember, in retrospect, what order moments happened in (with the possible exception of finale scenes). An audience member's story, when considered as a linear journey with its own events and structure, is formed in the meeting place between their decisions (what door to go through, etc.), and the production's own choreography, direction and layout. These events might be remembered merged together into a single three-hour "block" of immersive experience, with particular high points of specific scenes or "peak" immersive activity. This is similar to how immersion in gaming can be described: being engaged in the activity of play for a long time with a few intense, climactic moments of peak experience. The state of mind in those who have been intensely immersed in an activity for a long period might be one that cannot, in retrospect, describe every event in the order they happened. Ryan comments on the relationship between gaming and memory:

> For a game to inspire *specific* retellings, to be *narratively designed*, it must involve actions whose purpose is not just winning or losing, but fulfilling a concrete goal. [...] The greater our urge to tell stories about games, the stronger the suggestion that we *experienced the game narratively*. (2006: 284; original emphasis)

As discussed in Chap. 4, immersive productions can create the urge to tell stories, the communication a means to share and claim ownership of experience. These stories may be more about the audience member as an individual (the crafting of their own narrative score, their enjoyment or frustration with the mechanics and logistics) than an objective description of the storyworld or story the production created. Immersive experience happens in the meeting place between the perspective of the individual and the sense of a larger production design at work. Considering shows like *Sleep No More* or *The Drowned Man* as systems that invite ludo-narrativism allows for a more nuanced perspective on analysis than if the two approaches are modelled as a binary, destined to be ever at odds with each other during a performance. Barriers to immersive experience may be raised if ludology and narrative appear to be at odds: if (for example) following a specific quest is contradicted by an invitation to freely wander.

A ludo-narrativist approach to immersive theatre allows gaming mechanics and story elements to be considered separately, but not taken as mutually exclusive. Answering the question of what an audience member is immersed *in* becomes a means explore how craft and structure facilitate immersive experience. Gordon's discussion of audience behaviour in *Sleep No More* makes an interesting connection to the kind of game the production resembles, and the notion of linking two participants (real-world and long-distance):

> the classic adventure/quest games that are the closest model for Punchdrunk's immersive environments are typically not played as networked multiple player games. The behavior of other players in these frameworks is distracting and incongruous (unlike in first person shoot 'em ups) precisely because, unless the game is simulating a search-and-ransack, the behavior of players (trying every door and drawer) clearly denies immersion. Modeled on this type of game, Punchdrunk's website reinforces an immersion in task, rather than environment. (2012: n.p.)

The physical *Sleep No More* environment and the virtual game world created as part of the MIT project suggest different types of games, each with different gaming mechanics and the potential to immerse in different—possible contradictory—ways. "Trying every door and drawer" might be precisely what creates (or at least facilitates) immersion in a first-person exploratory adventure or quest game, a game style the physical structure of the production does resemble. If this model jarrs with another reading of the shows as a site of connected or networked multiplayer gaming, the behaviour of other "players" (audience members) becomes the cause of a potential barrier to immersion, if their way of "playing" the show results in them treating it a story instead of a treasure hunt, or vice versa. The *Sleep No More* project sought to replicate visiting the production for the remote player in the (re)creation, not just of the exploratory structure and the multi-sensory, visceral atmosphere, but the sensation of having an apparently *individual* experience. Successful interactions via the Portal Objects appeared to be happening just for the participants, in the same way successful one-on-one scenes feel bespoke rather than tightly scripted. Whether it is narratology or ludology that engages an audience member in play, the illusion of individuality (for both players) and the sensation of presence in a space (for the long-distance player) are even more important aspects of what is deemed a "successful" immersive experience. Connection between players becomes the site for immersive experience, instead of the solitary journey implied by the production's physical environment.

Conclusion: "Level Design Is More like Theatre Design Than Anything"

> We're experimenting with technology, with wearables, with how you can almost make a theatre *playable*...
>
> (Barrett 2014: talk at "Experience Economy" Remix Summit)

This chapter focused on the *Sleep No More* project between Punchdrunk and MIT Media Lab to consider immersion, gameplay and story in an explicit site of overlap between immersive theatre and computer game forms, but the project is one event in a longer history of interaction between theatre and game for the company. *The Masque of the Red Death* contained gaming aspects explicitly in the Gold-Bug treasure hunt as well as implicitly, with its exploratory/sandbox design and audience invitation being reminiscent of adventure and quest games. Punchdrunk's later productions continued to open themselves up to readings as games (Green 2013 draws a comparison between Punchdrunk shows and *Myst*) with consequences for theorising how immersion is created, facilitated and maintained throughout performance. The narratology/ludology model offers a way of thinking about the relationship between the immersive potential of theatre and games. It is a relationship that will repay further investigation, and a recent interview with a game designer shows influence going both ways. *Gone Home* is "directly influenced by *Sleep No More*":

> Just as in a Punchdrunk production, players in Gone Home are let loose in a beautifully-realised world—in this case, a suburban family home in the mid-1990s—and tasked with discovering its stories and secrets for themselves. And, just as in a Punchdrunk production, players are unable to influence the story, but are instead given a great deal of freedom over how they choose to unearth it. "Level design is more like theatre design than anything," notes [its designer] Steve Gaynor. "Because when you're designing a space to be playable, you have to design it in the same way that someone designs a stage, where there could be someone on the balcony, there could be someone up front on the left, or on the right. Especially something like [*The Drowned Man*]. I mean, this entire experience is level design. Lighting directs you to stuff that's important, there are main thoroughfares, etc. This is a videogame level, period." (Jakob-Hoff 2014: n.p.)

Punchdrunk's future plans also suggest this trajectory of enquiry might continue:

> Barrett and his team are currently looking closely at how they can exploit more explicit game mechanics in future productions. Earlier shows like *The Masque of the Red Death* and *Sleep No More* experimented with puzzle solving and treasure hunts, but Barrett feels these game-like elements disturbed the balance of the show too much. "I think we've learned that one discipline has to be your lead—so with *The Drowned Man, The Masque of the Red Death*, it's theatre. We started putting game mechanics into it, putting a square peg into a round hole, and it didn't quite fit. So I think if we were to do a project using game mechanics now, it would be a game primarily.
>
> "Now we're aware of games, and the similarities, and the similar aspirations, we've literally started to break down game mechanics and just take them out." He is interested in how casual games like Clash of Clans or Candy Crush Saga balance accessibility with a "level of difficulty that stays just attainable. How do you do that theatrically? [...] What I'm fascinated by is: what happens when you level up? What happens when you know that you can only access this room and this one-on-one when you're a level five player?" (Jakob-Hoff 2014: n.p.)

The narrative/ludology model will enable further explorations into the relationship, between gaming mechanics and immersive experience in theatrical performance, that is being hinted at here. Gaming concepts such as "levelling up" and gradually increasing levels of difficulty can potentially facilitate immersion or raise barriers to it. They are evocative of the psychological state of mental immersion or "flow," partly defined by experiencing a positive correlation between a player's sense of challenge and her sense that she has the skills to match it. These aspects are the domain of ludology and might deny immersion to other "players" in a theatrical space, who (for whatever reason) have not reached "level five." The relationship between ludic and narrative elements is not one of straightforward opposition, although the previous quote implies this dynamic. The approaches to structure and forms of gaming in *The Masque of the Red Death, Sleep No More* and *The Drowned Man* overlap with theatrical elements. The results could be interpreted as unequal, the elements off-balance: treasure hunters or puzzle solvers jostling with paratelic wanderers who are trying to enjoy a space's atmospheric worldbuilding, raising barriers to immersion for everyone (in Gordon's terminology: a player's immersion in task becoming detrimental to a spectator's immersion in environment). However, ludology and narrative are not mutually exclusive. As interplaying approaches, the ludo-narrativist approach to immersive theatre proposed here provides a useful and more nuanced consideration of how future productions might be crafted to allow both gaming elements and narrative elements, without throwing themselves out of balance.

References

Aarseth, Espen. 1997. *Cybertext: Perspectives on Ergodic Literature*. Baltimore: John Hopkins University Press.
Atkins, Barry. 2003. *More Than A Game: The Computer Game as Fictional Form*. Manchester: Manchester University Press.
Barrett, Felix. 2014. Felix Barrett, Artistic Director, Punchdrunk. Speaking at Remix Summit: *Experience Economy: Creating Extraordinary Moments and Stories that Get People Talking*. https://www.youtube.com/watch?v=xCRcuHiDEYs. Accessed March 2014.
Bartle, Richard. 1996. Hearts, Clubs, Diamonds, Spades: Players who suit MUDs. *Journal of MUD Research* (1). http://mud.co.uk/richard/hcds.htm. Accessed April 2014.
Bartle, Richard. 2003. *Designing Virtual Worlds*. San Francisco: New Riders.
Dickinson, Dan. 2011. Games of 2011: Sleep No More. The Primary Vivid Weblog. Accessed July 2012.
Frasca, Gonzalo. 2003a. Simulation versus Narrative: Introduction to Ludology. In *The Video Game Theory Reader*, ed. Mark J.P. Wolf and Bernard Perron, 221–235. New York: Routledge.
Frasca, Gonzalo. 2003b. Ludologists Love Stories, Too: Notes From a Debate That Never Took Place. In *Level Up: Digital Games Research Conference Proceedings*, ed. Marinka Copier and Joost Raessens. Utrecht: DiGRA and University of Utrecht.
Gordon, Colette. 2012. Pedestrian Shakespeare and Punchdrunk's Immersive Theatre. *Cashiers Elizabethains*, Autumn 2012, 43–50.
Green, Adam. 2013. Immersive Theatre and the Freedom of Choice. TGC Circle.
Hide&Seek. 2008. Last Will: Enter a World Where the Virtual and the Real are Two Sides of the Same Door. Accessed July 2012.
Higgin, Peter. 2012. Innovation in Arts and Culture #4: Punchdrunk—Sleep No More. Guardian Culture Professionals Network, 5 May 2012.

Higgin, Peter and Colin Nightingale. 2012. Remote and Real World Interconnected Theatrical Immersion. Talk given at StoryCode Forum May 2012.
Jakob-Hoff, Tristan. 2014. At the Gates of Temple Studios: Where Gaming and Theatre Collide. Eurogamer, 235 Accessed 2 May 2014.
Jenkins, Henry. 2004. Game Design as Narrative Architecture. In *First Person: New Media as Story, Performance, and Game*, ed. Noah Wardrip-Fruin and Pat Harrigan, 118–130. Cambridge, Mass: MIT Press.
Jenkins, Henry. 2007. Narrative Spaces. In *Space Time Play: Computer Games, Architecture and Urbanism: The Next Level*, ed. Friedrich von Borries, Steffen P. Waltz, and Matthias Böttger, 56–60. Basel: Birkhäuser.
Juul, Jesper. 2001. Games telling stories? A brief note on games and narratives, Game Studies (1) http://www.gamestudies.org/0101/juul-gts/. Accessed April 2014.
Klich, Rosemary E. 2017. Playing a Punchdrunk Game: Immersive Theatre and Videogames. In *Framing Immersive Theatre: The Politics and Pragmatics of Participatory Performance*, ed. Frieze, James. London: Palgrave Macmillan (forthcoming).
Laurel, Brenda. 1991. *Computers as Theatre*. Reading, Mass: Addison-Wesley.
Leino, Olli, Hanna Wirman, and Amyris Fernandez. 2008. *Extending Experiences: Structure, Analysis and Design of Computer Game Player Experience*. Vaajakoski: Gummerus Printing.
McMullan, Thomas. 2014. The Immersed Audience: How Theatre is Taking its Cue From Video Games. Guardian, Tuesday 20 May. Accessed May 2014.
Murray, Janet H. 1997. *Hamlet on the Holodeck: The Future of Narrative in Cyberspace*. New York, NY: The Free Press.
Punchdrunk. 2012. *Sleep No More/MIT project feedback materials*. Punchdrunk Archives, London.
Ryan, Marie-Laure. 2006. Computer Games as Narrative: The Ludology versus Narrativism Controversy. In *Avatars of Story* (Electronic Mediations Series, Vol. 17). University of Minnesota Press.
The Golden Amulets of Agnes: A Sleep No More Point System. Delirium Dog. March 8, 2012. Accessed July 2012.

CHAPTER 8

Environment and Site-Specificity: Space, Place and Immersion

> *Punchdrunk's Barrett admits that he's not a fan of the term ""immersive theatre". "We would never use it ourselves, although I'm delighted if our audiences are totally immersed," he says. "We used to call it 'site sympathetic'—because it's all about the building."* (Masters 2013: n.p.)

Although theatremakers may have a range of responses to the question of whether the term *immersive* applies to their own work—including suspicion, partial acceptance or active resistance, all of which might be found in the quotation above—the use and manipulation of performance space is one of the clearest indicators that a piece of theatre might define itself (or end up being defined by others, whatever the artist's own preferences) as *immersive*. White defines *immersive theatre* in relation to environment (2012); Nield describes it as a form where "the audience inhabit the space of the play alongside the actors [...] within a tricked-out space" (2008: 531). Alston defines *immersive* to emphasise audience engagement rather than any particular theatrical form or shape, but that engagement remains unavoidably framed by spatial boundaries, occurring in reaction to the performance space: "[*immersive*] is a term that can be applied to a range of practices in a range of contexts, so long as an audience engages with an environment that prompts the perception of immersion's cues" (2016: 71). Environmental innovations signify that a production is a piece of *immersively* shaped theatre—*immersive* implying that a space has been created for the audience to wander about in (large and open-plan or smaller and maze-like, or some combination of the two): perhaps scenographically detailed and musically rich, certainly demonstrating some quality of deliberate design or curation on the part of the makers. Use of the term *immersive* is often, as Barrett puts it, "all about the building."

This chapter considers immersive experience in relation to environment and space. While acknowledging that environment and narrative are connected (see Horton 2003 on geography and/as narrative power), this chapter explores immersive experience when defined as the product of site. The production site is where narrative events are enacted and where interactivity takes place: the relationship between performer, spectator and space is one of the ways a production might be considered *immersive*, and in the context of space and environment the state of *immersion* exists in negotiation between the found setting (the original building or site) and the designed set (the design, mise-en-scene, etc., created and installed by the artists).

The chapter begins with an overview of approaches to space, before discussing immersive experience with relation to two Punchdrunk shows with differing approaches to environment. *The Borough* (2013) was a linear outdoor audiowalk drawing heavily on its location (the village of Aldeburgh). *The Drowned Man* (31 London Street/Temple Studios, 2013–2014) was a space in more typical "immersive" mode, with finite clear boundaries for visitors and clear indicators of Punchdrunk's design authority over the original building, as the audience navigated Punchdrunk's trademark environmental and logistical signifiers through a heavily modified site. Both shows negotiated a complex relationship between the original site of performance and the fictional world created within and/or on the site, and between the spectator and the performance space.

INTRODUCTION TO THEORIES OF ENVIRONMENT AND IMMERSION

Cognitive Studies and Neurobiology: The Environment of the Embodied Mind

The model of a clear Cartesian body/mind dichotomy has long been discredited (Varela et al. 1993; Lakoff and Johnson 1999; Turner and Fauconnier 2003). The mind is no longer the superior of an arbitrary binary hierarchy: the way we perceive, think and act in the world is connected to the way our bodies evolved as part of the earth. McConachie explicitly applies this non-distinction to the field of theatre: "The mind is embodied" (2013: 1) and cognition continues to be applied to performance with fascinating results (McConachie and Hart 2006; McConachie 2008, 2013; Blair 2008; Cook 2010; Lutterbie 2011). If immersive experience can be defined by levels of brain activity and their effects on the body, *environment* in this context is the stimulus to which the body reacts.

Cognitive enquiry is a particularly attractive lens through which to consider the ephemerality of theatregoing, since it can be attributed to and measured by equally ephemeral but very real brain activity that can be recorded and tracked: *immersion* as cognitive phenomenon defined by high engagement, emotional investment, rapt attention, sensory stimulation, emotion, empathy or make-believe. A more specific phrase for make-believe is *conceptual blending*, a theory concerned with the way an audience member is able to hold multiple truths or images in her mind: "Spectators also engage in conceptual integration" (McConachie 2013: 23), blending an actor's performance with their own concepts, which might include the space, their relationship to the actor or (as in Carlson 2003) memories of earlier theatrical experiences. Conceptual blending seems to provide a cognitive explanation for Rebellato's question of how we are able to conceive an actor and a character at the same time (2009). Rebellato considers the problem of blending and believing in theatre, suggesting theatrical representation ultimately functions as metaphor. An audience member can hold multiple concepts in mind and blend them because, in the performative moment, one concept "is" the other. One concept acts, quite literally, as a metaphor for the other. A spectator blending two or more concepts in mind is useful for considering the relationship between "real-world" and "fictional/theatrical" environments, and how those fictional environments are created in, or over, an existing site. An outline of cognitive approaches to multisensory stimulus clarifies my approach further.

Welton (2011) uses a phenomenological perspective to consider feelings and emotion in theatre, and sensory stimulus such as being in the dark. Di Benedetto (2010) considers the senses in contemporary theatre from a neurobiological approach. His multidisciplinary approach to the theatrical event draws on cognitive science, neurology and phenomenology to consider how theatre stimulates the senses, considering visual perception, olfaction and aural stimulation (noise, vibrations, etc.) as well as physical touch. The provocation of the senses in theatre is considered at a cellular level: empathy, for example, can be illustrated at the level of the brain by the fact that seeing two performers hit each other on stage (for example) will make the same mirror neurons associated with that action fire in a spectator's brain (76). Immersive experience in a show such as Punchdrunk's *The Drowned Man* could certainly be considered from the perspective of appeals to multiple senses in the created environment: light/darkness and olfactory stimulation as well as the physical structure of performance spaces and detailed mise-en-scene create an overwhelmingly "total" effect that seems designed to allow for immersion at a cognitive level. Indeed, the stimulation of multiple senses in response to a surrounding environment could be considered a defining aspect of immersive theatre. McKinney and Butterworth (2009) note that many reviews of *The Masque of the Red Death* mention multiple scenic details: description and/ or review, and this multisensory aspect could be considered from a neurobiological perspective. It would be possible to track brain activity of fear or excitement, or when smelling roses or embalming fluid, or experiencing other sensory stimulus reminiscent of much immersive theatre such as darkness, sudden sounds or disorientation: a positive consequence of this approach would be the level of (physical, atomically precise) detail that could be reached for describing and defining sensory immersion.

However, a cognitive or neurobiological approach to immersion and environment has some problematic aspects. The primary risk is reductionism. Cognitive studies allow for unprecedented levels of scientific detail, but nuanced social consequences of any theatregoing experience become inconsequential if response becomes instinctive flashes of our animal brains that are near-identical from person to person. Studies of performance that draw on cognitive science do not imply cognition is the only approach to adopt; Cook (2010) states early on that cognitive science does not separate body from mind (3–4) and draws on cultural contexts in her analysis of neuroscience and Shakespeare. Sensual perception is of course an important aspect of theatre, and particularly in work where attempts to stimulate the senses of audience members directly are forefronted in its form. But the approach risks a reductive description of the theatrical process, implying that artists make work with their audience's brain cells in mind, considering "the ways in which theatre practitioners have manipulated physiological traits to keep us stimulated and interested in what is happening on stage" (Di Benedetto 2010: xi). This chapter is interested in the constructed environment of immersive theatrical space, and the interplay between this environment and the real-world site. While remaining aware of the potential for examining immersive experience as direct cognitive response to sensory stimulation, my discussion in this chapter adopts model(s) drawn from site-specificity in performance to theorise theatrical environment and immersive experience in that environment. I look forward to future studies applying the technical advances of neuroscientific approaches to immersive theatre.

Memory provides a bridge between neuroscience and theatre studies. Carlson's study of the importance of memory on performance reception (2003) describes how a spectator's memories—of earlier performances, of individual performers and so on—affect how a performance is received. These memories "ghost" the current performance being experienced and influence a spectator's response. Site-specific theatre incorporates the resonances of the pre-existing performance site:

> In [site-specific] productions, already written texts are placed in locations outside conventional theatres that are expected to provide appropriate ghostings in the minds of the audience, or, in more extreme cases, new works are created that are directly inspired by the extratheatrical associations of these locations. (2003: 134)

Responses that evoke memories of previous experiences can occur in any performance space: as Carlson comments, "how important for us, and yet how underrated, are the ghosts of our previous theatregoing.... any theatrical production weaves a ghostly tapestry for its audience" (164–165). But site-specific or site-sympathetic theatre (as the quote at the beginning of this chapter has it, work that is "all about the building") is particularly interesting to consider in the framework of "ghosting." *Ghost* begins to take on multiple meanings: in Carlson's model memories are ghosts, haunting a current production; in site-specific theatre the production *itself* is the "ghost" that haunts the "host" of the performance site (for the origins of this terminology see discussion of Pearson 2010, later in this chapter). *Ghosts* takes on further meaning in the context of Punchdrunk, who have described the masked spectator as allowing the audience to "become ghosts walking through the building" (Barrett in Sooke 2007), and this sensation of not-quite-belonging to the environment continues themes of transgression and exploration that may characterise part of the excitement of experiencing a production that calls itself *immersive*. The concept of memory influencing spectatorship is also interesting to consider in the context of multiple visits to the same show.

Site-Specific and Environmental Theatre: Memory, Ecology and the Theatrical Event

The relationship between environment and spectator is a site for ethical enquiry. Zaiontz notes that audience members within site-specific performance events "often serve as the equivalent of an 'animate' mise en scene" (2012: 167), and these ambulatory or otherwise active spectators bring a spatial dimension to the theatrical environment and function as co-creators or facilitators of the work. Encounters with(in) the work build a sense of role or responsibility within the production and can lead to an environment in which "strangers produce binding ethical relationships with each other" (167). Considering subjectivity in so-called intimate theatre practice, Iball brings up the politics of individuals and relationships as worthy of consideration, noting that "there is evidence of UK-based practitioners using site-specific strategies for an ethical imagining of audience participation" (2012: 201). Considering audience members as individuals impacts an idea of "the audience" as a whole group, a process that comes particularly clear if the structure of a show enables spectators to be more explicitly aware of each other.

Pearson (2010) issues an invitation for further site-specific practice rather than proposing a rigid definition of site-specific performance, and suggests an "immersive" model as a means for the reader to imagine themselves into a site. The relationship between performance and environment can refer to a defined geographical area, approaching a piece of work "horizontally across the terrain and simultaneously vertically through time: performance becomes a topographic phenomenon of both natural history and local history" (Pearson 2006: 3). Drawing on methodologies and metaphors of archaeology and geology (excursions; strata), and social sciences, Pearson can consider "performance and landscape, biography and locality, memory and place" (2006: 3). *Memory, history* and *ghost* are concepts that suggest ways a spectator or audience member might become immersed in an environment. Immersive experience is a specific, time-bound (temporary) state, and a non-binary phenomenon that can be experienced at varying levels of intensity. *Memory, history* and *ghost* contribute to this model of immersive experience as a series of graded states by complicating the idea that a spectator might be(come) completely "lost" in a created theatrical world. Instead of totally forgetting about the real world, memories of previous performances or an awareness of the history of the space contribute to the experience of immersion by throwing the temporary nature of the created environment into further relief.

Pearson credits McLucas of Brith Gof as first theorising *the host and the ghost* in the early 1990s:

> [McLucas began to] characterize site-specific performance as the coexistence and overlay of two basic sets of architectures: those of the extant building or what he called the host, that which is at site—and those of the constructed scenography and performance, or the ghost, that which is temporarily brought to site. (2012: 70)

Other metaphors of making in site-specific work include *bricolage* (Pearson 2010: 119) and *palimpsest* (Turner 2004: 373; Kaye 2000: 11), and as Kaye notes, "site-specific art frequently works to trouble the oppositions between the site and the work" (2000: 11) (See Étienne [2016] for further application of the term site-specificity to outdoor immersive performance). The theorisation of *host* and *ghost* provides a framework for considering the ways immersive productions might use existing buildings and spaces to create their theatrical environments. The case studies in this chapter consider the relationship between what is already at site and what Punchdrunk brings to site in order to enable immersive experience. *Environment* can refer to both the original host and the Punchdrunk ghost: interplay between awareness of the pre-existing site and consciousness of Punchdrunk's creation of another site over/above/on top/within that site, contributes to theatrical immersion.

As previously mentioned, Pearson resists providing a rigid definition of site-specific work. Hodge offers a continuum of site-specific performance "types": at one extreme is performance in a theatre building; followed by outside theatre (i.e., outdoor Shakespeare); site-sympathetic work which is an "existing performance text physicalized in a selected site"; site-generic work which is "performance generated for a series of like sites" (i.e., car parks, swimming pools); and at the other end of the scale is site-specific work, "performance specifically generated from/for one selected site" (in Wilkie 2002: 150). The continuum lists common features, methods or techniques that may occur in site-specific work in order to reveal "layers of the site," including historical documentation; found text, objects, actions or sounds; personal association; and site morphology, physical and vocal explorations of site. Drawing on these models it is possible to conclude that Punchdrunk shows are not site-specific, and furthermore that much of their work tends to resist readings from the perspectives of local history or individual memory by making the pre-existing or "real-world" site invisible beneath the created theatrical world.

Hunter provides a useful perspective on the importance of influence and affect in the creation of site-specific dance performance, based on a reciprocal relationship between choreographer/dancer, space of performance and a spectator watching: "interaction between site, performance and observer results in the creation of a new 'space', the conceptual space of performance, which exists only temporarily, yet brings a new dimension to the architectural location" (2009: 413). Site-specific dance takes influence from its location, and also has the potential to influence how that location is perceived. Hunter's definition of site-specificity emphasises the importance of the original environment:

> in site-specific theatre, there is a specific interdependence between the site and the performance. Move the performance from the location and its significance will be either lost completely or weakened dramatically. (2009: 399)

The possibility that an immersive theatre production could theoretically be moved raises questions about the appropriateness of a site-specific or site-sympathetic designation. Punchdrunk's Aldeburgh-specific *The Borough* couldn't move without considerable changes to the performance text, and certain resonances of the setting would be lost—as the show was built into the landscape and historical resonances of that setting (or, alternatively, the show could move to a new performance site with "pretend you're in Aldeburgh" added to the audience's required imaginative heft—in effect adding a layer of fictional site-specificity to a new host site). *The Drowned Man* was dependent on its host building for its physical layout and structure, but the world created inside was entirely self-sufficient, and could theoretically be moved without significant changes to the content: the spaces that were inspired by the original building could be recreated in another. Barrett has commented on both the temptation and the possible difficulties of moving to a new host location:

> "I'd love to do *Drowned Man* again in a different building," Barrett says. "It would evolve hugely due to the findings we've made this iteration. [...]

But I don't think it would be possible for us to replicate a show somewhere else. In fact, it's not. Physically, there's always going to be different buildings, different flows, different tempos, different atmosphere." (in Jakob-Hoff 2014: n.p.)

As Hunter suggests, "works [that move, even between unconventional performance spaces] cannot be deemed 'site-specific' in the true sense of the word as the essence of the work remains constant from location to location" (2009: 408). The two case studies in this chapter illustrate this tension between original site and created environment, raising different answers to the question of whether it is purely in the created world that a spectator becomes immersed, or whether the interplay between the sensation of original host environment and theatrical ghost creates immersive experience.

Schechner's "Six Axioms for Environmental Theater" (1967, revised 1987) emphasise a reciprocal relationship between the space and the gaze of a spectator:

1. The theatrical event is a set of related transactions;
2. All the space is used for the performance;
3. The theatrical event can take place either in a totally transformed space or in "found space";
4. Focus is flexible and variable;
5. All production elements speak their own language;
6. The text need be neither the starting point nor the goal of a production. There may be no verbal text at all. ([1973] 1994: ix–li)

For Schechner, a relationship between, and dialogue across, the space, performers and audience are central to the creation of the performance itself. Interactions between audience members, and between audience members and performers, are part of the energy of the performance—and unplanned moments of conflict or tension in the space contribute the energy and atmosphere as much as rehearsed events. Environment, performance and audience behaviour are allowed, or even invited, to inform and affect each other. Harding and Rosenthal suggest "[Schechner's] highly controversial and now legendary production of *Dionysus in 69*" could be considered "the quintessential environmental theatre piece" which "exploded the boundaries between performers and spectators" (2011: 5). However, Bottoms notes that *Dionysus in 69* was branded, packaged and marketed to a similar extent as other successful pieces of mainstream theatre (in Harding and Rosenthal 2011: 23–38).

A social assumption of space in Environmental Theatre is that it is fundamentally more democratic for its audience. There are no "best" seats with an officially sanctioned better view, a system in opposition to theatre's long history of segregated seating. Instead the audience is free to control its own view, directing its own gaze and how (multi- or local-focus) it looks. This assertion does not sit easily with the possibilities of discomfort or manipulation suggested by moments of tension in performance. It is possible for theatre of this type to allow audience behaviours that affect the experience of others, resulting in a "better" view for some. Behaviours within an apparently democratic performance space might easily recreate oppressive or problematic dynamics that draw on knowledge or social structures from outside the space. Considering immersion and environment from this perspective raises questions of freedom(s) and agency, leading to ethical and social implications of the manipulation of spectators' and performers' movement: on the level of the role of structure, design and direction, but also on a more personal level of individual well-being. It is of course also possible for theatre of this type to have a segregated pricing system, as *Dionysus in 69* did originally (Bottoms 2011: 30), or as Punchdrunk's *The Drowned Man* did with its VIP ticket option: democratically "empty" spaces are not free from other outside pressures.

Environmental theatre is concerned with the agency of individuals, be that performers or spectators. Aronson describes the defining trait of environmental theatre as "any form of theatre in which a spectator cannot apprehend the total performance space within the normal frontal lines of vision" and suggests that "[a]udience incorporation may be achieved in several ways and in varying degrees" (2012). Environmental theatre forefronts the relationship between actors, audiences and the space of performance: a general truism of environmental theatre is that the audience and the performers occupy the same space and there is no "make-believe" that the performers are elsewhere. Environmental theatre works to diminish the literal distance between audience and performers; the question therefore becomes one of whether a fictional distance is maintained. Anonymous masked audience members are in many ways distant from the performers they may be physically close to, separated from the environment they temporarily inhabit: the rules of the mask (no touching, no talking) and the performance style of the performers (ignoring the audience members except during one-on-one scenes) may emphasise this distance within physical proximity.

Wider social and cultural approaches to environmental theatre enable discussion to include *the theatrical event*. Aronson traces environmental theatre's lineage back to "processional and church-based productions of medieval theatre in Europe, as well as many forms of traditional Asian theatre and various folk performances" (2012), noting that the use of the environment in productions might be created by the manipulation of atmosphere only, or involve a more drastic (re)structuring or organisation of the space. In this way, pageants, processions and parades can also be considered environmental theatre. A spectator cannot take the entire event in at once, and the route through the city is part of the event, making the background/setting take on theatrical significance of its own. Wiles proposes that the political implications of civic processional events are connected to the shape of the route through the environment: "The spatial order is an order of power. A linear movement through the streets defines the shape and order of the town and of its processing inhabitants" (2003: 21). Immersion in these contexts becomes tied to a sense of inclusion, of belonging to a particular group or community—a concept that quickly becomes problematic if it is celebrated (or otherwise experienced) in a manner exclusive to the group(s) that are not deemed, be definition and default, to be "outside" or "other." If environmental theatre has in its lineage this kind of civic or political event, the purpose of audience inclusion into the work takes on an extra social resonance. The political implications of a single defined route or strictly demarcated performance space suggest, rather than the freedom of audience members to wander, the power of those who first demarcate the space.

Environmental theatre's relationship with illusion and fiction also has interesting implications for immersion. As already mentioned, the audience's incorporation into the production is a central aspect of the form, either by being merely permitted to wander or given greater freedom for interaction or co-creation. Although environmental theatre is occasionally used to achieve levels of greater levels of naturalism, Aronson notes that "More often artists have used environmental staging as a means of *thwarting conventional illusion*, as in various productions of Meyerhold, Barba, Mnouchkine, [and] the Bread And Puppet Theatre" (2012; my emphasis). Thwarting conventional illusion is almost directly contradictory to the idea of creating immersive experience by fashioning a fictional world at a high level of detail and encouraging an audience member to lose themselves in its exploration.

Environmental work is deliberately crafted and directed to call attention to the site where the performance takes place, or to commence or continue a negotiation with that space. In "Six Axioms for Environmental Theater," Schechner argues that "Every space has its own given character. [...] An environmental theatre design should not be blindly imposed on a site" (xxxvi). In larger productions such as Punchdrunk's *The Drowned Man* and their other shows created to a similar template, the building itself, set and props design, lighting design, actor- and audience-direction, and musical score are the means to an immersive end for its audiences. The performance environment calls attention to itself, and moments where these elements seem out of sync will adversely affect immersive experience. Environments are designed to create both a fictional dreamworld and the very real structural and logistical means for an audience member to experience that world. Scenography provides a useful perspective: in their discussion of immersion, participation and exchange in the work of Punchdrunk, McKinney and Butterworth note that "scenography effectively provides the dramaturgical through-line" of some contemporary theatre practice situated outside traditional theatre spaces (2009: 192–195). Reviews of Punchdrunk's *The Masque of the Red Death* (2007–2008) responded to a range of scenographic elements as well as the performances, including sights and smells and stage/space pictures: "Ultimately, the quality of participation in the Punchdrunk production was determined by individual audience members who made choices about the way they viewed the performance" (McKinney and Butterworth 2009: 194). The presence and manipulation of multisensory stimuli might seem more pronounced in work where an emphasis is placed on design aspects. When there is no performer present, the space is composed entirely of such elements.

The frames of environmental theatre and the theatrical event have consequences for the question of audience empowerment. Aronson suggests that environmental theatre finds its modern-day equivalent in site-specific work: "as in much environmental theatre, the environment itself often becomes the central aspect of [site-specific] performance and incorporates performer and spectator equally" (2012). Twentieth-century happenings took place at an intersection of performance, fine art and progressive political ends—such as attempts to interrupt mass political speeches; their "structure and content are a logical extension of [their] environments" (Kaprow in Henri 1974). However, in the historical trajectory of the "revered gaze" in large other-worldly spaces (Griffiths 2008), immersive experience is more suggestive of a highly *unequal* relationship between performer and spectator, and/or between environment and spectator. Rather than deliberately all-encompassing multisensory atmospheric environments designed to overwhelm the spectator, site-specificity returns to the anti-immersive idea of deliberately refusing or *thwarting illusion*: instead drawing on real-world environments as the stimulus, asking a spectator to see the real world anew. An analysis of how immersive experience is created or experienced in a production needs to address this tension between the created world and the site already present, and the consequences for how "empowered" a production therefore wants its audiences to be, seem or feel (and whether each of those has a different answer.)

The perspectives of cultural geography and ecocriticism can also further approaches to the wider consequences of creating immersive spaces in/on/over original sites, and the question of power implicit within them. Kershaw discusses the challenges to, and the role of, theatre and performance in the context of a changing ecological situation; of particular relevance is his description of "the late-twentieth-century paradigm shift towards performance that confirmed the spectacular as an especially potent phenomenon in the realms of excessive power" (2007: 206). Large-scale immersive environments could certainly be considered part of the far end of this trajectory of spectacle, power and individuality. Drawing on cultural geography and ecocriticism more broadly would require too large a geographical and critical scope for this chapter, but an approach to Punchdrunk and immersive theatre from these fields would greatly reward further enquiry.

As a final concept concerning space and spectator, Giannachi proposes a distinction between environment and *ecology*:

> an environmental interpretation of presence foregrounds the set of circumstances that surround the occurrence of presence, while an ecological reading of presence foregrounds how presence may operate as a relational tool between organisms. (2012: 50)

The reciprocal relationship described by McAuley of "energy exchange" in performance is also suggestive of a kind of ecology: "In the theatre, due to the live presence of both spectators and performers, the energy circulates from performer to spectator and back again, from spectator to performer and back again" (2003: 246). Kaye suggests that work containing architectural and sculptural elements might contain "bodily confrontations with materials or an acting out of place and space, a 'performed ecology' of the subject" (in Giannachi and Stewart 2006: 269). This metaphor of ecology emphasises the interconnectedness of spectator, performer and space: "performance becomes the means by which the individual's relationship with the built and found material environment is understood, realised and reproduced" (282). If an immersive performance environment lends itself to being considered an ecology, it is interesting to posit the audience member as one element of a wider ecology of immersive experience, part of a reciprocal energy exchange between spectator, performer(s) and aspects of the performance environment.

The case studies for this chapter have different relationships between spectator and space. *The Borough* (2013) was a soundwalk through Aldeburgh for a single participant at a time, a narrator inviting the participant to follow a prescribed path through the village. *The Drowned Man* (2013–2014) continued the trajectory of work that began with *Faust* and *The Masque of the Red Death*, being the largest to date of their large-scale productions containing looping action in buildings through which audience members were invited to wander. My discussion is interested in the relationship between the original site and the created theatrical environment, and the consequences for immersive experience in the relationship between spectator, host and ghost.

Immersion and Environment in *The Borough*

> Punchdrunk's gift has always been the ability to make it feel as if you've been plunged into a parallel universe. The spooky beauty of this latest work is that they achieve it, not within an enclosed space, but on the streets of Aldeburgh in broad daylight. [...] The show disrupts the everyday and yet is also woven into the fabric of daily life, and it exists simultaneously in the mind and out on the streets. You walk among the living, but when you catch a glimpse of your own face, reflected in a window, it looks oddly spectral. (Gardner 2013: n.p.)

Gardner's review defines the key way *The Borough* was considered atypical for Punchdrunk. The immersive experience of this production was not contained within the physical walls of a building but within more porous boundaries. *The Borough* was produced in June 2013 as part of the Benjamin Britten festival in Aldeburgh, Norfolk, its story inspired by George Crabbe's poem which, in turn, influenced Britten's *Peter Grimes*. The show's narrator guided participants through the village on a predetermined route, providing a rhythm for their footsteps, and moving them through scenes in hidden spaces (the route involved exploring a bedroom and a fishing hut) and at other times guiding along village streets. The soundscape was composed of the rhythm of footsteps (a practical means of keeping to time, and actors also matched their actions to footsteps), natural sounds of sea waves and music from Britten's opera. Although the show did not have physical walls adopting the headphones served to demarcate a clear moment of "entering" or beginning the journey and Aldeburgh itself functioned as a site with physical boundaries; especially given the show's story of paranoia in a small village, building to its climax along themes of scrutiny, watching, rumours, guilt and blame. Some indoor scenes were evocative of the designed environments of indoor immersive productions but in general the show's form places *The Borough* closer to site-specific work, pervasive performance and audiowalks. It was also atypical for much of Punchdrunk's work by deviating from a structure where the audience is clearly identifiable, either by wearing masks or simply by virtue of being in the space: the show created a tension between the participants experiencing the show and the people who were not as *The Borough*'s participants shared the streets with non-participants, and at times the show played with this ambiguity.

The Borough might also be considered atypical in its treatment of story, chronology and narrative by being a very linear experience in a literal sense. The earphones played a single hour-long mp3 soundtrack which could not be paused or rewound. This took the participant through the show without the appearance of choice regarding when and where to walk. (Making these choices in *The Borough* would manifest as mistakes or refusals that threaten to break or stop the show.) *The Borough*'s soundtrack was non-linear in the sense that chronology was recounted in an impressionistic way that allowed for a gradual accumulation of details ("there was another boy") which lead to a final climactic reveal in the second fishing hut. The linearity of the score emphasised that these gradual reveals were a choice of the structure of the narrative, pre-authored by Punchdrunk, rather than occurring as a result of an audience member's own exploration.

Structural aspects of *The Borough* demonstrate immersive qualities, even as the show was not typically structurally "immersive" in the sense of occurring entirely in a dark, indoor space. The second fishing hut, where the finale of the show took place, was constructed in the middle of a field rather than on the shoreline, appearing to be much more isolated but otherwise identical to one the audience member explores early in the show. As argued in Chap. 6 in relation to endings, by returning to a same-but-different space the spectator literally sees the environment differently, following all the events that have occurred since the previous visit. A boy performer in the second fishing hut also made the act of watching a very different experience to exploring an empty space: and, rather than being ignored by the performers, the presence of the spectator was central to the climactic scene, acknowledged and directly stared at by multiple actors. Changes in the sound quality also emphasised the final culmination of the narrative as the music played through speakers as well as the earphones, the sound quality literally giving resonance to the story's final events.

Immersion and environment in *The Borough* is connected to structure and form. The show's ability to lower barriers to immersive experience was provided by the interplay between the real environment of the village and Punchdrunk's created scenes and story.

The participants' route was controlled in terms of direction and pace, the narrator drawing attention to certain landmarks. The audience members were never actually alone: although they often seemed to be and the story and soundtrack suggested isolation, they were always in the sight of a performer or non-character steward. Many characters were not seen at length but only glimpsed briefly, which both created the illusion of a larger world and further blended the real life of the village—actual shoppers and so on—with the fictional story of *The Borough*—in which a character, who gradually comes to be identified with the participant, is increasingly isolated in the town. The stewards, in contrast, fulfilled a more pragmatic function and were hidden throughout. Noticing this aspect of the structural framework of the show would break the illusion of the world. The tension between the structural logistics of the show and its fictional environment, therefore, were present throughout *The Borough*—boundaries of the piece were hidden in order to allow for a more potent immersive experience inside them. In its form, the piece was a deliberately isolating experience, experienced individually (Gardner commented that by the end of the piece "I began to feel as if even the seagulls had a grudge against me" 2013: n.p.) but the show also enabled a sensation of (a more positive, inclusive) community and measures of care and safety in terms of how route and pace were mediated. Sensations of long-held grudges and the accusing stares of performers were part of the fictional world, while in real life each participant was well looked after. The show used the village as both a real and a fictional space. The immersive environment in this context becomes one created between the participant, the village of Aldeburgh, the Punchdrunk-created fictional spaces (such as the fishing hut) and the fictional story of *The Borough*, which itself draws on other existing texts.

The Borough was part of Aldeburgh's Benjamin Britten festival, making explicit the production's link to a historical and cultural heritage. The show also drew on Punchdrunk's own heritage in terms of the history of the company, by appearing to take a very different form to much of their other work. The show demonstrated that immersive experience can be created and maintained outside, although the site of *The Borough* still had very clearly defined boundaries: the route taken, the length of the soundtrack. The participant of *The Borough* was immersed in terms of the technological and physical setup—constantly surrounded by sound effects, their journey through the village always the "centre" of their experience of the production. Immersive experience in *The Borough* occurred on the boundary between the real world and the fictional world. The show consisted of created, performed and performative elements mixed with the everyday layout and life of the village. If the gap between these worlds is less noticeable—so even seagulls seem sinister by the end and one is on the lookout for accusatory stares all the way home—the conclusion might be drawn that the whole world, for a while, seems to carry with it the flavour of the production. Pervasive gaming does not have rigorous geographical boundaries in the way traditional immersive environments do: the show bleeds, spatially or temporally, or in any case is perceived to. In *The Borough*, the gap between the experience of the fictional environment and the real one—the one without headphones—may lead to paranoid conclusions about society and surveillance, or a feeling of relief that society is not like that after all.

Site-specific performance is characterised by two co-existing architectures: the host of the original site; the ghost which is temporarily brought to site (Pearson 2012: 70). The host site of Aldeburgh had its own ghosts before *The Borough* arrived, in its musical heritage and nautical history. The show's content weaved in and out of an already multilayered host. The narrator pointed out landmarks as they evoked memories, as well as being a pragmatic aid to navigation. Host and ghost blurred in the show's form as well as content, which took its participant past real village buildings and through purpose-built fictional spaces.

The Borough was designed as a simple experience with a straightforward operating system, maintaining a low-tech aesthetic to experiencing the show even as it was entirely produced and framed by technology. These decisions enabled a lowering of initial barriers to immersion by making the interface easy to access and operate: a single hour-long mp3 file with no need to pause, stop or rewind; route and walking pace mediated by the narrator; ushers present throughout to correct mistakes or deal with any discomfort or disorientation. The fictional (ghost) environment of props, buildings, costumes and landmarks blended into the surrounding (host) landscape. Some sites were made into fictional spaces with great attention to detail, and at other times the fictional world of *The Borough*'s story was created by the audio score alone, combined with the landscape of Aldeburgh, and the participant's own imaginative input. Indoor scenes of detail and darkness presented a contrasting atmosphere to the experience of moving through the outdoor site. Immersed in the story and the narrative/musical score of the show, *The Borough* also used environmental immersion within the wider landscape of Aldeburgh to create immersive experience in small, dark spaces. The climax made this relationship between environment and immersion explicit, as the audience member was pushed out of the final encounter in the dark, into wide space and accusatory silence.

The experience of immersion in *The Borough*'s various fictional/real environments required mediation and control. It would be a technical or organisational failure that would cause an audience member to walk into a room just as the action has ended (rather than being simply par for the course, as is the case for *The Drowned Man* and its antecedents). The phrase "the role of the audience" has a double meaning in *The Borough*, since as well as placing them centre logistically, the fictional narrative slowly revealed their place within the society described in the story. The audience members begin as a stranger having a tour of the village, but eventually the narrator goes beyond this. *The Borough* slowly turns its audience members into maligned outsiders who other villagers know and glare at. The centrality of the audience member's fictional role is gradually revealed corresponds to a gradual building up of immersion. The immersive experience technically began as soon as the headphones are turned on to play the opening sound effect of ocean waves—a very definite, finite boundary. But it was through a slow build-up of both fictional story elements and literal aspects, such as the set, number of actors and sound quality, that *The Borough* was able to manipulate levels of audience immersion as it guided its participants through Aldeburgh.

IMMERSION AND ENVIRONMENT IN *THE DROWNED MAN*

> As with all Punchdrunk work, in whatever we do, the space always comes first. And actually the first time I walked around this building, about right where we are now [Studio 3], it was completely open-planned. A huge void, an empty open wasteland. And it had very few architectural details of note. The source and the show always comes from the space, and because it was so barren, it sort of screamed out "film studio". (Barrett 2013, *The Drowned Man* pre-show talk)

The making of *The Drowned Man* (2013) saw a building become an open-plan, emptied site become a series of constructed spaces. The production turned 31 London Street into Temple Studios, and this renaming symbolises an attitude towards site. As discussed previously, immersive experience in *The Borough* occurred in the interplay between the real and the constructed. According to Wilkie, site-specificity occurs when performance is "specifically generated from/for one selected site" (2002: 150). In the earlier quotation, *The Drowned Man* fits this definition of site-specific in the sense of being informed by its environment; the show was literally built for the building, its layouts unavoidably informed by the original architecture of the space. However, immersive experience in this show relied on the creation of a totally self-contained fictional world. The mise-en-scene of the production was more prominent than the original site: the interior of 31 London Street was neutralised and the new design installed. (The same happened in New York, *Sleep No More* turning West 27th Street into The McKittrick Hotel.) *The Drowned Man* is more representative of *site-generic* work than *site-specific*; though informed by 31 London Street's geography, Temple Studios could be recreated/rebuilt in another large open-plan building. This case study is interested in the relationship between environment and immersive experience in a show that is fundamentally less "sympathetic" to its host site than *The Borough*. As argued in relation to *The Borough*, immersive experience can occur in the interplay between the real and the fictional—this is where barriers to immersive experience might be lowered and a sensation of transgression becomes key to the structure of the show. Immersive experience is defined by a paradoxical awareness of the boundaries of the sensation: being aware of boundaries leading to the pleasure of their being broken or transgressed. The relationship between the "real" and the "fake" was central to *The Drowned Man*'s story as well as its form, given its Hollywood setting and the themes of disorientation, performativity and increasing madness of many of its characters. The production was "immersive" in its having finite physical and temporal boundaries, but being inside an immersive-shaped production does not in itself guarantee immersive experience. Atmospheric and design elements work to create a world that is wholly self-contained, but it is an awareness of the temporary nature of the production that leads to immersive experience in the created environment. *The Drowned Man* began with an invitation to the audience to "steer your own course" through the world: although perhaps not site-specific due to its neutralisation of the original space, a key aspect of immersive experience in the production was a sense of interplay between the "real" sensation of exploring a theatrical production, and the verisimilitude of the fictional environment. The created fictional environment of *The Drowned Man* could almost be read as a host site, in itself, the audience becoming coded as the ghost.

Many Punchdrunk shows played with the line between modification and neutralisation of their original spaces. *The Masque of the Red Death* (2007–2008) spread through Battersea Arts Centre including its spaces not traditionally designated for performance, such as the foyer staircase. *The Duchess of Malfi* (2010) drew on the venue's earlier purpose as an office block, using computer wires to create parts of a new fantasy landscape. For *The Drowned Man* the building's architecture influenced the design of the show in a literal sense, but the overall effect was of neutralising the original atmosphere and dynamics of the space. The performances of the actors and dancers could also be considered site-specific, as performances are created and rehearsed in response to the specific fictional landscape created by the designers. Finally this relationship between modification and neutralisation of the original space, and transgression of the boundaries between these two processes, was mirrored in the content of the production itself. The relationship between "host" building and the "ghost" brought to site was mirrored in the interplay within the fictional environment and the building, and the story enacted upon and embedded within the fictional environment: retelling Buchner's *Woyzeck* in a *Day of the Locust*-inspired corrupt Hollywood world leads to blurred lines abound between the "real" and the "fake," the "real-life" and the "acting," the "genuine" and the "pretending." Although the relationship between the original site and the ghost was less one of equal exchange and mutual influence (as in *The Borough*) and more a flat overlaying, interplay between created environment and host site remains a key component of the potential for immersive experience in the space. It is not the parallel universe in itself that allows for immersive experience, but the relationship between the parallel universe and a sense of the "real world," whatever the power dynamic between them.

The Borough's fictional story weaved through the real geography and landmarks of Aldeburgh. *The Drowned Man* announced the creation of a whole and complete fictional world in (re)naming of the site. The environment in *The Drowned Man* was designed to create a feeling of wholeness and allow for a sense of getting lost in the fiction/setting. As mentioned in this chapter's introduction, a defining pre-occupation of environmental theatre is the attempt to deliberately thwart illusion. This pre-occupation is in opposition to immersive experience, as defined as the process of losing oneself in a fictional environment: immersion coming from the highly detailed, atmospheric, and strategically structured internal space. The interplay between tiny winding corridors and secret passages, opening out into much larger spaces and sudden shifts between very different spaces (light/dark, cosy/sinister, naturalistic/abstract) contribute to the creation of a rich fictional environment, designed and created inside the host building. The structure of the environment creates immersive experience—through a sense of being lost, disorientated, free to wander—and commences an active negotiation with the environment—choice-led exploration, following characters. If immersive environment is a dreamworld, its means of navigation makes it a lucid one. The purpose of illusion and fiction in this context encourages audience members to get lost (literally) in the "real" (highly detailed, tactile, etc.) fictional world that has been installed inside the host building. Furthermore, the characters who occupy this fictional world absolutely belong to it: performers in *The Drowned Man* do not leave the building to blend into the real-world landscape and crowds in the way that *The Borough* encouraged. The actors and dancers are also part of the environment, their characters' stories and journeys able to be explored by a visiting audience member, just as much as the space itself.

The relationship between immersive experience and physical environment can be considered from a scenographic, design perspective and a more structural, logistical perspective. A scenographic lens allows all design elements to be considered. Sight, smell and touch played a part in creating *The Drowned Man*'s various environments and atmospheres (such as the church of the Dust Witch, which smelled strongly of herbs and smoke; or the sand coating the floor on the highest level). Discussing the use of darkness in Shunt's 2009 production *Money*, Welton suggests when "actors and audiences [are] forced to feel their way through darkened places both real and imagined, these explorations of theatrical darkness blur physical and fictional domains" (2012: 14). The creation of environment has the potential to lower barriers to immersion by manipulating scenographic elements. Chapter 6 described the action of opening a door as an example of how engaging with environment functions as a narrative event, in the context of an immersive space. Opening a door is also as an event in the exploration of environment, and in the facilitation of immersive experience in that environment. Opening a door, pushing aside a curtain or otherwise crossing a threshold into a new and previously unexplored space provides a new set of scenographic stimuli. It is an act that can potentially further exploration—adding information to a gradual picture of the show's physical layout—or increase disorientation.

From a structural and logistical perspective, *The Drowned Man* faced the challenge to lower barriers to immersion by its treatment of the layout of the rooms and floors of 31 London Street, and in its arrangement of architectural features and organisation and design within the space. The site of *The Drowned Man* suggested size but also maintained the potential for individual interactions; an important challenge of making the show was to ensure that immersive experience could still be achieved for a larger audience, and how the show responded to that challenge demonstrates how *immersive experience* is being defined. The building was the biggest single space the company had yet used, with the biggest audience capacity. The possibilities for immersive experience were great, but potential barriers to immersion were also more numerous and difficult to lower. The physical environments included larger spaces and visual spectacle as well as smaller rooms with detailed settings and an atmosphere of intensity: immersive experience can be facilitated by these spaces on their own, and by moving between them. The number of people in the space increased the challenge of making the atmosphere one of tension, interest and excitement rather than a feeling of simply being lost in a crowd; an increase in scale also raises the challenge to create and maintain an experience of moving about the show predicated on secrecy, exploration, intensity, individual viewpoints, one-on-one interactions and solo moments.

The mise-en-scene and design of Punchdrunk's created environments is described on the company's website as employing a "cinematic" level of detail to immerse the audience in the world of the show. Bartley recognises the importance of environment in *Sleep No More*: "Though Barrett and Doyle frame their work with rhetoric of interpersonal exchange, *Sleep No More* is fundamentally object-based and space-based rather than performer-based" (2013: n.p.). *The Drowned Man* had a similar emphasis on spatial elements, with the performers acting and dancing across and within it. The invitation to explore the detailed sets remained central to *The Drowned Man*'s facilitation of immersive experience. Both quotations below refer to *The Drowned Man*:

> "The audience is the camera floating around this dream," says Barrett. "All we are doing is presenting loads of content like the unedited rushes for them to cut together." [...] The mask, he adds, is the 'fourth wall' that enables the audience to become anonymous and get closer to the action. "They can almost feel the breath of the performers on them. The mask enables them to become the camera." (Masters 2013: n.p.)

> "For audiences, it's like directing your own film," explains Punchdrunk founder and artistic director Felix Barrett [...] "They become a living Steadicam and they're shooting their own director's cut of the show. They float down corridors and choose which characters they want to have close-ups with, where they want spectacle. They are in charge." (Lukowski 2013: n.p.)

The language of film is invoked regarding the show's environment and the means to engage with that environment: the creation of a fictional space with "a cinematic level of detail" and the invitation to navigate it with "director's cut" approach and level of power.

The relationship between "real" and "fake" becomes even more multilayered when considering that the production is based around a fictional film company: some spaces are film sets, deliberately designed to look fake, while some have a grimy, crumbling, gothic aesthetic that looks more "realistic" in comparison to the film sets. In *The Drowned Man*, one room contained large sloping piles of fake snow: deliberately fake snow, film-set looking snow, with glitter among the white and a solid surface to run about and dance on. The room next door to this space is a decadent dressing room, and in one corner is a smaller fake snow-hill that appears to be coming through the wall. This detail might be a means of linking together two parts of the site, and as such it may suggest that the artificiality of the film-making world is encroaching on the real world of the studio's actors, with consequences for the relationship between fiction and reality for these characters, or the mental health or wellbeing of these characters—or it may, as I heard one audience member wonder out loud through their mask, be "all about cocaine." Depending on which room is experienced first, it may become a navigational clue: providing a hint at what is to come or a reminder of what is next door. Horton suggests that film landscapes can clue an audience into the type or genre of story they are watching, or even become a character in its own right (2003: 77–81). The relationship between the snow-scape and the dressing room in *The Drowned Man* allows various interpretations of the fictional world, and the rules (or lack thereof) of that world. This interruption across the two spaces—a place where the real and the fake, the (relatively) realistic dressing-room and the explicitly theatrical snow—is a site of the possible breaking of immersion in environment as it makes obvious the boundary between these two spaces and these two aesthetic states. Becoming aware of this boundary allows for further immersion as the limits of the experience are felt. RWD allows for an interruption between two spaces to become, in itself, a site for immersive experience: made more intense by the awareness of an interruption followed by the decision to dismiss the interruption.

Immersive experience is defined by its limits: intense and overwhelming because it is temporary. *The Drowned Man* and other immersive productions of its shape are strongly bordered and with definite boundaries of both time—three hours, tonight, this moment—and space—this building, this room. There is a considerable, noticeable gap between the world outside the building and what is inside. *The Borough* used immersive experience to blend the real and the fictional to the point where it became possible to respond to elements of the real-world environment within the tone of the fictional narrative. The gap between these worlds in *The Drowned Man*, on the other hand, could be seen as one that allows for total escapism: the show provides a puzzling dreamworld that is temporarily gone into, explored and then left behind. Its themes and characters might provide ways of thinking about corruption and poverty, dreams and exploitation, fame and rivalry, trauma and war, that still have contemporary relevance: or perhaps the production invites you to see its atmospheric world as totally self-contained, an adventure to explore for a finite time, a world that is removed from our own. Of course, form reveals itself to be even more invariably political in efforts to communicate an apolitical existence. Individual rooms, scenes, encounters and props could spark many imaginative or artistic interpretations concerning its in-world story or characters: but they might also be a catalyst for considering the production itself, the amount of artistic imagination and physical labour that went into the creation of the environment, and any wider political, social, ethical or economic ramifications of form.

CONCLUSION: IMMERSIVE ENVIRONMENT(S)

> The whole thing with Punchdrunk is it's always for the individual. So even if it was a larger scale show, an audience of two thousand people, it's still about each one as an individual, and we'd still want to make sure every single one of them had their own experience they had ownership of, and there were enough beats of intimacy and that panic-inducing alone time. Because without that, we might as well just do it in a theatre. (Barrett 2013, *The Drowned Man* pre-show talk)

This quote demonstrates the centrality of environment towards a conception of immersive experience. Emotion and sensation, panic and intimacy, alone time and exploration, are all theorised as explicitly connected to, and derived from, the way a production manipulates space: it is integral to the desired effect that a production occurs in a non-theatre space, and issues an invitation to the audience to experience an individual journey through that space. Such a definition relies on an awareness of the contrast between what is seen here as an "immersive" use of space, and its inferior opposite, "just do[ing] it in a theatre." The interplay between the sensation of experiencing a created theatrical world, and an awareness of the real world outside, facilitates immersive experience in environment. An awareness of the temporary nature of the experience is required to allow the sensation of feeling lost. Graded states of immersive experience can be made or represented in the existence of a production's fictional world over different floors of a building or across a village (which may encompass both indoor and outdoor sites). Variation between larger spectacles and smaller, detailed settings also lowers barriers to immersion in environment within the space.

Immersive theatre is not necessarily site-specific, and immersive experience may depend on the relationship between host and ghost. While relying on the architecture and layout of 31 London Street for its structure, *The Drowned Man* neutralised the site rather than allowing for "articulate exchanges between the work of art and the places in which its meanings are defined" (Kaye 2000: 1); the spaces of the original building were overlaid by the production's own technologies and design elements. The relationship between host and ghost was more porous in *The Borough*, as the landscape and history of the village was incorporated into the fictional narrative of the soundwalk, and performers and constructed spaces were hidden within real-world locations. In both cases, the relationship between the original host and the created ghost allowed for an interplay that facilitated immersive experience in environment, either in the detail of the created environment itself or in the ways Punchdrunk has acted on the original building/site. This allows for what Griffiths names "a 'revered gaze', a response marked as much by recognition of the labor and effort involved in creating the spectacle as in the spectacle itself" (2008: 286). The construction and craft of creating *The Borough* and *The Drowned Man* involved making this "labour and effort" invisible: the technology unobtrusive; a gradual layering up of fictional world and story; the introduction to, and navigation through, the performance spaces. As much as a maker might will their construction to be unnoticeable, moments of awareness invariably occur. This may interrupt immersion, or it may facilitate a "revered gaze" that is not necessarily contradictory to immersive experience. In either case, in quotations like the one above, immersive experience is inherently connected to environment, space and site.

References

Alston, Adam. 2016. Making Mistakes in Immersive Theatre: Spectatorship and Errant immersion. *Journal of Contemporary Drama in English* 4 (1): 61–73.

Aronson, Arnold. 2012. Environmental Theatre. In *The Oxford Companion to Theatre and Performance*, ed. Dennis Kennedy. Oxford: Oxford University Press.

Barrett, Felix. 2013. Burn the Seats: Audience Immersion in Interactive Theatre. Promotional Video for Future of StoryTelling Summit, New York, 2–3 October.

Barrett, Felix. 2014. Felix Barrett, Artistic Director, Punchdrunk. Speaking at Remix Summit: *Experience Economy: Creating Extraordinary Moments and Stories that Get People Talking*. https://www.youtube.com/watch?v=xCRcuHiDEYs. Accessed March 2014.
Barrett, Felix, and Maxine Doyle. 2013. The Drowned Man Pre-Show Talk: Meet the Directors. December 1.
Bartley, Sean. 2013. Punchdrunk: Performance, Permission, Paradox. *Borrowers and Lenders*, Athens: Oct 2013, 7 (2).
Blair, Rhonda. 2008. *The Actor, Image, and Action: Acting and Cognitive Neuroscience*. London: Routledge.
Bottoms, Stephen. 2011. In Defence of The String Quartet: An Open Letter to Richard Schechner. In *The Rise of Performance Studies: Rethinking Richard Schechner's Broad Spectrum*, ed. James Harding and Cindy Rosenthal, 23–38. Basingstoke: Palgrave Macmillan.
Carlson, Marvin. 2003. *The Haunted Stage: The Theatre as Memory Machine*. Ann Arbor: The University of Michigan Press.
Cook, Amy. 2010. *Shakespearean Neuroplay*. London: Palgrave.
Di Benedetto, Stephen. 2010. *The Provocation of the Senses in Contemporary Theatre*. London: Routledge.
Étienne, Anne. 2016. Challenging the Auditorium: Spectatorship(s) in 'Off-site' Performances. *Journal of Contemporary Drama in English* 4 (1): 74–89.
Gardner, Lyn. 2013. The Borough. *Guardian*, June 11 2013. Accessed June 2013.
Giannachi, Gabriella. 2012. Environmental Presence. In *Archaeologies of Presence: Art, Performance and the Persistence of Being*, ed. Gabriella Giannachi, Nick Kaye, and Michael Shanks, 50–63. London: Routledge.
Giannachi, Gabriella, and Nigel Stewart (eds.). 2006. *Performing Nature: Explorations in Ecology and the Arts*. Oxford: Peter Lang.
Griffiths, Alison. 2008. *Shivers Down Your Spine: Cinema, Museums and the Immersive View*. New York: Columbia University Press.
Harding, James M., and Cindy Rosenthal (eds.). 2011. *The Rise of Performance Studies: Rethinking Richard Schechner's Broad Spectrum*. Basingstoke: Palgrave Macmillan.
Henri, Adrian. 1974. *Environments and Happenings*. London: Thames and Hudson.
Horton, Andrew. 2003. Reel Landscapes: Cinematic Environments Documented and Created. In *Studying Cultural Landscapes*, ed. Iain Robertson and Richard Penny, 71–92. London: Hodder.
Hunter, Victoria. 2009. Experiencing Space: The Implications for Site-Specific Dance Performance. In *Contemporary Choreography: A Critical Reader*, ed. Jo Butterworth and Liesbeth Wildschut, 399–415. London: Routledge.
Iball, Helen. 2012. My Sites Set on You: Site-Specificity and Subjectivity in Intimate Theatre. In *Performing Site-Specific Theatre: Politics, Place, Practice*,

ed. Anna Birch and Joanne Tompkins, 201–218. Basingstoke: Palgrave Macmillan.

Jakob-Hoff, Tristan. 2014. At the Gates of Temple Studios: Where Gaming And Theatre Collide. *Eurogamer*, 2 May 2014 235 Accessed May 2014.

Kaye, Nick. 2000. *Site-Specific Art: Performance, Place and Documentation*. London: Routledge.

Kershaw, Baz. 2007. *Theatre Ecology: Environments and Performance Events*. Cambridge: Cambridge University Press.

Lakoff, G., and M. Johnson. 1999. *Philosophy in the Flesh: The Embodied Mind and Its Challenge to Western Thought*. New York: Basic Books.

Lukowski, Andrzej. 2013. Open the Door to The Black Room and Punchdrunk. *Time Out*, 16 July 2013. Accessed July 2013.

Lutterbie, John Harry. 2011. *Toward a General Theory of Acting: Cognitive Science And Performance*. Basingstoke: Palgrave Macmillan.

Masters, Tim. 2013. Punchdrunk's The Drowned Man is Theatre on a Grand Scale. *BBC News*. 19 July 2013. Accessed July 2013.

McConachie, Bruce and F. Elizabeth Hart (Eds.). 2006. *Performance and Cognition: Theatre Studies and the Cognitive Turn*. London: Routledge.

McConachie, Bruce. 2008. *Engaging Audiences: A Cognitive Approach to Spectating in the Theatre*. New York: Palgrave Macmillan.

McConachie, Bruce. 2013. *Theatre & Mind*. London: Palgrave Macmillan.

McKinney, Joslin, and Philip Butterworth. 2009. *The Cambridge Introduction to Scenography*. Cambridge: Cambridge University Press.

Nield, Sophie. 2008. The Rise of the Character Named Spectator. *Contemporary Theatre Review* 18 (4): 531–544.

Pearson, Mike. 2006. *In Comes I: Performance, Memory and Landscape*. Exeter: University of Exeter Press.

Pearson, Mike. 2010. *Site-Specific Performance*. Basingstoke: Palgrave Macmillan.

Pearson, Mike. 2012. Haunted House: Staging the Persians with the British Army. In *Performing Site-Specific Theatre: Politics, Place, Practice*, ed. Anna Birch and Joanne Tompkins, 70–83. Basingstoke: Palgrave Macmillan.

Rebellato, Dan. 2009. When We Talk of Horses: Or, What Do We See When We See a Play? Performance Research 14, no. 1 (March): pp 17–28.

Schechner, Richard. [1973] 1994. *Environmental Theatre*. New York: Applause Books. ['Six Axioms For Environmental Theater' (1967, revised 1987) pp xix-li].

Sooke, Alistair. 2007. Adventures in a Parallel Universe. Telegraph, 15 September 2007. Accessed April 2014.

Turner, Catherine. 2004. Palimpsest or Potential Space? Finding a Vocabulary for Site-Specific Performance. *New Theatre Quarterly* 20 (4): 373–390.

Turner, Mark, and Giles Fauconnier. 2003. *The Way We Think: Conceptual Blending and the Mind's Hidden Complexities*. New York: Perseus.

Varela, Francisco J. et al. 1993. *The Embodied Mind: Cognitive Science and Human Experience*. Cambridge, MA: MIT Press.
Welton, Martin. 2011. *Feeling Theatre*. Basingstoke: Palgrave Macmillan.
White, Gareth. 2012. On Immersive Theatre. *Theatre Research International*, 37(3) October, 221–235.
Wiles, David. 2003. *A Short History of Western Performance Space*. Cambridge: Cambridge University Press.
Wilkie, Fiona. 2002. Mapping the Terrain: A Survey of Site-Specific Performance in Britain. *New Theatre Quarterly* 18(70) May, 140–160.
Zaiontz, Keren. 2012. Ambulatory Audiences and Animate Sites: Staging the Spectator in Site-Specific Performance. In *Performing Site-Specific Theatre: politics, Place, Practice*, ed. Anna Birch and Joanne Tompkins, 167–181. Basingstoke: Palgrave Macmillan.

CHAPTER 9

Conclusion

Immersive performance is increasingly prevalent, and ever more its forms, assumptions and values merit further investigation. By defining immersive experience and immersive theatre as interrelated concepts, it is easier to consider how relationships between spectator, performance, performer, story, space and site are constructed and maintained: and how each of these aspects might, or might not, contribute to the visceral/ emotional/exciting audience experience that might, or might not, be a theatremaker's ultimate goal. Interactivity, narrative and environment all have the potential to create, influence or intensify immersive experience. They also have the potential to become barriers to immersion if they seem to be at odds with other aspects of the work or do not feel themselves, for whatever reason in the moment of performance, to be properly understood. A piece of theatre may choose to hold any of these aspects in major. Or they might all be given equal weight. When separate elements become greater than the sum of their parts the effect can be powerful, and it can be difficult (in retrospect as well as in the heat of the moment) to consider precisely what is going on when someone is "immersed," by the very nature of the experience. Considering how various aspects of a production might, or might not, contribute to a quality of immersive experience allows the phenomenon to be explored in greater detail.

Punchdrunk's work, and especially their larger-scale shows, can be called physically immersive in their shape, and they offer an implicit (or, given the company's reputation, increasingly explicit) promise to be highly immersive in terms of the atmospheric, spectacle-filled adventure the audience will encounter inside. All "immersive theatre," in being so called, promises to facilitate a certain visceral or overwhelming or otherwise exciting response in its participants. But use of the term is often connected, not directly to an emphasis on audience experience, but on the basis of a production's shape, layout and/or its audience logistics. *Immersive* is used to refer to a promise of interactive (or interactive-seeming) elements requiring varying levels of participation; or to indicate the use of certain aesthetic and atmospheric tropes (scenographic, sensory and environmental innovations, not to mention darkness and gloom); or a production's use of a non-linear or fractured narrative structure. Although these things may be defining tropes of the form, interactive elements and experimental approaches to story and space have a complex relationship to immersion, and their use does not in itself guarantee any particular kind of experience or level of immersion in an audience member. And just as interactivity and narrative innovations do not automatically lead to immersive experience, neither does merely being surrounded by a spatially innovative or painstakingly decorated environment. The notion that immersive performance is by definition site specific can also be contested: immersive productions have varying relationships with their host site. Immersive experience can be constituted, created, facilitated, troubled or blocked by spatial or logistical signifiers, unwritten rules or conventions of play, or a production's wider political landscape and social positioning. The relationship between immersive experience and immersive theatre opens up a wide area for further investigation into their various forms, politics, purposes, audiences and aesthetics.

Immersive experience exists as a series of graded states. It is a temporary phenomenon rather than a felt/not-felt binary that exists in relation to, and as a result of, the overcoming of various barriers. This definition of *immersion* allows for further exploration of its creation, maintenance or curation in immersive performance, including productions that seek to test the boundaries or capabilities of the form. It might be particularly rewarding to conduct practical research into immersive- or interactive-identifying work, or to apply the theoretical models proposed here to related forms including pervasive gaming or participatory performance, or any work using "unnatural" narratives (cf. Alber et al. 2013), and/or digital storytelling. Real World Disassociation (RWD) is also a helpful concept for thinking critically about the relationship between immersive experience and an audience member's awareness of the "real world" beyond the fictional/immersive one. The topics of interactivity, narrative and environment are fruitful areas of further research in themselves with complex relationships to immersive experience, each capable of either facilitating or providing difficulty in getting, and then staying, immersed.

I do not wish to imply a value judgement on immersive experience or suggest that it is always by default better to achieve it than to miss out. Rather, the approaches in this book are intended to aid a discussion of *why* something was or was not felt to be immersive: its aim is to unpick the "it" that we might talk about being achieved or missed, through which we can then further investigate the implicit value judgements at play. What is going on in a question like "what did you think: did you get the story?" which was asked of me by a member of Punchdrunk moments after the finale of *The Drowned Man*? Was "getting the story" (however that is defined) supposed to be integral to my enjoyment or opinion of the show? And, if it was, what does this reveal about what is valued in an immersive production—both in an audience member's understanding in the moment and during the wider processes of how it has been designed, directed, and marketed?

An emphasis on audience experience, combined with immersive theatre's increasing popularity as a genre, creates further problems for makers. In this summary, for example, Punchdrunk are credited not only with responsibility for the form's popularity but also for establishing its defining aspects in the first place: "Punch-drunk are generally credited as pioneering immersive theatre in the 2000s—a form of promenade theatre which is defined by the audience being able to choose what to watch and where to go" (Merlin Events, 2016). Of course this description is somewhat lacking in historical nuance. But if a piece's effectiveness—its ability to create immersive audience *experience*—is dependent upon surprise, suspense or a general defamiliarisation of form, the question arises: how to make further work that achieves this effect now that the template is increasingly familiar, and *immersive* is a form with easily describable signifiers and audiences who may be fully aware they are "able to choose what to watch and where to go"? Can this very structural awareness—the expectation of, and openness to, certain forms of surprise—become the springboard for further innovation, further surprise? Punchdrunk's own intentions are to prioritise audience experience by playing with perceived boundaries of form:

> What we're doing now is we're trying to [ask] how can we shift that heightened state and that theatricalised experience, how can we take it outside of the confines of a building, and how can you extend the evening of theatre over a number of days, weeks, months.... (Barrett 2014: talk at "Experience Economy" Remix Summit)
>
> The work that I'm really excited about, the future for us as a company, is the use of the real world as set and creating the same sort of immersive responses, sensibilities and reactions that we can in a completely controlled, designed space. (Barrett in Machon 2013: 163)

By not taking the tropes of immersive theatre for granted, it becomes possible to tap further into their potential.

The underlying purposes—be they artistic, political or economic—that influence a decision to make a piece of immersive theatre should not go unexamined. The form's political implications remain a relevant area of enquiry, including its positioning in the experience economy and the relationship between immersive media, audience experience and the wider context of global capitalism. Punchdrunk have attracted particular criticism in this context (Alston 2012, 2016) and immersive theatre as a whole continues to raise urgent discussion in terms of ethics, integrity and honesty towards audiences (Goode 2015: 223). It remains vital to continue to consider immersive work from these angles. Awareness of the financial and ethical positioning of immersion and the various responsibilities (or lack thereof) of those working in the form must remain a high priority for both researchers and artists.

If a certain cynicism or scepticism is a growing part of the critical landscape around immersive theatre (as in the "tired and hackneyed already?" suspicions of Higgins in 2009, variations of which have been regularly repeated since), the approaches outlined in this book are intended to foster an attitude towards immersive theatre that is generally more optimistic, and to open up a series of investigations—by theatremakers as well as academic researchers—into how work that calls itself "immersive" might be constructed with ever more sophistication, hope, integrity and complexity. Is it possible to make a piece of immersive theatre that imagines existence outside the logic of capitalism; or a piece of immersive theatre that allies itself to women's rights; or a piece of immersive theatre that's fundamentally comedic? Experiments with form are possible, as well as with content.

My focus has been the work of Punchdrunk, but it is my hope that the modes of enquiry in this project will allow for further research on other companies and productions that define as immersive, or otherwise play about with immersive tropes. This book's definition of immersion can be applied to other media, as well as other shapes, genres or forms of theatre that might not immediately appear to include popular signifiers of "immersive" performance. Applying the approaches outlined in this book to practical research may allow further exploration of the creation of immersive experience, as well as its critical examination. Masked audience members, the freedom to roam, interactive(-seeming) elements, messed-about chronologies and certain environmental or aesthetic trademarks, might not be the defining elements of immersive theatre after all—opening up further possibilities for artists and theatremakers, and, through them, for audiences.

REFERENCES

Alber, Jan, Skov Nielsen, Henrik, and Richardson, Brian. (eds.). 2013. *A Poetics of Unnatural Narrative*. Columbus: The Ohio State University Press.

Alston, Adam. 2012. Funding, Product Placement and Drunkenness in Punchdrunk's *The Black Diamond*. *Studies in Theatre & Performance* 32 (2): 193–208.

Alston, Adam. 2016. *Beyond Immersive Theatre: Aesthetics, Politics and Productive Participation*. London: Palgrave Macmillan.

Barrett, Felix. 2014. Felix Barrett, Artistic Director, Punchdrunk. Speaking at Remix Summit: *Experience Economy: Creating Extraordinary Moments and Stories that Get People Talking*. https://www.youtube.com/watch?v=xCRcuHiDEYs. Accessed March 2014.

Goode, Chris. 2015. *The Forest and the Field: Changing Theatre in a Changing World*. London: Oberon.

Higgins, Charlotte. 2009. Immersive Theatre: Tired and Hackneyed Already? *Guardian Theatre Blog*, December 7.

Machon, Josephine. 2013. *Immersive Theatres: Intimacy and Immediacy in Contemporary Performance*. London: Palgrave Macmillan.

Merlin Events. 2016. All the World's a Stage: The Rise of Immersive Theatre. Events London.

BIBLIOGRAPHY

Babbage, Frances. 2009. Heavy Bodies, Fragile Texts: Stage Adaptation and the Problem of Presence. In *Adaptation and Contemporary Culture: Textual Infidelities*, ed. Rachel Carroll, 11–22. London: Continuum.
Barton, Bruce, and Windeyer, Richard. 2012. Immersive Negotiations: Binaural Perspectives on Site-Specific Sound. In *Performing Site-Specific Theatre: Politics, Place, Practice*, ed. Birch and Tompkins, 182–199. Basingstoke; New York: Palgrave Macmillan.
Bennett, Jane. 2010. *Vibrant Matter: A Political Ecology of Things*. Durham, NC: Duke University Press.
Bennett, Jane. 2012. Powers of the Hoard: Further Notes on Material Agency. In *Animal Vegetable Mineral: Ethics and Objects*, ed. Jeffrey Jerome, Cohen, 237–269, 228. Washington, DC: Oliphaunt Books.
Biggin, Rose. 2015. Reading Fan Mail: Communicating Immersive Experience in Punchdrunk's Faust and The Masque of the Red Death. *Participations* 12 (1): 152–169.
Birch, Anna, and Joanne Tompkins (eds.). 2012. *Performing Site-Specific Theatre: Politics, Place, Practice*. Basingstoke, New York: Palgrave MacMillan.
Blackadder, Neil. 2003. *Performing Opposition: Modern Theatre and the Scandalized Audience*. Westport, CT: Praeger.
Briginshaw, Valeria A. [2001] 2009. *Dance, Space and Subjectivity*. Basingstoke: Palgrave Macmillan.
Broadhurst, Sue, and Josephine Machon (eds.). 2009. *Performance and Technology: Practices of Virtual Embodiment and Interactivity*. Basingstoke: Palgrave Macmillan.
Brooks, Peter. 1992 [1984]. *Reading for the Plot: Design and Intention in Narrative*. Harvard: Harvard University Press.

Burland, Karen, and Stephanie Pitts (eds.). 2014. *Coughing and Clapping: Investigating Audience Experience.* Surrey: Ashgate.

Butterworth, Jo, and Liesbeth Wildschut. 2009. *Contemporary Choreography: A Critical Reader.* London: Routledge.

Crawford, Chris. 2003. Interactive Storytelling. In *The Video Game Theory Reader*, ed. Mark J. P. Wolf and Bernard Perron. New York: Routledge.

Cremona, Vicky Ann, Eversmann, Peter, van Maanen, Hans, Sauter, Willmar, and Tulloch, John (eds.). 2004. *Theatrical Events: Borders, Dynamics, Frames.* Amsterdam: Rodopi.

Currie, Mark. 1998, 2011. *Postmodern Narrative Theory.* London: Palgrave Macmillan.

De Jongh, Nicholas. 2007. Interactive Black Tie and Tails. *Evening Standard*, October 3.

Deleuze, Gilles. 2007. *Francis Bacon: The Logic Of Sensation.* trans. Daniel W. Smith. London: Continuum.

Diamond, Elin. 1991. The Violence of 'We': Politicizing Identification. In *Critical Theory and Performance*, ed. Janelle Reinelt and Joseph R. Roach, Rev. ed, 402–412. Ann Arbor: University of Michigan Press.

Eagleton, Terry. 1990. *The Ideology of the Aesthetic.* London: Blackwell.

Fischer-Lichte, Erika. 2012. Appearing as Embodied Mind—Defining a Weak, A Strong and a Radical Concept of Presence. In *Archaeologies of Presence: Art, Performance and the Persistence of Being*, ed. Gabriella Giannachi, Nick Kaye, and Michael Shanks, 103–118. London: Routledge.

Gardner, Lyn. 2010. Wisdom of the Crowd: Interactive Theatre is Where it's at. *Guardian Theatre Blog*, March 2 2010. Accessed July 2012.

Glusker, Anne. 2006. The Best Seats for This Play Are Moving Fast. *New York Times.* December 17, 2006.

Gruber, William. 2010. *Offstage Space, Narrative, and the Theatre of the Imagination.* New York: Palgrave Macmillan.

Herman, David (ed.). 2011. *The Cambridge Companion to Narrative.* Cambridge: Cambridge University.

Jenkins, Henry. 2002. Game Design as Narrative Architecture. In *First Person: New Media as Story, Performance, and Game*, ed. Noah Wardrip-Fruin and Pat Harrigan, 118–130. Cambridge: MIT, 2004.

Jennett, C., Cox, A., and Cairns, P. 2009. Being in the game. In *Proceedings of the Philosophy of Computer Games 2008*, ed. S. Gunzel, M. Liebe, D. Mersch, 210–227. Potsdam University Press.

Kattwinkel, Susan (ed.). 2003. *Audience Participation: Essays on Inclusion in Performance.* Westporn, Conn.: Praeger.

Kaye, Nick. 2006. Performed Ecologies: Body, Material, Architecture. In *Performing Nature: Explorations in ecology and the arts*, ed. Gabriella Giannachi and Nigel Stewart, 269–284. Oxford: Peter Lang.

Konijn, E. 1991. What's on Between the Actor and His Audience? Empirical Analysis of Emotion Processes in the Theatre. In *Psychology and performing arts*, ed. G.D. Wilson, 59–74. Amster-dam/Lisse: Swets & Zeitlinger.

Koumarianos, Myrto, and Cassandra Silver. 2013. Dashing at a Nightmare: Haunting 'Sleep No More'. *TDR* 57 (1): 167–175.

Lacey, Nick. 2002. *Media Institutions and Audiences*. London: Palgrave Macmillan.

Lancaster, Kurt. 1997. When Spectators Become Performers and Theater Theory: Contemporary Performance-Entertainments Meet the Needs of an 'Unsettled' Audience. *Journal of Popular Culture* 30 (4): 75–88.

Machon, Josephine. 2011. *(Syn)aesthetics: Redefining Visceral Performance*. London: Palgrave Macmillan.

Macintosh, Iain. 1993. *Architecture, Actor and Audience*. London: Routledge.

McAuley, Gay. 2000. *Space in Performance: Making Meaning in the Theatre*. Ann Arbor: University of Michigan Press.

Metro. 2013. Punchdrunk's Hugely Ambitious The Drowned Man Takes Their Immersive Theatre to a New Level. Accessed June 2013.

Nacke, Lennart, and Craig Lindley. 2008. Flow and Immersion in First-Person Shooters: Measuring the Player's Gameplay Experience. In *Future Play '08: Proceedings of the 2008 Conference on Future Play*, ACM, Toronto, Canada, 81–88.

Oddey, Alison, and Christine White (eds.). 2009. *Modes of Spectating*. Bristol: Intellect Books.

Parsons, Michael J. 1987. *How We Understand Art: A Cognitive Developmental Account of Aesthetic Experience*. Cambridge: Cambridge University.

Phelan, James, and Peter J. Rabinowitz (eds.). 2008. *A Companion to Narrative Theory*. Oxford: Blackwell.

Postlewait, Thomas, and Bruce McConachie (eds.). 1989. *Interpreting the Theatrical Past: Essays in The Historiography of Performance*. Iowa: University of Iowa Press.

Punchdrunk. 2014. About. https://www.punchdrunk.org.uk/about/. Accessed July 2014.

Ravaja, Niklas, Timo Saari, Marko Turpeinen, Jari Laarni, Mikko Salminen, and Matias Kivikangas. 2006. Spatial Presence and Emotions During Video Game Playing: Does It Matter With Whom You Play? *Presence* 15 (4): 281–392.

Rayner, Alice. 1993. The Audience: Subjectivity, Community and the Ethics of Listening. *Journal of Dramatic Theory and Criticism* 7 (2): 3–24.

Richardson, Brian. 1987. Time is Out of Joint: Narrative Models and the Temporality of the Drama. *Poetics Today* 8: 299–309.

Richardson, Brian. 2011. Drama and Narrative. In *The Cambridge Companion to Narrative*, ed. David Herman, 142–155. Cambridge: Cambridge University.

Rimmon-Kenan, Shlomith. [1983] 1989. *Narrative Fiction: Contemporary Poetics*. London: Routledge.

Roose, Henk, Daniëlle De Lange, Filip Agneessens, and Hans Waege. 2002. Theatre Audience on Stage: Three Experiments Analysing the Effects of Survey Design Features on Survey Response in Audience Research. Marketing Bulletin, 2002, 13, Article 1.

Roose, Henk, Hans Waege, and Filip Agneessens. 2002. Response Behaviour in Audience Research: A Two-Stage Design for the Explanation of Nonresponse. In *Developments in Social Science Methodology*, ed. Anuška Ferligoj and Andrej Mrvar Metodološki zvezki, 18. Ljubljana: FDV.

Ruddock, Andy. 2000. *Understanding Audiences: Theory and Method*. London: Sage.

Sanders, T., Cairns, P. 2010. Time perception, Immersion and Music in Videogames. BCS HCI, Accessed December 2010.

Seiter, Ellen. 1999. *Television and New Media Audiences*. Oxford: Oxford University Press.

Shaughnessy, Robert. 2012. Immersive Performance, Shakespeare's Globe, and the 'Emancipated Spectator'. *The Hare*: 1.1.

Swift, Elizabeth. 2016. What do Audiences Do? Negotiating the Possible Worlds of Participatory Theatre. *Journal of Contemporary Drama in English* 4 (1): 134–149.

Tavinor, Grant. 2009. *The Art of Videogames*. London: Wiley-Blackwell.

Tomlin, Liz (ed.). 2015. *British Theatre Companies 1995–2014: Mind the Gap, Kneehigh Theatre, Suspect Cultre, Stan's Cafe, Blast Theory, Punchdrunk*. London: Methuen.

Truman, Matt. 2010. Immersive Theatre: Take us to the Edge, But Don't Throw us in. *Guardian*, April, 7.

Tulloch, John. 2000. Approaching Theatre Audiences: Active School Students and Commoditised High Culture. *Contemporary Theatre Review* 10: 85–104.

Turnbull, Olivia. 2016. It's All about You: Immersive Theatre and Social Networking. *Journal of Contemporary Drama in English*. 4 (1): 150–163.

Turner, Mark (ed.). 2006. *The Artful Mind: Cognitive science and the Riddle of Human Creativity*. Oxford: Oxford University.

Welton, Martin. 2011. *Feeling Theatre*. Basingstoke: Palgrave Macmillan.

White, Gareth. 2016. Theatre in the Forest of Things and Signs. *Journal of Contemporary Drama in English* 4 (1): 21–33.

Wolf, Werner. 2013a. Aesthetic Illusion. In *Immersion and Distance: Aesthetic Illusion in Literature and Other Media*, ed. Werner Wolf, Walter Bernhart, and Andreas Mahler. Amsterdam: Rodopi, 1–62.

Wolf, Werner. 2013b. Unnatural Metalepsis' and Immersion: Necessarily Incompatible?. In *A Poetics of Unnatural Narrative*, ed. Jan Alber, Henrik Skov Nielsen, and Brian Richardson, 113–141. Columbus: The Ohio State University Press.

Wozniak, Jan. 2015. The value of Being Together? Audiences in Punchdrunk's *The Drowned Man. Participations* 12 (1): 318–332.

Zaiontz, Keren. 2014. Narcissistic Spectatorship in Immersive and One-on-One Performance. *Theatre Journal*, 66 (3): 405–425.

INDEX

A
Aarseth, Espen, 158, 159
Abbott, H. Porter, 114, 116–119, 137
Abercrombie, Nicholas, 17, 98
Aebischer, Pascale, 152, 153
Agarwal, Ritu, 38
Aldeburgh, 6, 178, 184, 190, 191, 193–195, 197
Alston, Adam, 3, 7, 18, 26, 60, 68, 71, 93, 177, 210
Ang, Ien, 18
Arnott, Jack, 2
Aronson, Arnold, 23, 186–188
Arts and Humanities Research Council (AHRC), 2
Arts Council England (ACE), 6
As You Like It, 8
Atkins, Barry, 160
Audience, 48
    fans. *See* Fan communities
    in film, television and cultural studies, 10
    in theatre and performance studies, 8
Auslander, Philip, 16
Avatar, 45, 67

B
Babbage, Frances, 141
Baptism, 27, 28
Barker, Martin, 10, 18, 98
Barnum Museum. *See* The Millhauser, Steven
Barrett, Felix, 3–5, 13, 19, 26, 82, 84, 90, 103, 135, 169, 170, 174, 174, 184, 195, 199, 201, 210
Barriers to immersion, 15, 38–40, 47, 63, 68, 73, 81–83, 86, 87, 91–93, 120, 123, 126, 130, 131, 166, 167, 175, 194, 198, 201, 207
Barthes, Roland, 122
Bartle, Richard, 161
Bartley, Sean, 66, 136, 144, 199
Bayes, Honour, 91
Bennett, Susan, 10, 12, 16, 26
Billington, Michael, 150
Bishop, Claire, 9, 19
Blair, Rhonda, 179
Blood feud, 159
Bramer, M.A., 59
Brook, Peter, 9
Brooks, Peter, 122, 137

Büchner, Georg, 79, 135
Burke, Edmund, 35–37
Burton, Tara, 37, 93
Butsch, Richard, 18
Butterworth, Philip, 60, 180, 188

C

Cairns, Paul, 23, 38–40, 44–46, 84, 144
Carlson, Marvin, 11, 179, 181
Chatman, Seymour, 19, 119
Childlikeness, 106
Choice, choices, 2, 15, 37, 40, 48, 74, 80, 88, 89, 91–94, 109, 124, 125, 153, 159, 162, 188, 191, 197
Cinema, cinematic, 33, 140, 199
Clapp, Susannah, 87
Cobley, Paul, 113, 114, 116, 120
Cocaine, all about, 200
Cognition, 179, 180
Cognitive turn, the, 17
Comedy, 5
Computer games
 and emotion, 179
 and interactivity, 2, 33, 50, 61, 68, 94, 161
 and puzzles, 71
 and Sleep No More, 170, 174
 immersion in, 15, 22, 38, 41–46, 111, 125, 130, 159, 168, 171, 172, 175
 immersive fallacy, the, 42, 43
 narrative/ludology debate, 158
Conceptual blending, 13, 30, 31, 179
Cook, Amy, 179, 180
Crawford, Chris, 59, 70, 71
Csikszentmihalyi, Mihaly, 28
Cultural participation. *See* Interactivity, Beyond-the-object
Curtis, Adam, 147

D

Dark Knight. *See* The Why So Serious?
Dark twisted love, 97
Day of the Locust. *See* The West, Nethaneal
Di Benedetto, Stephen, 130, 179, 180
Dickinson, Dan, 157
Dinesh, Nandita, 7, 13
Disorientation, 28, 82–84, 87, 120, 142, 149, 153, 180, 194, 196, 198
Dixon, Steve, 21, 61–64, 74
Doctor Who, 114, 115, 125, 127–132
Dovey, Jon, 59
Doyle, Maxine, 17
Duffett, Mark, 98
Dusinberre, Juliet, 8
Dyson, Frances, 21

E

Ecocriticism, 189
Ecology, 10, 189, 190
Eglinton, Andrew, 7, 93
Empathy, 14–17, 39, 41, 43, 93, 159, 168, 179, 180
Empowerment, 2, 25, 26, 34–37, 48, 59, 61, 62, 72, 80, 90, 94, 111, 136, 188
Enrivonmental Theatre, 8, 10
Environment
 and cognition, 179
 and immersion, 50, 62, 172, 178, 181, 186, 189, 192, 194, 195
 and structure, 118, 171, 184
 and The Borough, 6
 and The Drowned Man, 6, 174, 202
 host and ghost, 183, 190, 193, 202
 site-specific, 181–184, 188, 193, 195
 site-sympathetic, 181, 183, 184
Erikson, Jon, 143

Experiece economy, 8, 210
Exploration, 7, 9, 42, 46–48, 50, 65, 80, 83, 84, 90, 94, 98, 99, 101, 111, 115, 116, 126, 131, 137, 140, 145, 160, 163, 165, 169, 181, 187, 191, 197–199, 201, 208, 211

F
Fan communities, 48, 66, 69, 100
Fan mail, 48, 99, 100, 103, 111
Fans. *See* Fan communities
Fan studies, 98
Fernandez, Amyris, 161
Film. *See* Cinema
Fischer-Lichte, Erika, 21, 23
Flow, 17, 28, 29, 31, 32, 36, 37, 40, 41, 65, 70, 90, 120, 128, 142, 144, 153, 161, 174
Fludernik, Monika, 114
Forster, E.M., 121, 122
Frasca, Gonzalo, 158, 159, 165
Freeman, David, 41
Freshwater, Helen, 8, 10, 21, 24, 98, 101, 111
Frieze, James, 7, 49, 157
Frome, David, 41

G
Games. *See* Computer games
Gaming mechanics, 41, 42, 45, 46, 50, 60, 158-160, 163–165, 168, 170–172, 174
Gardner, Lyn, 1, 7, 125
Genette, Gérard, 138
Giannachi, Gabriella, 22, 23, 189, 190
Gilbert, Ron, 42
Gillinson, Miriam, 7
Gold Bug, The (treasure hunt), 169
Golden Amulets of Agnes, The, 157

Goodall, Jane, 23
Goode, Chris, 11, 12, 18, 210
Gordon, Colette, 7, 23–25, 86, 93, 98, 157, 171, 175
Graded states, 16, 21, 47, 72, 83, 89, 94, 116, 118, 142, 182, 201, 208
Grau, Oliver, 32, 33, 35
Green, Adam, 49, 157, 173
Griffiths, Alison, 21, 23, 32–34, 37, 60, 188, 202
Grounded theory, 38

H
Hare, David, 1
Hemming, Sarah, 135
Henri, Adrian, 188
Herman, David, 113, 115, 116, 126, 139
Higgin, Peter, 6, 50, 63, 163, 162, 210
Higgins, Charlotte, 8
Hills, Matthew, 98
Hitchcock, Alfred, 164
Hogan, Patrick, 143, 144
Hoggard, Liz, 3, 82, 84
Horton, Andrew, 178, 200
Host and ghost. *See* Environment
Huizinga, Johan, 59
Hunter, Victoria, 184, 185
Hurley, Erin, 14
Hutcheon, Linda, 152

I
Iball, Helen, 3, 182
Idealised spectator, 8, 13, 17, 19, 20
Imagination, 25, 91, 109, 118, 159, 201
Immersion
 and presence, 22, 23, 44, 46
 as pedagogy, 27

in computer games, 45, 158
in performance art, 17, 21, 138, 160, 181, 186, 189
in story, 42, 115, 125, 136
in Virtual Reality, 9, 22, 63, 117
Immersive experience
  defining, 44, 207
  in cognitive science, 1, 16
  in computer games, 45, 158
  in philosophical aesthetics, 35
Immersive theatre
  criticism of, 11
  definitions of, 45, 71
  histories of, 13, 25
In philosophical aesthetics, 35. . *See also* Sublime
Interactivity
  beyond-the-object interactivity in *The Drowned Man*, 75
  cognitive interactivty in *The Drowned Man*, 74, 80, 83
  explicit interactivty in *The Drowned Man*, 74, 80, 89, 90, 92, 124
  fan activity. *See* Fan mail
  functional interactivty in *The Drowned Man*, 74, 80
  in computer games, 45, 158
  in digital and multimedia performance, 59, 60
  in improvisatory theatre and pervasive gaming, 48, 64, 65, 193
  in the experience economy and Theatrical Event, 13, 20, 33, 68, 187
  in Virtual Reality, 22, 48
  Multivalent Model, 48, 79
  on-on-one performance, 25
Interpretive participation. *See* Cognitive interactivity
Interval, 69, 89, 147
Izzo, Gary, 64

J
Jakob-Hoff, Tristan, 110, 173, 174, 185
Jenkins, Henry, 13, 18, 98, 100, 159, 163–165
Jennett, Charlene et al., 38, 40, 44–46
Jubb, David, 66
Juul, Jesper, 158, 159, 165, 166

K
Kant, Immanuel, 35–37
Kaye, Nick, 22, 23, 183, 202
Kelly, Guy, 90
Kershaw, Baz, 21, 23, 26, 189
Kinaesthetic empathy, 17
Klich, Rosemary, 22, 60
Knowles, Richard, 13
Krasner, David, 15

L
Laurel, Brenda, 39, 158
Lewis, Lisa, 98
Longhurst, Brian, 17, 98, 101
Lorentz, Diana, 21
Ludology, 49, 158–160, 163–166, 168–175
Ludo-narratavism, 158
Lukowski, Andrzej, 199
Lutterbie, John, 179

M
Macbeth, 5, 164
Machon, Josephine, 3, 11, 19, 21, 23–25, 61, 63, 80, 103, 131, 210
Maples, Holly, 25
Masked spectators, 82
Masters, Tim, 177, 199
McAuley, Gay, 189

McConachie, Bruce, 13–16, 30, 47, 178
McGonigal, Jane, 59
McKee, Robert, 124, 146, 147
McKenzie, Jon, 21
McKinney, Joslin, 16, 17, 60, 180, 188
McMahan, Alison, 23, 42, 43, 45
McMullan, Thomas, 157
Memory, 48, 102, 111, 171, 181, 182, 184
Millhauser, Steven, 46
MIT Media Lab, 50, 160, 173
Montola, Markus, 60, 64, 65
Morgenstern, Erin, 110
Moser, Mary Ann, 21
Multimedia, 22, 59–61, 63, 67
Murray, Janet, 71, 73, 159
Myst, 173

N
Narrative/ludology debate. *See* Computer games
Narrative
 and *It Felt Like A Kiss*, 147–149
 and *The Crash of the Elysium*, 6, 49, 114, 115, 121, 125, 126
 and The Duchess of Malfi, 6, 136, 141, 146, 149, 151
 Aristotle (Poetics), 123, 137
 causality, 115, 117, 122, 126, 153
 character, 41, 126
 chronology, 137, 140, 153, 191
 discourse, 119, 120, 123, 126, 138, 142, 145–147, 149, 153, 165, 167, 170
 endings, 49, 146, 148, 192
 frame and embedded narratives, 138, 140
 linearity, 129
 mimesis and diegesis, 140
 plot, 118, 120, 122, 126, 137, 146, 147, 149, 153
 showing vs telling, 140
 storyworld, 115–117, 139, 167, 170, 171
 structure, 19, 131, 149
 suspense, 118, 168
 time, 49, 135–137, 141, 166
Narrator
 heterodiegetic/homodiegetic, 138
 narrator-visitor, 66, 144
 real/implied, 19
Nell, Victor, 32
Newman, James, 39, 43, 59, 70, 72
Nield, Sophie, 3
Night Circus. *See* The Morgenstern, Erin
Nightingale, Virginia, 18, 160

O
One-on-one. *See* Interactivity
Optimal performance. *See* Flow
O'Grady, Alice, 60, 63, 64, 74

P
Pace, Steven, 40
Packer, Randall, 61
Participation. *See* Interactivity
Participations (journal), 7, 67
Passivity, 8, 19, 80
Peak experience. *See* Flow
Pearson, Mike, 181–183, 193
Perron, Bernard, 59
Pervasive gaming. *See* Interactivity
Play, 1, 3, 12, 24, 30, 39, 40, 42, 47, 59, 62, 64, 65, 69–74, 86, 87, 90, 110, 120, 124, 125, 137, 146, 150–153, 158–161, 164, 168, 170–172, 177, 194, 208, 209, 211

Popat, Sita, 63, 65, 100
Portal Objects, 162, 165–168, 172
Postlewait, Thomas, 20
Premium tickets, 85, 86, 93
Presence, 3, 9, 13, 14, 17, 21–24, 31, 32, 38, 40–42, 44–46, 49, 68, 127, 131, 144, 172, 188, 189, 192
Primary data, 13, 24
Punchdrunk
  commercial projects, 7, 68
  Faust, 6, 48, 97
  It Felt Like A Kiss, 6, 49, 63, 136
  Punchdrunk Enrichment, 6, 25
  Punchdrunk International, 6
  Punchdrunk Travel, 6
  Sleep No More, 2, 6, 7, 24, 37, 48, 50, 69, 75, 90, 110, 135, 144, 160, 173
  The Borough, 6, 50, 178, 190, 191, 193, 202
  The Crash of the Elysium, 6, 49, 63, 114, 121, 125, 129, 131, 138
  The Drowned Man: A Hollywood Fable, 25, 48, 50, 59, 75, 87, 92, 180
  The Duchess of Malfi, 6, 136, 137, 147, 151–153
  The Firebird Ball, 5
  The Masque of the Red Death, 6, 48, 69, 75, 97, 103, 106, 135, 141, 168, 174, 180, 188, 190, 196
  Tunnel 228, 6
Purcell, Stephen, 26

R

Rancière, Jacques, 8, 136
Real World Disassociation (RWD), 38, 40, 84, 144, 208

Reason, Matthew, 2, 13, 17, 21, 27, 35–37, 63, 102, 107, 122, 161, 167, 207
Rebellato, Dan, 179
Revered gaze, 26, 34, 35, 37, 60, 82, 92, 188, 202
Ricoeur, Paul, 140
Ridout, Nicholas, 24, 60
Romeo and Juliet, 5
Rose, Frank, 67
Ruddock, Andy, 18
Rules of engagement, 25, 30, 49, 83, 87, 88, 91, 94, 99, 104, 109, 158
Ryan, Marie-Laure, 116

S

Salen, Katie (Rules of Play), 42, 59, 73, 74, 80, 85, 89, 93
Sauter, Willmar, 20, 33
Schani, Hadassa, 60
Schechner, Richard, 185
Scheer, Edward, 22, 60–62
Seiter, Ellen, 18
Shaughnessy, Robert, 8, 11, 23
Shaw, Philip, 37
Silvestre, Agnes, 93, 98, 110
Site-specific, sympathetic. *See* Environment
Smith, Matthew, 32, 33, 125
Sooke, Alistair, 181
Space. *See* Environment
Spectator-Participation-as-Research (SPaR), 3, 9, 13
Spectatorship. *See* Audience
Staiger, Janet, 18
Story. *See* Narrative
Sublime
  and the beautiful, 36
Superfans, 110, 114

T

Technology, 21, 22, 38, 60, 61, 63, 67, 160, 162, 166–169, 194, 202
Temple Studios, 79, 81, 83, 85, 88, 93, 139, 178, 195
Tetris, 42
Theatrical Event, 13, 20, 33, 59, 60, 68, 69, 74, 85, 143, 179, 185, 187, 188
Tulloch, John, 13
Turner, Catherine, 30, 178, 183

U

Ubersfeld, Anne, 26
Ushers, 11, 87, 88, 104, 194
Utilitarian participation. *See* Interativity, Functional

V

Varela, Francisco, 30, 178
Videogames. *See* Computer games
VIP. *See* Premium tickets
Virtual Reality, 9, 22, 63, 117, 161
Voyeurism, 24, 25, 86, 93

W

Warren, Jason, 7
Welton, Martin, 179, 198
West, Nethaneal, 79
White, Gareth, 22, 24, 25, 86, 98, 111, 163, 177, 199
Why So Serious?, 67
Wilkie, Fiona, 183, 195
Worthen, W.B., 11
Woyzeck. *See* Büchner, Georg

Z

Zaiontz, Keren, 182
Zimmerman, Eric. *See* Salen, Katie